The
Life
Book

Nina Grunfeld is the founder of Life Clubs, weekly 90-minute self-development workshops around the UK and Canada that give you a clearer way of thinking. The workshops are very structured, focusing on a different topic each week and have been proven to give you the confidence and courage to live the life you want to live. Life Clubs are also held in corporates as part of their learning and development and are used by the NHS.

Contact us on 0207 22 22 199 or visit www.lifeclubs.com

Nina Grunfeld

The Life Book

Laugh more
Love more
Play more
Earn more

entice Hall Life
an imprint of

rlow, England • London • New York • Boston • San Francisco • Toronto • Sydney • Singapore • Hong Kong
kyo • Seoul • Taipei • New Delhi • Cape Town • Madrid • Mexico City • Amsterdam • Munich • Paris • Milan

PEARSON EDUCATION LIMITED

Edinburgh Gate
Harlow CM20 2JE
Tel: +44 (0)1279 623623
Fax: +44 (0)1279 431059
Website: www.pearsoned.co.uk

First published in Great Britain in 2010

ISBN: 978-0-273-72888-7

British Library Cataloguing-in-Publication Data
A catalogue record for this book is available from the British Library

Library of Congress Cataloging-in-Publication Data
A catalog record for this book is available from the Library of Congress

10 9 8 7 6 5 4 3 2 1
13 12 11 10 09

Text design by Two Associates
Typeset in 10/14 Minion by Two Associates
Printed and bound in Great Britain by Ashford Colour Press Ltd, Gosport

The publisher's policy is to use paper manufactured from sustainable forests.

To Genevieve

cont

ents

Acknowledgements

I wrote my second book when I was living in New York, and I shall never forget my mortification when, back in England, my brother read out to a group of friends in his best American accent my page-and-a half of gushing acknowledgements. I have tried to learn some English self-restraint but I'm not sure it's worked.

This book is rooted in my experience with Life Clubs. So many people have helped me in that project that I cannot thank them all individually. The biggest thank you is to Henry Morris who has helped and inspired me from the start and continues to do so. Also to Genevieve Hawes who has been my right-hand for the past two years. Special thanks to Haji Chana, Anna Elcock, Carol Faculjak, Lynne Irwin, Simon Jones, Maurits Kalff, Julia Lloyd-Evans, Gordon Melvin, James Miller, Pat Morden, Ruth Needham, Dan Price, Cyndy Walker and everyone who has ever hosted or visited a Life Club. I'd also like to thank Charlotte Style for having spent a year of her life studying Life Clubs and how they affect the happiness of those participating in them.

Sam Jackson, my editor at Pearson, first suggested that I write *The Life Book,* which was a thrilling (if daunting) idea. I am indebted to her for trusting me. I want to thank her and her team. I had great help with the writing from Laura Barnicoat, Andrea Blundell, Annie Lionnet and Tiffany McCall. Welcome support came from Adrian Brooks, Lowri Glain, Jacob Laurent and William Ward; and, in the final stages some much-needed help from Michael Underhill and Alice White. Thanks also to David Eldridge, Kevan Westbury and everyone else at Two Associates for their wonderful graphics and Ursula Underhill and Lucy Sisman for the use of their photos.

I'm also grateful to the many journalists who have supported Life Clubs and me, especially Casilda Grigg and Jon Stock (*The Daily Telegraph*), Rosie Ifould (*Psychologies*), Hilly Janes (formerly *The Times, Body & Soul*), Emily Murray (*More!* magazine), Charles Howgego (*Big Issue*), Ginny Dougary (*The Times*) and Harriet Griffey and many other freelance journalists.

On a personal note, I'd like to thank Ira, Miranda, Neia (and my wonderful neighbours, Sally and Matt Marlow/Durdy) for looking after me so that I can do what I enjoy; and my family, Nicholas and our children, Michael, Frances, Ursula and Tommy whom I love more than they'll ever know.

I've enjoyed self-development since I was 16 and wrote the astrology column for our school magazine, based on the little I then knew about the signs of the Zodiac – and life. This book feels like a wonderful culmination of what I've learnt from all of you in the interim. I hope I, in return, can pass some of that knowledge back to you.

Foreword

When in 2007 Charlotte told me that, inspired by Life Clubs, she was going to be one of the first intake in the Positive Psychology course in the University of East London, I was thrilled for her. Little did I know then that she was going to write her thesis on the effects of Life Clubs on its participants. The thesis was immensely time-consuming for Charlotte, but for me it's been a fascinating process and a good way of getting to know Charlotte and her wonderful enthusiasm for life better. Plus the final result was a great endorsement for everything I've done. – Nina

I have spent much of my adult life examining the subject matter of this book; academically in the study of philosophy and positive psychology, practically as a wife, friend and mother and, for the last 10 years, professionally as a coach.

When I heard of Nina's Life Clubs in 2006 I was immediately curious. I signed up mainly to check out what sounded a great idea: inexpensive workshops available immediately to those who wanted to get more from their lives, but I was almost at once forcefully reminded of the power of regularly attending to one's own life.

Through the simple, supportive structure of the clubs, I was prompted to remember that, however good life is, really living the life we want, a good life, needs constant quiet and simple attention. After just a few attendances my life took off again after a period of stagnation because I had rediscovered the importance of sustained, supported examination and challenges to accepted thinking and behaviour.

When, through the University of East London Positive Psychology Department, I got the opportunity to conduct an academic study on happiness and wellbeing I chose to measure and examine the effects of Life Clubs.

The study was carried out over a six-week period. The participants were split into two groups. One group attended six Life Clubs, while a control group met on the same occasions, in the same location and were invited to discuss their happiness and wellbeing (or anything else they wanted to talk about) but were given no direction or structure of any kind. The participants from both groups answered questionnaires at the beginning of the study, at the end of the six-week period and three months later. The answers to these formed the basis of my conclusions.

The results of the research showed that Life Clubs has a positive effect on a significant number of factors by which psychologists measure wellbeing. The most significant effects were on 'orientation to happiness' and 'self-acceptance'. 'Self-efficacy' and 'hope' also increased, as did 'purpose in life' and 'satisfaction with life'. These effects remained over time.

Nina's Life Clubs are visionary. They are a practical way to give yourself an hour-and-a-half a week to attend to those things that make up the life you are living and to grow and change with the support of others. This book will be a great tool for all those who want simple ideas and reminders of how to take small and large steps towards living a happier and more fulfilled life. Like the clubs, *The Life Book* can be read and used with an immediate issue in mind or, more generally, to encourage and support challenges and change in your life.

Keep this book to hand, notice the words that resonate and more especially those that don't. Use Nina's encouragement and wisdom and see where it takes you. This book will give you back as much as you choose to put into it.

Charlotte Style, Positive Psychologist

'A book is like a garden in the pocket.'

Indian proverb

Getting the most out of *The Life Book*

As you'll discover, I really enjoy metaphor. I have enjoyed thinking of *The Life Book* like a garden, a combination both of your own back garden and of a glorious garden of the kind that you would go to visit. I wanted to create a garden for your pocket – a book that would help you get more out of yourself and your life in whatever way you wanted to.

In the first place I wanted it to have something in it for everyone – whether you wanted simply to smell the roses, or instead take a leisurely stroll or long run around the perimeter. There would be both flowering borders and tall majestic trees. I wanted you to be able to uncover whatever you wanted in it.

One of the joys of gardening is discovery – stumbling across a new plant, watching your bulbs spring into life, feeling the soil between your hands, learning how to make plants thrive. While this book will clear the pathways for you, nudging you off in new directions, it is all about you finding things out for yourself. Think of these pages as your gardening tool kit, ready to boost you with expert advice, techniques and knowledge, so that you can get the most out of you and your garden.

Life is as varied, complex and fascinating as a garden. And, like a garden, you too never stop growing, changing, and evolving. *The Life Book* will help you to get to know yourself as you are now and as how you would like to be. It introduces you to all the different facets of yourself, perhaps in a way you had never thought about before, or in ways you never had time to explore – or maybe never knew how to. Like a herbaceous border that you can change every year, so that it becomes more and more as you want it to be, *The Life Book* will help you become whatever you want, whether it's more outgoing, more in control, or more fulfilled. Like a garden manual, this book will allow you to discover the answers to questions you may not have been previously sure how to find the answer to – only this time you're the expert. You'll discover how the answer is already within you.

In *The Life Book* you'll find ways of focusing on the whole garden – the whole of life – but also of focusing on one blossom at a time. Gardening, like life, is not about following a strict regimented plan – it's a process of learning and relearning. You'll find *The Life Book* is a series of reminders aimed to keep you going along smoothly.

When I founded Life Clubs in 2004, I imagined them full of gardeners coming together to discuss their own gardens – reporting what was and wasn't thriving, sharing plans and exploring how to achieve them – a place (leaving metaphor behind) where anyone could come and meet other people who were also questioning what they wanted from life, and where there would be a spirit of openness and non-judgement. This book is for you to use alongside the clubs or, as an alternative, if you can't get to them. You'll enjoy asking questions that you've longed to know the answer to and discovering more about yourself in the process.

I hope you like the proverbs I chose. My last two books had quotes throughout, but proverbs seemed more universal for a book all about life. The collages are fun too. We use a lot of visual metaphors in Life Clubs and I wanted the book to reflect that.

To me the ultimate garden experience is the Internet. There's so much to discover, so much to learn, so much to see. You search a question and then come up with a whole load of answers. Each answer has links to another place and on and on you go, caught up in a voyage of discovery. I wanted *The Life Book* to be as much like surfing the net as a book can be.

I hope you enjoy using *The Life Book* as much as I've enjoyed writing it.

How to use *The Life Book*

Small beginnings

Start this book by filling in your Balance Chart, page xvii. Use a pencil or draw a quick version of your own so you can fill in a Balance Chart again and again. Each time you fill it in, you'll have taken a snapshot of your life as it is at that point, which you can use to find out where in your life there's something you'd like to change. You can then turn to the relevant section of *The Life Book*, pages 3–50, to start exploring that area of your life a little more.

When you're filling in your Balance Chart, be totally honest. There's no point in doing it otherwise, and you don't have to show it to anyone. Read the paragraphs about each area below and then score your life by thinking about how you feel right now – your score will change every time you fill in the Balance Chart.

Ask yourself 'How satisfied am I with each area of my life?' Ten is most satisfied and one is least. Then join up the numbers you've scored and you'll have your shape for the day. Your aim is to see how you feel about life right now. It's not about scoring the maximum in every area. Sometimes it's fine for one area to outscore all the others: if you've just fallen in love and are scoring 10 on 'Love & Romance' and very low on everything else, that might be perfect, at least for a while. But if you wanted to run the next marathon and were scoring low on 'Health & Fitness' it would be a wake-up call that you want to start doing something about it.

Each of us sees our life differently. Some of us are high 8/9/10 scorers, others score ourselves in the 1/2/3 zone. It doesn't mean we necessarily have different lives or different degrees of happiness, we just have a different visual response. If you score what you feel is 'low', see it as an opportunity to grow. If you've scored 'high', see it as an opportunity to keep growing.

Areas of life
You'll already be aware of what these areas mean to you, but these brief descriptions might open your mind to a new perspective.

Home: Does your home feel like 'home' to you? Is it affordable or are you constantly worried about further expenses? Do you enjoy the people you're sharing with? Are you happy with your neighbours and the location? Do you have enough privacy? (See page 3.)

Creativity: Creativity isn't just about classic creativity (art, music, words). It's about being open to explore (such as by reading this book), doing things differently, expressing yourself. Do you have the time to be creative? Are you confident about your creativity? (See page 7.)

'From small beginnings come great things.'

Health & Fitness: Are you treating your body well? Do you respect your body? Do you have regular check-ups? Do you listen to it? Do you do what it wants? Do you trust it? Do you know what kind of food and exercise it likes? (See page 11.)

Rest & Relaxation: Do you sleep well and wake up rested? Do you take enough and regular holidays? Do you worry a lot? Do you often feel stressed? (See page 15.)

Friends & Social Life: Do you have time for friends and do they have time for you? Do you have a variety of friends? Do your friends allow you to change? Do you go out to have fun? (See page 19.)

Work: Does what you do feel like a job or what you want to do? If you don't have a job do you know what work you want to do? Do you feel satisfied with your working environment, your colleagues, the recognition you receive? Would you like further training? (See page 23.)

Family: *(You may want to circle two numbers in 'Family' – one for the family you were born into and another for the family that you've created.)* Do your family appreciate that you're a grown-up with your own life? Do they support you? Are there feuds going on in your family? Are you blaming your family for everything that's gone wrong in your life? Do you enjoy your family? (See page 29.)

Money: What relationship do you have with money – are you constantly in debt or do you save? Would you like to be better informed? Do you give to charity? Do you frequently buy things and then regret it? (See page 34.)

Spirituality: Do you have a religion and, if not, do you feel the lack? Are you living life according to your values? Do you have faith that you're being looked after? Do you feel grateful? Do you feel love for others and a connection to them? (See page 39.)

Love & Romance: *(You may want to circle two numbers in 'Love & Romance' – one for you and your feelings towards yourself and the other for the way you feel about another or, if there isn't anyone else in your life, how much that matters.)* Are you looking after yourself as you would a best friend? Do you feel you deserve love? Are you aware of your own sexuality? Are your expectations too high/ low? Do you always pick the same type of person to fall for? Are you able to commit? Are you happy in a relationship and, if not, does it matter? (See page 44.)

Once you've completed your Balance Chart, you'll probably find an area you'd like to think about – either because you've scored 'high' or 'low'. Turn over and, in the following few pages, find the area you'd like to think about or work on and find the question there that is most similar to the one you would like the answer to.

Then follow the links to discover your answer.

My Balance Chart

Date.......................

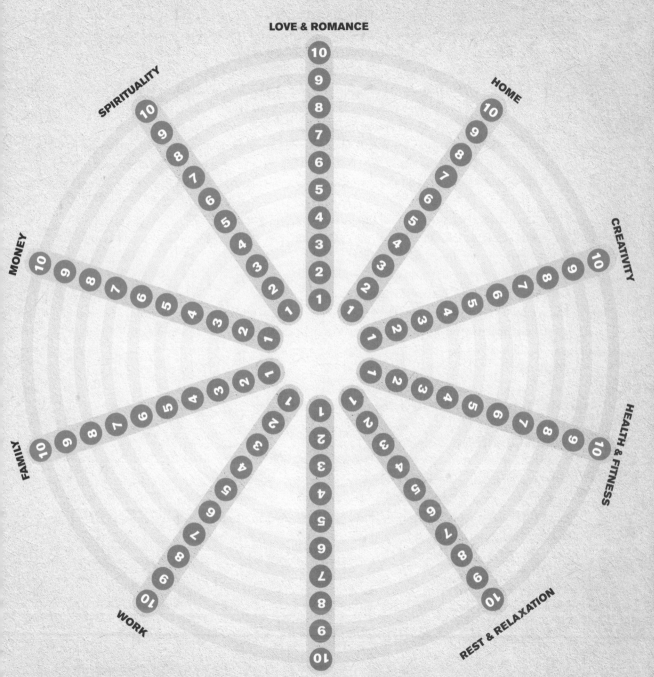

LOVE & ROMANCE

SPIRITUALITY

HOME

MONEY

CREATIVITY

FAMILY

HEALTH & FITNESS

WORK

REST & RELAXATION

FRIENDS & SOCIAL LIFE

Moving along : what to do next

Now you've completed your Balance Chart, you'll know which part of your life you'd like to explore. Over the following pages are fuller introductions to each of the 10 areas of the Balance Chart. Each introduction is followed by lots of questions, one of which will hopefully address the concern or interest you've got at the moment or, at least, be similar to it.

Rather than repeat questions, they're in one area or the other. So, if, for example, you and your partner are having some disagreements about decorating your home, look in both the 'Creativity' and 'Love & Romance' sections for a suitable question. You'll find the question *'Do you have different taste from your partner?'* in one of them – in this case in 'Love & Romance'.

Once you've found the question that best suits your line of enquiry, you'll see it can be answered with a simple 'Yes' or 'No'. No matter what you answer, you'll notice underneath it lots of words ('links') with page references. Each of these links is one of the topics in *The Life Book*. Turn to the one that feels the most relevant to you and read it. Then follow up the others. You'll learn something from each topic you read.

Each topic follows a similar format:
The coloured dots ● ● ○ ● ● ● ● ● ● ● let you know which areas of the Balance Chart the topic is pertinent to. You'll find that a few of the topics are applicable to all areas of life.

The topic

A story from my life to illustrate the concept

A more **dictionary-style definition** of the concept

The concept used colloquially in one or two sentences

More information about the concept plus lots to think about and (more often than not) some exercises or a quiz to do

Either:
● **Things to do:** or
● **Your Lightbulb Moment:** or
● **Project:**

At the end of each topic there will be **links**. These **links** will take you to other topics that are also relevant. You can either follow them up then and there or later in your own time. Just imagine you're surfing the net, travelling as and where you want.

'You always miss if you don't shoot.'

Dutch proverb

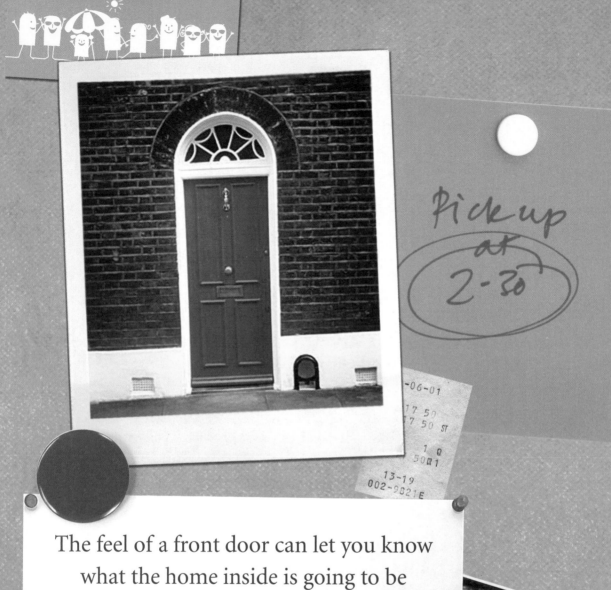

Pick up at 2-30

-06-01
17 50
17 50 ST
1 Q
50 0 1
13-19
002-9021E

The feel of a front door can let you know what the home inside is going to be like. I remember my daughter, when she was quite small and highly attuned to atmosphere, refusing to go into the home of a friend of hers because she didn't like their front door. As you might expect, their friendship didn't last.

Home ●

Many of us think of home as the place we come back to every day, but home could equally be where your parents or children live, or where you go every year on holiday. We can create homes anywhere. Your local swimming pool might be a favourite 'home' as might the neighbouring park. You may be someone to whom location doesn't matter, so long as you have your laptop with you and are free to use your imagination.

And what about your home – the place where you live. Do you think of your home as a sanctuary – a nurturing environment where you can relax and enjoy time alone or with friends and family? How do you feel when you walk through the front door – happy to be home or feeling sad that it's not as you want it? Do you enjoy your living space and feel that it reflects your personality, lifestyle and needs or does your heart sink when you contemplate the expense that will be needed to make it the way you want it?

Whether or not we think we are sensitive to atmosphere, most of us can sense when a home is friendly, warm and welcoming. Without necessarily knowing why, we want to spend time in it – we feel good, relaxed and comfortable and take pleasure in simply being there. If you have created this kind of ambiance in your home it's almost certainly because you love where you live and this gives your home a heart. Your home feels cared for and it's a joy for you to inhabit and for others to visit.

Not all of us feel this way about our homes. For some of us our home is just a place to live. It might not be ours or we know it's only a temporary base or perhaps we don't feel confident about making it ours and so we don't put any of ourselves into it. We neglect to buy flowers or nice things that would enhance our living space and, as a result, the energy becomes stagnant and we may feel stuck or depressed. We can also feel saddened by the neighbourhood we live in and the people we live with. Both can have a big impact on how we feel about our homes. A neighbourhood you thrive in will make you feel you're coming home long before you reach your home, whereas one you feel fearful in may well pervade the atmosphere of your home even when you close the front door behind you. Harmonious relationships in which each person enjoys each other and the home that they share create a happy environment. But sour relationships can make life difficult and home a place to avoid rather than enjoy. If your home isn't a place you want to be, you may want to start thinking about how you could change that or even move. There may be big decisions to be made, but sometimes just putting a little time and attention into your home right now can immediately give you a sense of lightness and clarity.

On a functional level our homes are a place of safety and refuge from the outside world. But our homes represent far more to us than simply shelter. Visualise your dream home and what that would look like. Begin by imagining what colours you'd like to paint the walls. Or how you'd organise the space to better suit you and those you live with. Turning your house into a home takes time, energy and money, but just think how you'll feel when you've done it.

Which area of 'Home' are you interested in: Comfort, Community, Moving, Organisation, Sharing or Style? Find the area and then the question that feels right for you below it. Follow the links.

Comfort

Do you know when you feel 'at home'?

Belonging, p82, Confidence, p107, Play, p232, Relaxation, p251, Values, p298

Does your home feel like a 'home'?

Belonging, p82, Confidence, p107, Connection, p110, Intuition, p170, Relaxation, p251, Values, p298

Do you enjoy being on your own at home?

Confidence, p107, Fear, p141, Loneliness, p186, Relaxation, p251, Stress, p273, Values, p298

Are you more comfortable in someone else's home than your own?

Confidence, p107, Envy, p133, Mirroring, p194, Relaxation, p251, Role Models, p256, Style, p277, Values, p298

Do you want to invest in your home?

Big Picture, p83, Decisions, p121, Money, p196, Planning, p225, Prioritise, p234, Trust, p293

Community

Do you like your neighbourhood?

Belonging, p82, Compromise, p106, Fear, p141, Non-judgemental, p204, Trust, p293

Do you contribute to your community?

Accountability, p56, Belonging, p82, Comfort Zone, p105, Confidence, p107, Connection, p110, Giving, p152

Do you know how to choose a neighbourhood to live in?

Assumptions, p67, Belonging, p82, Compromise, p106, Intuition, p170, Perfectionism, p216, Values, p298

Moving

Would you like to move now or in the future?

Confidence, p107, Decisions, p121, Life Ambition, p179, Planning, p225, Prioritise, p234, Procrastination, p239

Are you always moving, or wanting to move?

Advantages, p62, Belonging, p82, Change, p99, Confidence, p107, Patterns, p212, Perfectionism, p216

Organisation

Have you got too many things?

Control, p111, De-cluttering, p122, Excess, p135, Fear, p141, Trust, p293

Does your home life feel disorganised?

Accountability, p56, Compromise, p106, Control, p111, De-cluttering, p122, Excess, p135, Stress, p273

Sharing

Do you want your own home?

Decisions, p121, Goals, p153, Money, p196, Prioritise, p234, Spider Diagrams, p269, Values, p298

Are you interested in sharing and do you know what kind of person you would like to live with?

Assumptions, p67, Boundaries, p94, Compromise, p106, Control, p111, Personality Typing, p219, Roles, p254, Values, p298

Do you find the people you live with easy to get on with (family or friends)?

Boundaries, p94, Compromise, p106, Control, p111, Forgiveness, p148, Planning, p225, Roles, p254

Do you have a space in the home that's yours?

Belonging, p82, Boundaries, p94, Compromise, p106, Relaxation, p251, Saying 'No', p262

Style

Do you know your style?

Confidence, p107, Creativity, p114, Intuition, p170, Style, p277, Values, p298

Does your home reflect your taste, or someone else's?

Compromise, p106, Confidence, p107, Control, p111, Style, p277, Values, p298

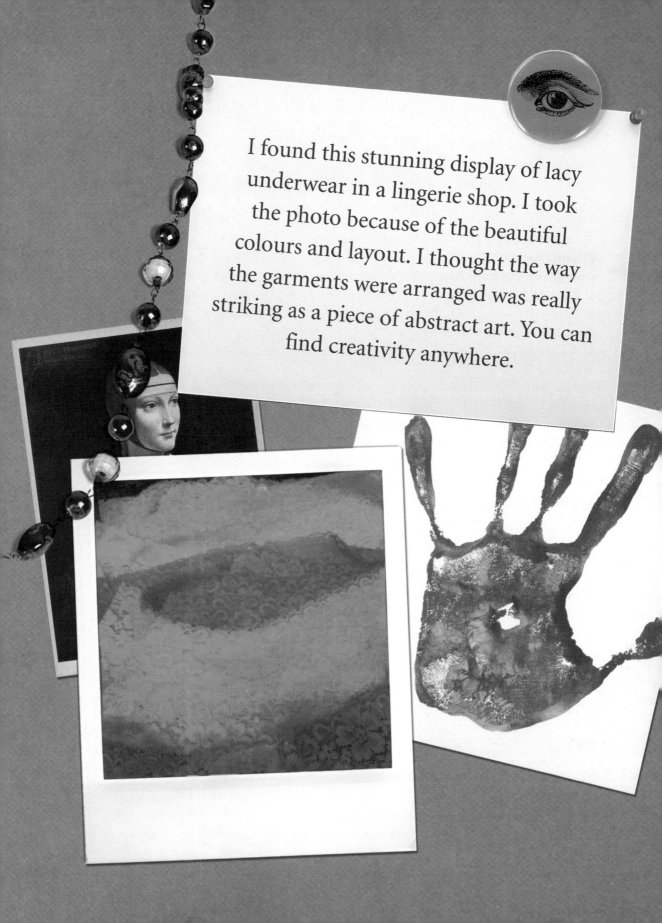

I found this stunning display of lacy underwear in a lingerie shop. I took the photo because of the beautiful colours and layout. I thought the way the garments were arranged was really striking as a piece of abstract art. You can find creativity anywhere.

Creativity ●

Being creative isn't a talent that belongs exclusively to artistic people. Whether we are aware of it or not, all of us possess an innate creativity which can be expressed in an infinite number of ways. Remember yourself as a child or watch a child now. Children are naturally creative – they continually use their imagination to invent games, make things and explore the world around them. They are free and spontaneous in their thinking as well as curious and open to life. They exist in the world of possibilities.

Some of us retain our creativity as we mature into adulthood and use it to make decisions, come up with solutions or create beautiful pieces of art, poetry or music. All too often, however, we lose touch with our creative side as we focus on making our way in the world. We stop tapping into our imagination and our capacity to dream up inspirational ideas. And when we block our ability to be creative, we deny ourselves the joy of developing our infinite potential.

Creative thinking is something that we can all relearn. But what does this really mean? It means giving yourself a free rein to let your imagination run wild. It means being open to new perspectives so that you are continually questioning your beliefs and ideas and willing to change your mind rather than getting entrenched in a point of view. It means being flexible enough to consider other ways of looking at a problem and brainstorming solutions. Creative minds never stop questioning, being curious, challenging themselves and everyone around them.

Creativity doesn't always involve a Lightbulb Moment, but there is something endlessly and wonderfully satisfying about having a creative breakthrough, whether it's discovering a secret ingredient to add to a gourmet meal you've made, or finding an original way of presenting a new idea at work. Sometimes you'll actively want to channel your creative thinking into a particular objective, such as how to market your business or plan the perfect holiday. Other times we'll just want to give our creative imagination the freedom to take flight and wait for something to emerge. Some of the greatest discoveries have come through dreams or by getting our rational minds out of the way and allowing a creative solution to arise spontaneously.

Think of yourself as a creative person and approach everything that you do without preconceived ideas or assumptions. If one approach doesn't work, be willing to take another one. Being creative isn't about being original, it's about adopting a relaxed, open and confident mindset and seeing what happens. When we live creatively we are open to the unexpected and we are less likely to feel threatened by change or uncertainty. We are alert and awake to everything around us and this enables us to respond immediately to whatever is going on around us. We are living creatively.

Keep thinking creatively. Reconnect with your talents and seek out new ones. Give yourself the time to explore your creativity and spend time with people who are naturally creative. Get excited about making new connections and associations and seeing where they lead. Make space in all areas of your life for creativity and see what happens. It might surprise you.

Which area of 'Creativity' are you curious about: Beliefs, Blocked, Confidence, Inspiration, Thinking or Time? Find the area and then the question that feels right for you below it. Follow the links.

Beliefs

Do you consider yourself a creative person?

Do you think creativity is only for certain types of people?

Do you know when you are being creative?

Would you like to feel more creative?

Blocked

Are you afraid to be creative?

Are you bored and tired of your day-to-day life?

Confidence

Are you afraid of other people's opinions regarding your creativity?

Do you set your standards too high?

Inspiration

Do you know what makes you feel creative?

Brainstorming, p96, Creativity, p114, Curiosity, p117, Emotions, p131, Happiness, p164, Intuition, p170, Luck, p187, Play, p232, Stories, p271, Synchronicity, p283

Do you try new things?

Brainstorming, p96, Change, p99, Comfort Zone, p105, Curiosity, p117, Habits, p162, Metaphor, p191, Perspectives, p222, Play, p232, Spider Diagrams, p269, Talents, p286

Thinking

Do you solve problems with creative solutions?

Big Picture, p83, Brainstorming, p96, Creativity, p114, Intuition, p170, Lightbulb Moment, p180, Metaphor, p191, Problem Solving, p235, Spider Diagrams, p269, Visualisation, p302

Time

Do you have time to be creative?

Accountability, p56, Balance, p75, Compromise, p106, Creativity, p114, De-cluttering, p122, Goals, p153, Prioritise, p234, Procrastination, p239, Routines, p259, Time Management, p290

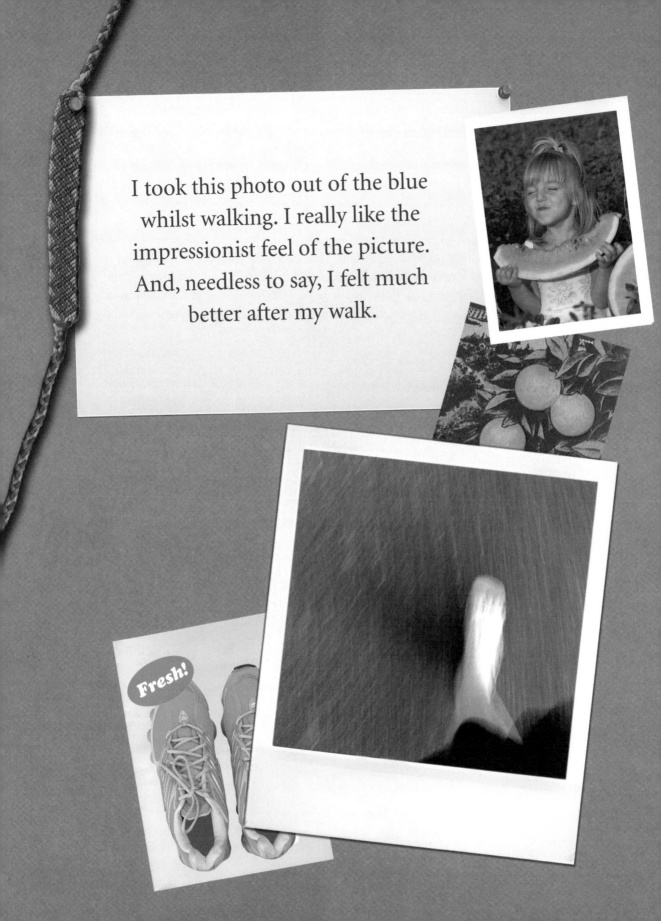

I took this photo out of the blue whilst walking. I really like the impressionist feel of the picture. And, needless to say, I felt much better after my walk.

Health & Fitness

Our bodies want us to listen to them, to let them play and have fun, to feel them as they stamp, curl and stretch. But we tend to focus on them visually and judge them for what they look like. If we pay attention to today's impossible standard of beauty, we'll never be at home in our own skin. To be fit, healthy and comfortable with our body, we want to look to the inside, not the outside.

Your body is unique to you. You are not like anyone else, neither in the way you look nor in what your body needs. Once you take the time to pay attention to the way your body feels and notice its strength and flexibility, you suddenly become aware of things that you can't believe you missed before. Our bodies communicate to us all the time. They tell us when they are tired and when they are full. They tell us when they want to stretch and when they're in pain. Our emotions are also communications from our body. You'll know whether you're angry or frightened or happy or stressed from what your body is telling you. Learning to listen to your body is a far more effective tool to finding good health than any diet or exercise regime can be.

The first part of becoming healthy is celebrating the internal beauty and strengths you do have. If you are in reasonable health that is definitely worth being proud of, no matter what your size. If you're tired or feeling poorly all the time you can't succeed at your goals and may not be taking an active part in life. Your physical health is at the heart of your wellbeing and connects to problems in many other areas.

Because your body is unique, you want to choose your own path to getting fit and healthy. Your body is an amazing machine that loves to be used, so find an activity that it likes and build it into your routine. When you are doing something you enjoy that's beneficial to your body you're far more likely to make time for it, stick to it and benefit from it. It pays to be creative too. Variety is important in life and our bodies respond well to it. The more activities you do, the more muscles get used. And if you keep the food you eat colourful and balanced you'll probably be eating most of the different nutrients that your body requires.

The way you prioritise your wellbeing says a lot about how you feel about yourself in general. The difficult part is that the worse we feel about ourselves, the harder it is to give up the unhealthy food or to get out there and enjoy activities that could make us happier. The opposite is true too. Just as we can neglect ourselves, we can overdo our workout regime and diet, which might mean we want to look at why we feel the need to push ourselves so hard.

The more you choose to respect your body and celebrate its strengths the greater you'll notice your self-confidence becoming. Like a positive circle, as well as your self-confidence growing, you'll notice the trust in your body increasing and you'll find yourself embracing the energised and joyful life that you have chosen to lead and the body that supports it.

Which area of 'Health & Fitness' do you want to do something about: Diet, Excess, Exercise, Lifestyle, Self-Image or Time Management? Find the area and then the question that feels right for you below it. Follow the links.

Diet

Do you eat healthily?

Control, p111, Emotions, p131, Excess, p135, Habits, p162, Intuition, p170, Listening, p181, Planning, p225

Excess

Do you do too much of anything?

Balance, p75, Control, p111, Excess, p135, Guilt, p159, Habits, p162, Inner Child, p168, Letting Go, p176, Relaxation, p251, Saying 'No', p262, Stress, p273

Exercise

Do you know what exercise you enjoy?

Beliefs, p79, Comfort Zone, p105, Creativity, p114, Happiness, p164, Intuition, p170, Laughter, p174, Personality Typing, p219, Play, p232, Talents, p286, Values, p298

Do you practise regular exercise?

Accountability, p56, Achievement, p58, Action, p61, Assumptions, p67, Balance, p75, Comfort Zone, p105, Forgiveness, p148, Goals, p153, Planning, p225, Routines, p259, Time Management, p290

Do you know what stops you from exercising?

Advantages, p62, Beliefs, p79, Comfort Zone, p105, Confidence, p107, Failure, p140, Fear, p141, Focus, p146, Motivation, p199, Perfectionism, p216, Procrastination, p239, Roles, p254

Do you know how to motivate yourself to exercise?

Accountability, p56, Confidence, p107, Goals, p153, Life Ambition, p179, Motivation, p199, Planning, p225, Prioritise, p234, Procrastination, p239, Success, p279, Time Management, p290, Visualisation, p302

Lifestyle

Are you happy with your general state of fitness and health?

Accountability, p56, Advantages, p62, Balance, p75, Breathing, p97, Change, p99, Excess, p135, Inner Child, p168, Perfectionism, p216, Procrastination, p239, Success, p279, Worrying, p307

Do you listen to your body?

Acceptance, p54, Body/Heart/Mind Types, p85, Breathing, p97, Control, p111, Curiosity, p117, Inner Child, p168, Intuition, p170, Lightbulb Moment, p180, Listening, p181, Trust, p293

Self-image
Do you like your body?

Acceptance, p54, Assumptions, p67, Body Image, p88, Body Language, p91, Change, p99, Confidence, p107, Envy, p133, Non-judgemental, p204, Perspectives, p222, Style, p277

Time Management
Do you make time for looking after your body?

Accountability, p56, Boundaries, p94, Choices, p102, Compromise, p106, De-cluttering, p122, Goals, p153, Habits, p162, Planning, p225, Prioritise, p234, Saying 'No', p262, Time Management, p290

Do you know how much time you want to commit to health and fitness?

Balance, p75, Big Picture, p83, Boundaries, p94, Choices, p102, Excess, p135, Goals, p153, Intent, p169, Life Ambition, p179, Motivation, p199, Planning, p225, Prioritise, p234, Time Management, p290

Do you want to change your routines?

Change, p99, Compromise, p106, Goals, p153, Optimism, p208, Outcome, p209, Planning, p225, Procrastination, p239, Routines, p259, Success, p279, Time Management, p290

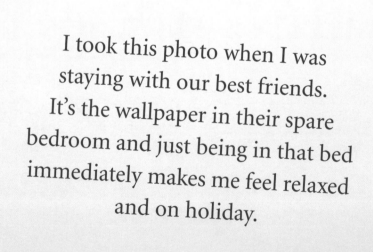

I took this photo when I was
staying with our best friends.
It's the wallpaper in their spare
bedroom and just being in that bed
immediately makes me feel relaxed
and on holiday.

Rest & Relaxation ●

Rest and relaxation is often the last thing we think of when we are on a mission to reorganise our lives and reach for new and better goals. Instead we choose to push ourselves to the limit. But think of a firework blazing across the sky; it soon vanishes with a disappointing puff.

Rest and relaxation are valuable tools. Taking time to schedule enjoyment into our lives, and creating rituals that ensure a good night's sleep, can do wonders to give our lives balance and energy. Proper sleep leads naturally to more productive days. Fun on holiday leads to a fresher mind. It might be that one of the best investments for our future success is a better mattress or a weekend away.

Modern living itself drives us to be up and about, constantly achieving and taking in information. Our bodies and brains are designed to work through the daylight hours, but still many of us persist in thinking that if we don't keep going, we'll miss something important.

The night can seem like an opportunity; hours more to achieve what we didn't quite have time for in the day. But without proper sleep, our days become a haze of unfocused thoughts and mood swings.

When we feel ourselves becoming angry, worried, unable to cope, even sad, rather than recognising that we need to rest, many of us take on even more commitments and responsibilities in the hope that we'll achieve more and feel better. We become part of the endless cycle of stress.

Once you know yourself and what relaxes and re-energises you, you can find ways of pacing yourself and move from feeling stretched and exhausted to energised and productive. Down time is an essential part of life. Value sleep and leisure and you'll find you'll be able to make better use of that brief commodity – time.

Which area of 'Rest & Relaxation' would you like to change: Laughter, Over-committed, Relaxation, Sleep or Stress and Worrying? Find the area and then the question that feels right for you below it. Follow the links.

Laughter

Do you know what makes you laugh?

Do you know who you laugh with?

Over-committed

Do you take on too much?

Do you spend more time on other people than yourself?

Are you too busy to relax?

Relaxation

Do you find relaxing difficult?

Does doing nothing make you feel guilty?

What sort of relaxation suits you?

Are you spending too much time doing nothing?

Accountability, p56, Balance, p75, Comfort Zone, p105, Confidence, p107, Depression, p128, Fear, p141, Loneliness, p186, Motivation, p199, Planning, p225, Procrastination, p239, Relaxation, p251, Routines, p259

Sleep

Do you sleep enough?

Balance, p75, Fear, p141, Habits, p162, Listening, p181, Planning, p225, Relaxation, p251, Routines, p259, Sleep, p266, Stories, p271, Stress, p273, Time Management, p290

Do you sleep better alone?

Advantages, p62, Blame, p83, Boundaries, p94, Compromise, p106, Feedback, p144, Sleep, p266, Stories, p271

Have you got a good environment to sleep in?

Boundaries, p94, De-cluttering, p122, Intuition, p170, Saying 'No', p262, Sleep, p266, Style, p277

Are you sleeping too much?

Assumptions, p67, Balance, p75, Beliefs, p79, Comfort Zone, p105 , Depression, p128, Loneliness, p186, Motivation, p199, Planning, p225, Routines, p259, Sleep, p266

Stress and Worrying

Do you feel stressed or worried?

Big Picture, p83, Blame, p83, Breathing, p97, Confidence, p107, Control, p111, Failure, p140, Fear, p141, Forgiveness, p148, Guilt, p159, Laughter, p174, Perspectives, p222, Planning, p225, Regret, p249, Stress, p273

Are you aware of when you're stressed?

Depression, p128, Emotions, p131, Patterns, p212, Stress, p273, Worrying, p307

Can you switch off?

Body/Heart/Mind Type, p85, Breathing, p97, Control, p111, Excess, p135, Laughter, p174, Meditation, p190, Relaxation, p251, Sleep, p266

There was something about this photo which really reminded me of those wonderful school friendships when you're young and in a gang, giggling and just having fun.

Friends & Social Life ●

Good friendships can often be the glue that holds our lives together. We can feel more intimate with our close friends than with anyone else and rely on them for everything – from being a shoulder to cry on to sharing our most joyful moments. Although we may have many people in our lives that we would loosely term as friends, those we consider our dear friends are more select. They are the ones that we know are unconditionally there for us no matter what.

True friendship can withstand all the ups and downs of life, the rites of passage such as marriage and parenthood and even months or years of separation. How many times have you been reunited with a long lost friend and simply picked up from where you left off? That old familiar feeling of intimacy and connection is still there.

Good friends are able to give and take and know that the balance will always be redressed. We never begrudge the time and energy that we spend giving to a cherished friend because we love them and we know that we are valued, loved and appreciated by them. And that they wouldn't hesitate to reciprocate.

Different friends bring out different facets of us. Some friends appeal to our more serious, thoughtful side while others reflect our extrovert, adventurous nature. You might chose to go on a trekking holiday in Nepal with one friend, go clubbing with another and discuss world politics with a third. The beauty of good friendships is that we can be ourselves even if we don't have everything in common or share the same taste in music or food. Often these differences enhance our friendships and help us to extend our boundaries and look at the world from a different perspective. Our friends help us see that each of us is unique and special.

Good friends make us feel energised, uplifted, valued and supported. But some friends can drain us and make us feel tired or even depressed. It's as if they suck the life force out of us and give nothing in return. We may not want to let go of a friendship, but just to no longer actively cultivate it and allow it simply to fade away, until we're ready to be reunited. Seeing less of friends we no longer feel a connection with leaves room in our lives for new friends. The more we discover about ourselves, the more likely we are to attract new friends into our lives who mirror those new qualities in us. Resist making assumptions about people you meet. Get to know them and you might be surprised at how much you get to like them. They could even become a best friend.

Or maybe you don't want as many friends. You're happy to go out on your own – whether travelling, to a film festival or to join in a game of netball. You may meet new people along the way or you may be so carried away by what's going on around you that you don't notice you're on your own. Whether you'd like to do more on your own or make time for being with friends, don't hesitate. Just get out there.

Which area of 'Friends & Social Life' would you like to be clearer about: Availability, Intimacy, Moving On, Social Life or Variety and Spontaneity? Find the area and then the question that feels right for you below it. Follow the links.

Availability

Are you too busy for friends and social life?

Advantages, p62, Balance, p75, Fear, p141, Planning, p225, Relaxation, p251, Routines, p259, Time Management, p290, Work/Life Balance, p305

Do you feel you make yourself too available to your friends and other people?

Boundaries, p94, Confidence, p107, Excess, p135, Feedback, p144, Giving, p152, Letting Go, p176, Saying 'No', p262

Do you think your friends and other people are too busy to spend time with you?

Assumptions, p67, Beliefs, p79, Blame, p83, Confidence, p107, Envy, p133, Loneliness, p186, Perspectives, p222

Intimacy

Do you think anyone would want you as a friend?

Advantages, p62, Assumptions, p67, Authentic, p72, Beliefs, p79, Comfort Zone, p105, Confidence, p107, Fear, p141, Intuition, p170, Loneliness, p186, Mirroring, p194, Regret, p249

Do you feel valued by your friends?

Anger, p66, Assumptions, p67, Beliefs, p79, Control, p111, Forgiveness, p148, Listening, p181, Loneliness, p186, Mirroring, p194, Perspectives, p222, Trust, p293, Values, p298

Do you find it difficult to trust your friends?

Assumptions, p67, Authentic, p72, Blame, p83, Confidence, p107, Fear, p141, Forgiveness, p148, Intuition, p170, Mirroring, p194, Trust, p293, Values, p298

Do you have a friend you think of as a soul mate?

Authentic, p72, Connection, p110, Gratitude, p157, Happiness, p164, Laughter, p174, Listening, p181, Luck, p187, Mirroring, p194, Synchronicity, p283, Trust, p293, Values, p298

Moving on

Are there any outstanding issues between you and your friends?

Acceptance, p54, Anger, p66, Blame, p83, Defensiveness, p125, Feedback, p144, Forgiveness, p148, Guilt, p159, Letting Go, p176, Listening, p181, Regret, p249, Worrying, p307

Are your friends preventing you from changing?

Assumptions, p67, Authentic, p72, Boundaries, p94, Change, p99, Fear, p141, Listening, p181, Problem Solving, p235 , Saying 'No', p262, Trust, p293

Have you outgrown any of your friends or have they outgrown you?

Action, p61, Authentic, p72, Big Picture, p83, Boundaries, p94, Change, p99, Choices, p102, Confidence, p107, Forgiveness, p148, Guilt, p159, Letting Go, p176, Mirroring, p194, Regret, p249, Saying 'No', p262

Social life

Do you need many people in your social circle?

Belonging, p82, Boundaries, p94, Confidence, p107, Connection, p110, Excess, p135, Laughter, p174, Loneliness, p186, Personality Typing, p219, Values, p298

Do you enjoy socialising and meeting new people?

Assumptions, p67, Beliefs, p79, Body/Heart/Mind Types, p85, Comfort Zone, p105, Confidence, p107, Fear, p141, Goals, p153, Loneliness, p186, Non-judgemental, p204, Trust, p293

Have you the confidence to expand your social circle?

Action, p61, Affirmations, p63, Beliefs, p79, Body Image, p88, Body Language, p91, Comfort Zone, p105 , Confidence, p107, Failure, p140, Motivation, p199, Perspectives, p222, Success, p279, Synchronicity, p283, Trust, p293

Do you spend too much time socialising?

Balance, p75, Compromise, p106, Giving, p152, Saying 'No', p262, Time Management, p290

Do you spend too much of your social life online?

Comfort Zone, p105, Confidence, p107, Excess, p135, Fear, p141, Loneliness, p186, Motivation, p199

Variety and Spontaneity

Have you got the right balance between work and play?

Balance, p75, Boundaries, p94, Compromise, p106, Laughter, p174, Play, p232, Relaxation, p251, Saying 'No', p262, Time Management, p290, Work/Life Balance, p305

Do you know what type of activities you enjoy?

Body/Heart/Mind Type, p85, Brainstorming, p96, Creativity, p114, Intuition, p170, Play, p232, Talents, p286, Values, p298

Do you find it difficult to try new social experiences?

Confidence, p107, Curiosity, p117, Fear, p141, Goals, p153, Habits, p162, Role Models, p256

One of the perks of my job is
going to fantastic offices and
seeing views of London that
no one ever gets to see.

Work ●

Our working life is a big part of our daily existence and many of us spend more time at work than we do with our friends and family. For some of us work is extremely fulfilling and gives us a sense of who we are and where our talents lie. It enables us to express ourselves creatively and intellectually and gives us a framework to our lives and a feeling that we are doing something worthwhile with our time. When we're doing work that we like we don't count the passing hours as we're totally absorbed. We may even sense that we have a natural vocation and that we are doing what we are meant to do and using all of our natural abilities. But for many of us work is a means to an end, at best something we know how to do and at worst, sheer drudgery which simply pays the bills.

Whether you enjoy your work or not, you may find yourself working long hours, especially in a new job, after a promotion or if there's been a lot of change in your department. No matter what the reason, it's important to get a good work/life balance if you're going to function at your optimum. If you are regularly focusing more on your professional life than your personal life something may be out of kilter. Ask yourself why that might be – could it be avoidance or escapism from other areas of your life? Discover your boundaries and learn to say 'No' to such long working hours.

As well as working long hours, you may be doing a job that doesn't fulfil you. Begin to ask yourself why that is and start questioning your beliefs and assumptions about work because they may be undermining your capacity to do the kind of work that you would love. If you doubt your abilities and don't give yourself credit for your talents and skills it's unlikely that anyone else will. Discover as well what motivates you, what you are passionate about. Align yourself with an industry that matches your core values and criteria. Whatever work you choose to do, if the ethos of an organisation is at variance with your own, it's unlikely that you'll gain any job satisfaction. When you limit yourself in this way you deny yourself the pleasure of doing something you could enjoy and excel in.

Believing in yourself and having the confidence to recognise your worth gives you a much better chance of identifying the right kind of work for you. Feeling confident enables you to perform well in your work, to hold your own and form good relationships with your colleagues. It also motivates you to go for a promotion or even change jobs if you don't feel valued or happy. Change at work can feel very threatening, but again, will be easier when you're feeling confident about yourself.

Before you can identify your dream job and start making it happen, recognise and acknowledge everything that you have to offer. Each of us is unique and we each have our own particular style and abilities. When we express these we are being true to ourselves and developing our potential. Keep asking yourself questions about who you are and how you really feel about your work; be open to discovering that you really can do what you love and love what you do.

Which area of 'Work' would you like to explore: Change, Career Development, Job Satisfaction, Performance, Relationships, Working Environment or Work/Life Balance? Find the area and then the question that feels right for you below it. Follow the links.

Change

Have you been fired from a job or made redundant?
Acceptance, p54, Accountability, p56, Anger, p66, Beliefs, p79, Big Picture, p83, Blame, p83, Change, p99, Confidence, p107, Depression, p128, Emotions, p131, Failure, p140, Forgiveness, p148, Letting Go, p176, Perspectives, p222, Planning, p225, Regret, p249, Stress, p273, Talents, p286, Trust, p293, Victim, p300, Worrying, p307

Have you chosen to quit a job?
Action, p61, Big Picture, p83, Change, p99, Confidence, p107, Decisions, p121, Focus, p146, Intent, p169, Life Ambition, p179, Motivation, p199, Optimism, p208, Patterns, p212, Planning, p225, Talents, p286, Values, p298

Are you unsure about the future of your job?
Assumptions, p67, Change, p99, Choices, p102, Confidence, p107, Fear, p141, Feedback, p144, Negotiation, p203, Perspectives, p222, Planning, p225, Questions, p246, Spider Diagrams, p269, Values, p298, Worrying p307

Are you putting off changing your job?
Action, p61, Big Picture, p83, Comfort Zone, p105, Fear, p141, Goals, p153, Intent, p169, Life Ambition, p179, Motivation, p199, Optimism, p208, Outcome, p209, Planning, p225, Procrastination, p239, Trust, p293

Have you got a new job/boss you find challenging?
Accountability, p56, Assumptions, p67, Beliefs, p79, Change, p99, Comfort Zone, p105, Confidence, p107, Goals, p153, Motivation, p199, Planning, p225, Stress, p273, Success, p279

Do you often leave jobs?
Accountability, p56, Advantages, p62, Belonging, p82, Change, p99, Confidence, p107, Excess, p135, Failure, p140, Life Ambition, p179, Patterns, p212, Perfectionism, p216, Regret, p249, Talents, p286

Is there a lot of change in your workplace?
Assumptions, p67, Beliefs, p79, Change, p99, Comfort Zone, p105, Compromise, p106, Control, p111, Decisions, p121, Fear, p141, Letting Go, p176, Planning, p225, Stress, p273, Trust, p293, Values, p298

Career Development

Have you been given more responsibilities?

Accountability, p56, Boundaries, p94, Change, p99, Compromise, p106, Confidence, p107, Decisions, p121, Feedback, p144, Negotiation, p203, Perfectionism, p216, Planning, p225, Prioritise, p234, Saying 'No', p262, Stress, p273, Time Management, p290

Are you aware of your potential?

Achievement, p58, Beliefs, p79, Body/Heart/Mind Types, p85, Curiosity, p117, Feedback, p144, Intuition, p170, Lightbulb Moment, p180, Personality Typing, p219, Talents, p286, Values, p298

Would you like a promotion?

Accountability, p56, Achievement, p58, Action, p61, Affirmations, p63, Body Language, p91 Confidence, p107, Feedback, p144, Focus, p146, Goals, p153, Intent, p169, Life Ambition, p179, Negotiation, p203, Optimism, p208, Planning, p225, Problem Solving, p235, Questions, p246

Would you like to have a clear career path?

Big Picture, p83, Choices, p102, Goals, p153, Life Ambition, p179, Planning, p225, Spider Diagrams, p269, Success, p279, Values, p298

Would you rather be self-employed?

Accountability, p56, Action, p61, Confidence, p107, Control, p111, Focus, p146, Goals, p153, Intuition, p170, Life Ambition, p179, Loneliness, p186, Motivation, p199, Planning, p225, Stress, p273, Success, p279, Talents, p286, Time Management, p290, Values, p298, Work/Life Balance, p305

Job satisfaction

Would you like to feel more fulfilled in your work?

Absorption, p53, Achievement, p58, Creativity, p114, Goals, p153, Life Ambition, p179, Money, p196, Success, p279, Talents, p286, Values, p298, Work/Life Balance, p305

Do you want to earn more money?

Accountability, p56, Action, p61, Affirmations, p63, Assumptions, p67, Big Picture, p83, Confidence, p107, Fear, p141, Intent, p169, Language, p173, Money, p196, Negotiation, p203, Outcome, p209, Perspectives, p222, Success, p279, Victim, p300

Performance

Do you get distracted easily?

Blame, p83, Body/Heart/Mind Types, p85, Bottom Line, p94, Boundaries, p94, Compromise, p106, Control, p111, Focus, p146, Goals, p153, Habits, p162, Intent, p169, Planning, p225, Prioritise, p234, Saying 'No', p262, Victim, p300

Do you find it hard to meet deadlines?

Accountability, p56, Compromise, p106, Control, p111, Decisions, p121, Focus, p146, Perfectionism, p216, Planning, p225, Prioritise, p234, Procrastination, p239, Time Management, p290

Are you aware of how you are performing at work?

Accountability, p56, Achievement, p58, Balance, p75, Blame, p83, Defensiveness, p125, Feedback, p144, Listening, p181, Patterns, p212, Perspectives, p222, Roles, p254, Success, p279

Do you feel that your colleagues underestimate you?

Accountability, p56, Assumptions, p67, Blame, p83, Confidence, p107, Defensiveness, p125, Feedback, p144, Listening, p181, Mirroring, p194, Questions, p246, Victim, p300

Would you like to be more creative?

Absorption, p53, Brainstorming, p96, Change, p99, Comfort Zone, p105, Creativity, p114, Curiosity, p117, Metaphor, p191, Perspectives, p222, Spider Diagrams, p269, Visualisation, p302

Is your performance affected by unresolved issues?

Anger, p66, Blame, p83, Compromise, p106, Control, p111, Defensiveness, p125, Fear, p141 Feedback, p144, Forgiveness, p148, Guilt, p159, Letting Go, p176, Negotiation, p203, Non-judgemental, p204, Perspectives, p222, Saying 'No', p262, Victim, p300, Worrying, p307

Do you know how to be your own boss?

Accountability, p56, Balance, p75, Confidence, p107, Decisions, p121, Focus, p146, Goals, p153, Life Ambition, p179, Motivation, p199, Outcome, p209, Planning, p225, Prioritise, p234, Routines, p259, Success, p279, Time Management, p290, Work/Life Balance, p305

Relationships

Do you get on well with your colleagues?

Assumptions, p67, Belonging, p82, Blame, p83, Compromise, p106, Curiosity, p117, Defensiveness, p125, Envy, p133, Feedback, p144, Gratitude, p157, Laughter, p174, Letting Go, p176, Listening, p181, Non-judgemental, p204, Personality Typing, p219, Role Models, p256, Values, p298, Victim, p300

Do you end up doing everyone else's work?

Accountability, p56, Advantages, p62, Blame, p83, Boundaries, p94, Confidence, p107, Control, p111, Giving, p152, Guilt, p159, Intent, p169, Negotiation, p203, Saying 'No', p262, Time Management, p290

Are you comfortable saying what you think?

Authentic, p72, Body Language, p91, Bottom Line, p94, Comfort Zone, p105, Compromise, p106, Confidence, p107, Defensiveness, p125, Feedback, p144, Language, p173, Listening, p181, Negotiation, p203, Questions, p246, Saying 'No', p262

Do you shy away from feedback?

Accountability, p56, Assumptions, p67, Blame, p83, Confidence, p107, Control, p111, Defensiveness, p125, Failure, p140, Fear, p141, Feedback, p144, Inner Child, p168, Listening, p181, Perspectives, p222, Trust, p293, Worrying, p307

Do you fancy one of your colleagues?

Big Picture, p83, Body Language, p91, Boundaries, p94, Decisions, p121, Intent, p169, Intuition, p170, Life Ambition, p179, Loneliness, p186, Outcome, p209, Patterns, p212, Perspectives, p222, Regret, p249, Saying 'No', p262, Trust, p293, Values, p298

Do you know what to do if your office romance ends?

Acceptance, p54, Anger, p66, Big Picture, p83, Blame, p83, Boundaries, p94, Change, p99, Confidence, p107, Failure, p140, Forgiveness, p148, Letting Go, p176, Loneliness, p186, Negotiation, p203, Victim, p300, Worrying, p307

Working environment

Do you know what your perfect working environment is?

Assumptions, p67, Balance, p75, Control, p111, Creativity, p114, De-cluttering, p122, Intuition, p170, Perfectionism, p216, Personality Typing, p219, Style, p277, Visualisation, p302

Do you feel overloaded with clutter – on your desk, in your computer, diary and mind?

Accountability, p56, Advantages, p62, Balance, p75, Blame, p83, Change, p99, Comfort Zone, p105, Control, p111, De-cluttering, p122, Habits, p162, Prioritise, p234, Procrastination, p239, Routines, p259, Time Management, p290

Work/Life Balance

Does your current work/life balance suit you?

Balance, p75, Balance Chart, p76, Boundaries, p94, Compromise, p106, De-cluttering, p122, Happiness, p164, Personality Typing, p219, Time Management, p290, Work/Life Balance, p305

Do you tend to work too hard?

Achievement, p58, Advantages, p62, Balance, p75, Balance Chart, p76, Belonging, p82, Big Picture, p83, Boundaries, p94, Comfort Zone, p105, Control, p111, Excess, p135, Failure, p140, Happiness, p164, Loneliness, p186, Perfectionism, p216, Relaxation, p251, Stress, p273, Values, p298

Do you find it difficult to prioritise work?

Absorption, p53, Action, p61, Big Picture, p83, Choices, p102, Comfort Zone, p105, Depression, p128, Focus, p146, Goals, p153, Motivation, p199, Outcome, p209, Planning, p225, Prioritise, p234, Procrastination, p239, Time Management, p290, Values, p298

My family at the beach at night.
What could be nicer? The noise
of the sea, the chattering of
family voices and a beautiful
starry sky.

Family ●

Whether you get on with your family or not, your family is with you from the day you are born to the day you die, and they don't go away, even if you choose to ignore them. These people are the family you were born into and they may also be the family you've created. Your family members can be inspirational and supportive or they can be destructive and oppositional – or a mixture of all of those – and they're a powerful presence in your life. Whether you choose to see them or not, you can't ignore them and their influence, but you don't want it to shape your life either.

You are an individual with your own life to lead, but if you have a good relationship with your family, your life can be enhanced. It's wonderful to have siblings and parents who support you. After all, they understand you like no other and have known you for longer than everyone else. And you can't swap your family so there's no point wishing your siblings were more like the sisters in *Little Women* by Louisa May Alcott – your family is what you've got. If they don't feel like the 'right' family for you, no doubt you're stronger as an individual for having to find your own way.

What you see as bad luck in life might be in part down to the way in which you were brought up and the relationship you have with your family, but move along from that. It can feel easier to remember back to the times you sobbed yourself to sleep rather than the times you bonded over ice creams at the beach. What's important is how you choose to react to your family and the role you find within it that works best for you. There's no point waiting for them to change, instead appreciate what they do have to offer you. And by accepting and forgiving them and changing yourself you will get back the energy you have depleted hoping they'll one day be different.

You may feel so disillusioned by your family that you consciously decide to reject them and their ways and be different, yet even by doing that you may find that you're behaving exactly the same way as they did. You may discover you've made choices and are repeating patterns that have been going on for generations. Even if you do exactly the opposite to them and choose a new pattern, you might unconsciously be following the script of another part of your family – the part that always broke the patterns. It is only by exploring your family and coming to terms with the fact that you cannot be an island that you can broaden your vision about who you can become.

Don't stop at your family. Look at other families you have known to help you discover your own identity and sense of uniqueness. Maybe you grew up always spending time with and admiring your best friend's family and it is those memories that hold the values that you now want to create in your life. Your family may have been kind and loving, but it's the wild freedom in your friend's family that you crave. Rather than blame your family for not having given you everything, embrace the good things that came out of your relationship and remember them.

Which area of 'Family' would you like to reflect on: Change, Children, Communication, Family, Growing Up or Loss? Find the area and then the question that feels right for you below it. Follow the links.

Change
Is there a lot of change in your family?

Anger, p66, Assumptions, p67, Belonging, p82, Blame, p83, Boundaries, p94, Change, p99, Compromise, p106, Confidence, p107, Control, p111, Depression, p128, Forgiveness, p148, Happiness, p164, Inner Child, p168, Letting Go, p176, Loneliness, p186, Perspectives, p222, Regret, p249, Roles, p254, Stress, p273, Victim, p300

Would you like your family to change?

Acceptance, p54, Anger, p66, Assumptions, p67, Blame, p83, Compromise, p106, Depression, p128, Forgiveness, p148, Listening, p181, Mirroring, p194, Negotiation, p203, Patterns, p212, Perfectionism, p216, Problem Solving, p235, Roles, p254

Children
Did you have a happy childhood?

Acceptance, p54, Anger, p66, Assumptions, p67, Belonging, p82, Blame, p83, Confidence, p107, Emotions, p131, Envy, p133, Forgiveness, p148, Inner Child, p168, Letting Go, p176, Patterns, p212, Perfectionism, p216, Play, p232, Regret, p249, Stories, p271, Victim, p300

Do you feel you are a good parent/child?

Anger, p66, Assumptions, p67, Beliefs, p79, Blame, p83, Boundaries, p94, Emotions, p131, Failure, p140, Forgiveness, p148, Giving, p152, Inner Child, p168, Intuition, p170, Laughter, p174, Listening, p181, Patterns, p212, Perfectionism, p216, Roles, p254, Role Models, p256, Stories, p271, Success, p279, Trust, p293, Worrying, p307

Communication
Are you able to communicate with your family?

Belonging, p82, Blame, p83, Body Language, p91, Boundaries, p94, Change, p99, Choices, p102, Compromise, p106, Connection, p110, Control, p111, Curiosity, p117, Defensiveness, p125, Feedback, p144, Inner Child, p168, Listening, p181, Negotiation, p203, Questions, p246, Roles, p254, Saying 'No', p262, Trust, p293, Worrying, p307

Do you feel that there are too many demands on you from your family?

Anger, p66, Blame, p83, Boundaries, p94, Compromise, p106, Control, p111, Giving, p152, Inner Child, p168, Letting Go, p176, Listening, p181, Mirroring, p194, Negotiation, p203, Saying 'No', p262, Stress, p273

Do you know how to ask for support from your family?

Assumptions, p67, Belonging, p82, Boundaries, p94, Comfort Zone, p105, Confidence, p107, Forgiveness, p148, Giving, p152, Intent, p169, Letting Go, p176, Negotiation, p203, Outcome, p209, Planning, p225, Success, p279

Family

Do you see your family often enough?

Balance, p75, Belonging, p82, Choices, p102, Connection, p110, De-cluttering, p122, Forgiveness, p148, Goals, p153, Guilt, p159, Intent, p169, Outcome, p209, Planning, p225, Prioritise, p234, Regret, p249, Time Management, p290, Work/Life Balance, p305

Are you embarrassed about your family?

Advantages, p62, Anger, p66, Blame, p83, Body/Heart/Mind Types, p85, Change, p99, Confidence, p107, Control, p111, Emotions, p131, Forgiveness, p148, Inner Child, p168, Letting Go, p176, Mirroring, p194, Personality Typing, p219, Values, p298, Victim, p300

Can you identify which values are yours and which values are your family's?

Body/Heart/Mind Types, p85, Inner Child, p168, Personality Typing, p219, Saying 'No', p262, Values, p298

Growing Up

Do you feel yourself when you're with your family?

Authentic, p72, Belonging, p82, Comfort Zone, p105, Confidence, p107, Connection, p110, Emotions, p131, Inner Child, p168, Life Ambition, p179, Mirroring, p194, Patterns, p212, Relaxation, p251, Roles, p254, Values, p298

Do you feel loved by your family?

Belonging, p82, Connection, p110, Depression, p128, Emotions, p131, Forgiveness, p148, Inner Child, p168, Laughter, p174, Loneliness, p186, Luck, p187, Perspectives, p222, Play, p232, Regret, p249, Roles, p254, Victim, p300

Do you find yourself repeating patterns from your family?

Beliefs, p79, Change, p99, Choices, p102, Comfort Zone, p105, Confidence, p107, Decisions, p121, Fear, p141, Forgiveness, p148, Guilt, p159, Mirroring, p194, Patterns, p212, Roles, p254, Stories, p271

Loss

Are you scared of leaving your nest?

Accountability, p56, Assumptions, p67, Beliefs, p79, Belonging, p82, Change, p99, Comfort Zone, p105, Confidence, p107, Connection, p110, Decisions, p121, Emotions, p131, Fear, p141, Goals, p153, Guilt, p159, Letting Go, p176, Motivation, p199, Planning, p225, Procrastination, p239, Roles, p254, Role Models, p256, Saying 'No', p262, Trust, p293, Worrying, p307

Are you scared of losing a member of your family?

Acceptance, p54, Assumptions, p67, Beliefs, p79, Change, p99, Comfort Zone, p105, Control, p111, Emotions, p131, Envy, p133, Fear, p141, Inner Child, p168, Letting Go, p176, Loneliness, p186, Optimism, p208, Synchronicity, p283, Trust, p293, Worrying, p307

Are you struggling to cope with loss in your family?

Acceptance, p54, Anger, p66, Blame, p83, Breathing, p97, Change, p99, Depression, p128, Emotions, p131, Fear, p141, Forgiveness, p148, Letting Go, p176, Loneliness, p186, Regret, p249, Roles, p254, Stress, p273, Victim, p300

Money ●

Money can be a very emotive subject. We need money to live, but how important is it to our essential happiness and wellbeing? Some of the richest people in the world have claimed that money doesn't make us happy and yet many of us act as if it's the answer to everything.

The reality is that money is just a simple tool – pieces of paper and coins – that we give or receive in exchange for goods or services and the reality is that it has no intrinsic value or meaning other than how we choose to perceive it. We give money its power by deciding how money makes us feel – good or bad, safe or anxious, optimistic or pessimistic.

What is your relationship with money? Do you covet it, hoard it, spend it, dream about it, fear the lack of it, feel you never have enough of it, worry how you are going to make it, feel anxious about how to hang onto it, worry about the responsibility of having too much of it? And what do you equate it with – freedom, comfort, prestige, kudos, security or power? If we don't have money we often believe that these things are not available to us.

Our beliefs and assumptions about money are almost always self-limiting and are often deeply rooted in our minds. For example, even though we consciously strive to acquire it, unconsciously we may believe that money is the root of all evil. Ambivalence like this can create conflict in us. Or we may assume that we don't have what it takes to make money and as a result we settle for less than we could. Needless to say, these negative beliefs perpetuate the lack of money that we fear.

By becoming more aware about your beliefs about money, you can start to change your thoughts and behaviours and develop a more positive relationship with it. Don't be afraid to challenge your assumptions about money. For example, if you believe that you have to hoard money because it's in short supply, ask yourself if that's really true. What would happen if you changed that belief and saw money as something that you could easily attract into your life?

If we have an attitude of wealth we trust that we will be provided for. That attitude then creates a positive energy around us that can attract more opportunities in all areas of our lives. In fact, the way you feel about money might even be a clue to how you feel about your life. If you don't feel deserving of financial abundance might you feel that way about other areas of your life?

By thinking about your attitude to money you will uncover all kinds of beliefs, assumptions and expectations that are creating your reality and experience around money. Once you've done that, you can start to change these patterns and develop a more confident, expansive and trusting mindset. See how wealthy you feel.

This is one of my favourite photos. I took it one day when I was being invited out to lunch at a very expensive restaurant. Can you believe the pods are loos and that there, in the middle of them, was this Japanese lady looking so beautiful. It's a scene that only money can buy. I felt lucky to have a camera, to be in that restaurant and to see such a stunning costume.

Which area of 'Money' would you like to get clear on: Beliefs, Confidence, Debt, Earning, Guilt, Relationships, Saving or Spending? Find the area and then the question that feels right for you below it. Follow the links.

Beliefs

Do you think money is the most important thing in life?

Achievement, p58, Assumptions, p67, Balance Chart, p76, Beliefs, p79, Belonging, p82, Big Picture, p83, Excess, p135, Fear, p141, Giving, p152, Happiness, p164, Intuition, p170, Life Ambition, p179, Money, p196, Prioritise, p234, Regret, p249, Success, p279, Values, p298

Do you know where your beliefs about money come from?

Assumptions, p67, Beliefs, p79, Money, p196, Patterns, p212, Perspectives, p222, Values, p298

Does money make you feel safe?

Advantages, p62, Assumptions, p67, Beliefs, p79, Belonging, p82, Big Picture, p83, Comfort Zone, p105, Confidence, p107, Connection, p110, Control, p111, Fear, p141, Happiness, p164, Inner Child, p168, Money, p196, Perspectives, p222, Trust, p293

Do you feel you have to spend money to have a good time?

Achievement, p58, Beliefs, p79, Brainstorming, p96, Creativity, p114, Happiness, p164, Laughter, p174, Money, p196, Play, p232, Relaxation, p251, Spider Diagrams, p269, Style, p277, Success, p279, Values, p298

Confidence

Do you worry about money?

Affirmations, p63, Assumptions, p67, Beliefs, p79, Big Picture, p83, Control, p111, Fear, p141, Life Ambition, p179, Money, p196, Optimism, p208, Perspectives, p222, Planning, p225, Spider Diagrams, p269, Stress, p273, Trust, p293, Visualisation, p302, Worrying, p307

Do you feel embarrassed talking about money?

Assumptions, p67, Beliefs, p79, Comfort Zone, p105, Confidence, p107, Guilt, p159, Metaphor, p191, Money, p196, Non-judgemental, p204, Perspectives, p222, Roles, p254, Stories, p271, Trust, p293, Values, p298

Debt

Is your debt out of control?

Accountability, p56, Big Picture, p83, Compromise, p106, Control, p111, Decisions, p121, Depression, p128, Excess, p135, Failure, p140, Fear, p141, Forgiveness, p148, Goals, p153, Money, p196, Motivation, p199, Prioritise, p234, Saying 'No', p262, Spider Diagrams, p269, Stress, p273

Do you find it difficult to ask for money when it is owed to you?

Action, p61, Anger, p66, Beliefs, p79, Blame, p83, Boundaries, p94, Confidence, p107, Failure, p140, Focus, p146, Forgiveness, p148, Goals, p153, Guilt, p159, Money, p196, Motivation, p199, Optimism, p208, Planning, p225, Success, p279, Trust, p293, Values, p298

Earning

Would you like to make more money?

Accountability, p56, Affirmations, p63, Beliefs, p79, Change, p99, Comfort Zone, p105, Confidence, p107, Creativity, p114, Envy, p133, Fear, p141, Focus, p146, Goals, p153, Listening, p181, Mirroring, p194, Motivation, p199, Optimism, p208, Planning, p225, Problem Solving, p235, Procrastination, p239, Role Models, p256, Success, p279, Talents, p286, Visualisation, p302

Do you believe you'll never earn enough money?

Advantages, p62, Assumptions, p67, Beliefs, p79, Confidence, p107, Fear, p141, Goals, p153, Money, p196, Motivation, p199, Planning, p225, Problem Solving, p235, Procrastination, p239, Success, p279, Talents, p286, Values, p298

Do you know your own worth?

Achievement, p58, Assumptions, p67, Beliefs, p79, Big Picture, p83, Confidence, p107, Depression, p128, Failure, p140, Gratitude, p157, Mirroring, p194, Money, p196, Optimism, p208, Perspectives, p222, Style, p277, Talents, p286, Trust, p293, Values, p298, Victim, p300

Do you know how much money you really need?

Assumptions, p67, Balance, p75, Belonging, p82, Big Picture, p83, Compromise, p106, Control, p111, Goals, p153, Life Ambition, p179, Money, p196, Perspectives, p222, Planning, p225, Prioritise, p234, Spider Diagrams, p269, Values, p298

Guilt

Do you feel guilty for having money?

Acceptance, p54, Assumptions, p67, Beliefs, p79, Confidence, p107, Defensiveness, p125, Envy, p133, Forgiveness, p148, Gratitude, p157, Guilt, p159, Inner Child, p168, Luck, p187, Money, p196, Perspectives, p222, Stress, p273, Values, p298, Worrying, p307

Do you feel guilty spending money on yourself?

Defensiveness, p125, Fear, p141, Gratitude, p157, Guilt, p159, Happiness, p164, Inner Child, p168, Money, p196, Trust, p293, Values, p298

Relationships

Can you talk about money with your partner?

Anger, p66, Assumptions, p67, Blame, p83, Compromise, p106, Control, p111, Defensiveness, p125, Feedback, p144, Listening, p181, Mirroring, p194, Money, p196, Negotiation, p203, Non-judgemental, p204, Questions, p246, Roles, p254, Saying 'No', p262, Trust, p293, Values, p298

Do you have more/less money than your partner?

Acceptance, p54, Advantages, p62, Big Picture, p83, Blame, p83, Compromise, p106, Envy, p133, Feedback, p144, Forgiveness, p148, Guilt, p159, Money, p196, Negotiation, p203, Perspectives, p222, Roles, p254, Values, p298

Saving

Do you tend to avoid thinking about your financial situation altogether?

Accountability, p56, Advantages, p62, Big Picture, p83, Comfort Zone, p105, Defensiveness, p125, Depression, p128, Fear, p141, Motivation, p199, Optimism, p208, Prioritise, p234, Procrastination, p239, Worrying, p307

Would you like to save more?

Accountability, p56, Affirmations, p63, Boundaries, p94, Compromise, p106, Excess, p135, Fear, p141, Focus, p146, Goals, p153, Guilt, p159, Habits, p162, Happiness, p164, Life Ambition, p179, Money, p196, Patterns, p212, Planning, p225, Prioritise, p234, Routines, p259, Success, p279

Spending

Do you spend too much?

Accountability, p56, Blame, p83, Boundaries, p94, Compromise, p106, Creativity, p114, Excess, p135, Forgiveness, p148, Giving, p152, Guilt, p159, Money, p196, Outcome, p209, Planning, p225, Regret, p249, Success, p279

Are you mean with your money?

Advantages, p62, Big Picture, p83, Comfort Zone, p105, Compromise, p106, Control, p111, Giving, p152, Goals, p153, Intent, p169, Planning, p225, Prioritise, p234, Procrastination, p239, Saying 'No', p262

In this photograph I connected with nature during a long walk. It was truly magnificent.

Spirituality ●

Spirituality is a word that all of us are familiar with, but sometimes we're unsure about what it truly means. It is often confused with religion and although many people discover their spirituality by following a religious path, there are an infinite number of other ways in which we can connect with this intrinsic part of our nature. So what is spirituality?

Simply put, spirituality is the part of us that desires to transcend the ordinary, mundane everyday world. It's our search for the sacred. What is sacred to you will be very personal and each of us will experience and express our spirituality in our own unique way. For some it will be communing with nature, listening to an exquisite piece of music, or appreciating a beautiful work of art. Whereas for others it may be sitting in meditation and experiencing deep, inner peace and stillness. In these heightened states we can feel an incredible sense of joy, aliveness and sense of being at one with everything. For that moment in time our everyday thoughts and preoccupations fall away and we are fully able to be in the present moment.

One simple way of embracing spirituality is by getting caught up in something you love and wholeheartedly enjoy – something that you can be totally absorbed in and that engages all of your being. This enables you to be in the moment, free of thoughts and judgements, and experience the joy of being at one with the experience. In our everyday lives we often forget to make room for the spiritual aspect of life. We are so hurried and busy and as a result we don't take the time to nourish our inner lives or nurture those around us. A big part of spirituality also includes the development of our inner life through such practices as meditation and prayer. Even sitting quietly in front of a sea of candles can quieten our busy minds and connect us to a feeling of stillness and inner peace.

We also connect with our spirituality when we are feeling lighthearted. Just spend some time around children to witness this part of our nature. Children have a sense of wonder and enthusiasm that we often lose as adults. Whether it's walking along the beach or laughing with friends, whatever makes you feel more joyful and enlivened is good for your spirit. When we start to feel good just being who we are, we instantly feel an empathy and connection for what is around us, whether that is nature, other people, or the great unknown.

The more we feel connected, the deeper we want to delve into our true selves, and the more we want to be a bigger part of the world around us. And this is where we find our spirituality. Although it is a very personal thing, we are being spiritual when we feel our life grounds us and connects us to something greater than ourselves. Begin with joy and ease, and move into connection. When we trust in something greater than ourselves or just acknowledge that perhaps there is a bigger pattern at work in our lives, we can stop trying to control things and life can start to unfold in ways we could not once imagine possible.

Which area of 'Spirituality' would you like to reflect on: Awareness, Experience, Faith, Gratitude, Live in the Present, Purpose or Self-knowledge? Find the area and then the question that feels right for you below it. Follow the links.

Awareness

Do you feel connected to others?

Assumptions, p67, Beliefs, p79, Belonging, p82, Connection, p110, Forgiveness, p148, Laughter, p174, Listening, p181, Mirroring, p194, Non-judgemental, p204, Role Models, p256, Synchronicity, p283, Values, p298

Do you have a sense of connection to something beyond yourself?

Absorption, p53, Connection, p110, Curiosity, p117, Gratitude, p157, Intuition, p170, Meditation, p190, Non-judgemental, p204, Synchronicity, p283, Trust, p293

Are you aware of your life unfolding?

Breathing, p97, Choices, p102, Connection, p110, Life Ambition, p179, Luck, p187, Synchronicity, p283, Trust, p293

Do you know what spirituality means to you?

Absorption, p53, Belonging, p82, Breathing, p97, Connection, p110, Forgiveness, p148, Gratitude, p157, Intuition, p170, Lightbulb Moment, p180, Meditation, p190, Patterns, p212, Synchronicity, p283, Trust, p293, Values, p298

Experience

Would you like to find rituals that support you?

Body/Heart/Mind Types, p85, Breathing, p97, Gratitude, p157, Habits, p162, Lightbulb Moment, p180, Meditation, p190, Routines, p259, Time Management, p290, Visualisation, p302

Do you know what gives you the deepest experiences?

Absorption, p53, Belonging, p82, Body/Heart/Mind Types, p85, Breathing, p97, Comfort Zone, p105, Connection, p110, Happiness, p164, Life Ambition, p179, Lightbulb Moment, p180, Meditation, p190, Personality Typing, p219

Would you like to have more time for spirituality?

Absorption, p53, Balance, p75, Breathing, p97, Choices, p102, Connection, p110, De-cluttering, p122, Habits, p162, Lightbulb Moment, p180, Planning, p225, Procrastination, p239, Routines, p259, Time Management, p290, Work/Life Balance, p305

Faith

Do you feel tied to family traditions?

Beliefs, p79, Belonging, p82, Boundaries, p94, Comfort Zone, p105, Fear, p141, Guilt, p159, Habits, p162, Patterns, p212, Perspectives, p222, Prioritise, p234, Questions, p246, Roles, p254, Saying 'No', p262, Values, p298

Would you like to find your own spiritual beliefs?

Authentic, p72, Body/Heart/Mind Types, p85, Boundaries, p94, Connection, p110, Curiosity, p117, Intuition, p170, Life Ambition, p179, Listening, p181, Personality Typing, p219, Questions, p246, Trust, p293, Values, p298

Have you lost your faith?

Acceptance, p54, Beliefs, p79, Belonging, p82, Blame, p83, Change, p99, Comfort Zone, p105, Failure, p140, Forgiveness, p148, Guilt, p159, Letting Go, p176, Loneliness, p186, Regret, p249, Roles, p254, Saying 'No', p262, Values, p298

Does your partner have a different faith?

Acceptance, p54, Assumptions, p67, Balance, p75, Compromise, p106, Curiosity, p117, Defensiveness, p125, Fear, p141, Listening, p181, Non-judgemental, p204, Perspectives, p222, Saying 'No', p262, Values, p298, Worrying, p307

Are you worried that if you find spirituality, too many things in your life will change?

Advantages, p62, Assumptions, p67, Change, p99, Choices, p102, Comfort Zone, p105, Control, p111, Fear, p141, Synchronicity, p283, Trust, p293, Worrying, p307

Do you have faith that your life will unfold as it should?

Confidence, p107, Intuition, p170, Optimism, p208, Synchronicity, p283, Trust, p293, Visualisation, p302

Gratitude

Do you have things you value in your life?

Absorption, p53, Connection, p110, Gratitude, p157, Happiness, p164, Laughter, p174, Optimism, p208, Success, p279, Talents, p286, Values, p298

Do you feel grateful?

Acceptance, p54, Confidence, p107, Connection, p110, Giving, p152, Gratitude, p157, Happiness, p164, Laughter, p174, Luck, p187, Talents, p286

Live in the present
Is there joy in your life?

Absorption, p53, Acceptance, p54, Body/Heart/Mind Types, p85, Connection, p110, Creativity, p114, Happiness, p164, Intuition, p170, Laughter, p174, Lightbulb Moment, p180, Luck, p187, Optimism, p208, Play, p232, Synchronicity, p283

Are you aware of what is important to you now?

Belonging, p82, Connection, p110, Goals, p153, Gratitude, p157, Life Ambition, p179, Planning, p225, Prioritise, p234, Routines, p259, Synchronicity, p283, Trust, p293, Values, p298

Can you forgive and let go of the past?

Acceptance, p54, Blame, p83, Change, p99, Defensiveness, p125, Emotions, p131, Failure, p140, Forgiveness, p148, Guilt, p159, Inner Child, p168, Intuition, p170, Letting Go, p176, Regret, p249, Trust, p293, Victim, p300

Purpose
Are you looking for meaning in your life?

Absorption, p53, Belonging, p82, Connection, p110, Goals, p153, Gratitude, p157, Intent, p169, Intuition, p170, Life Ambition, p179, Talents, p286

Are you looking for your life's purpose?

Authentic, p72, Beliefs, p79, Confidence, p107, Life Ambition, p179, Mirroring, p194, Personality Typing, p219, Role Models, p256, Talents, p286, Trust, p293, Values, p298

Self-knowledge
Are you at peace with yourself?

Acceptance, p54, Beliefs, p79, Blame, p83, Confidence, p107, Defensiveness, p125, Forgiveness, p148, Inner Child, p168, Letting Go, p176, Loneliness, p186, Non-judgemental, p204, Victim, p300

Do you know how to access your own wisdom?

Brainstorming, p96, Confidence, p107, Creativity, p114, Curiosity, p117, Intuition, p170, Listening, p181, Meditation, p190, Metaphor, p191, Mirroring, p194, Questions, p246, Problem Solving, p235, Stories, p271, Trust, p293

Do you know what you want from spirituality?

Acceptance, p54, Belonging, p82, Confidence, p107, Connection, p110, Forgiveness, p148, Life Ambition, p179, Questions, p246, Routines, p259, Values, p298

Love & Romance ●

Are you in the kind of relationship that you always dreamt of? Or do you feel that your relationship leaves much to be desired? And if you're currently single, what are your expectations around attracting a new relationship?

We live in a culture that is constantly fuelling our desire for romance and fulfilment. Finding the perfect partner who will sweep us off our feet and with whom we will live happily ever after can feel like the ultimate quest. As children the fairy tales we were told provided us with the romantic model of a handsome knight in shining armour who would rescue and adore us, and a beautiful maiden who would love us unconditionally. It's no wonder that we search for an ideal and inevitably set ourselves up for disappointment.

We project onto a potential or an existing partner all manner of qualities, hopes and dreams which are almost always impossible to live up to. And although those we fall in love with can give us just cause to feel let down, abandoned or betrayed, often it's our own expectations which can give us the most grief. When others fail to meet our exacting standards, we tend to see them as at fault and not look to ourselves for why we might be feeling so disappointed, hurt or angry. We can repeat these patterns and others over and over again. Sometimes we are aware of them but invariably we are not. Even when we think we have moved on, we can find ourselves in an all too familiar scenario without understanding how we got ourselves there. And again, rather than take responsibility for these, we blame our partners for the way we are feeling and the situation we find ourselves in. We fail to see that we are the common denominator for our experiences.

The more aware of yourself you become, the more control you have over your choices. With awareness also comes the realisation that although good relationships do indeed have the power to fulfil our desires and our deepest longings, perhaps one of their main gifts is to offer us a greater awareness and a deeper understanding of ourselves and the way in which we relate to others.

Take time to get to know yourself better – either in or out of a relationship – and to feel good about who you are. Know what you like and what you don't. Know where your boundaries are and what you'll enjoy doing. The happier you feel on your own, the more joy you'll bring to a relationship. Question your assumptions and beliefs about relationships too, because they will also influence your choices and experiences. If you expect to be rejected that will almost certainly become a self-fulfilling prophecy. Equally, if you believe that you deserve a loving relationship that is what you are likely to experience.

Loving relationships enrich our lives immeasurably and bring out the best in us. The world seems a more colourful place and we feel more connected to everyone and everything. Commit to discover more about yourself and you'll soon understand how you can enjoy greater intimacy and fulfilment in all your relationships.

This couple in the snow looked so absorbed in their conversation and completely and wholly together, mirroring each other with their matching hats and coats.

LOVE

Which area of 'Love & Romance' would you like to find out more about: Love: Self-love, Love & Romance: Behaviour, Commitment, Communication, Compatibility, Expectations: Love, Friends & Family, Jealousy, Living Together, Patterns or Sex? Find the area and then the question that feels right for you below it. Follow the links.

Love: Self-love

Do you have good self-esteem?

Body Image, p88, Confidence, p107, Forgiveness, p148, Happiness, p164, Intuition, p170, Letting Go, p176, Optimism, p208, Style, p277, Talents, p286

Do you look after yourself?

Balance, p75, Balance Chart, p76, Breathing, p97, Emotions, p131, Forgiveness, p148, Giving, p152, Gratitude, p157, Happiness, p164, Inner Child, p168, Intuition, Pp170, Laughter, p174, Meditation, p190, Optimism, p208, Play, p232, Relaxation, p251, Saying 'No', p262, Time Management, p290, Work/Life Balance, p305

Do you enjoy your own company?

Assumptions, p67, Beliefs, p79, Belonging, p82, Body/Heart/Mind Types, p85, Confidence, p107, Creativity, p114, Curiosity, p117, Depression, p128, Fear, p141, Inner Child, p168, Loneliness, p186, Personality Typing, p219, Talents, p286, Values, p298

Can you forgive yourself for mistakes you've made in the past?

Accountability, p56, Anger, p66, Blame, p83, Failure, p140, Forgiveness, p148, Guilt, p159, Inner Child, p168, Letting Go, p176, Non-judgemental, p204, Perfectionism, p216, Regret, p249, Stress, p273, Trust, p293, Victim, p300, Worrying, p307

Do you feel loved and cherished?

Acceptance, p54, Assumptions, p67, Beliefs, p79, Belonging, p82, Confidence, p107, Connection, p110, Envy, p133, Failure, p140, Forgiveness, p148, Giving, p152, Gratitude, p157, Happiness, p164, Inner Child, p168, Laughter, p174, Loneliness, p186, Perfectionism, p216, Trust, p293, Victim, p300

Love & Romance: Behaviour

Are you open to being loved?

Acceptance, p54, Beliefs, p79, Comfort Zone, p105, Confidence, p107, Connection, p110, Defensiveness, p125, Emotions, p131, Fear, p141, Non-judgemental, p204, Synchronicity, p283, Trust, p293

Do you only think about the other person when in a relationship?

Absorption, p53, Accountability, p56, Balance, p75, Boundaries, p94, Confidence, p107, Excess, p135, Inner Child, p168, Life Ambition, p179, Patterns, p212, Perspectives, p222, Saying 'No', p262

Do you tend to move the relationship on too fast too soon?

Balance, p75, Beliefs, p79, Belonging, p82, Boundaries, p94, Confidence, p107, Control, p111, Excess, p135, Fear, p141, Inner Child, p168, Loneliness, p186, Patterns, p212, Trust, p293

Do you often feel needy in a relationship?

Beliefs, p79, Boundaries, p94, Confidence, p107, Control, p111, Emotions, p131, Excess, p135, Fear, p141, Inner Child, p168, Loneliness, p186, Patterns, p212, Roles, p254, Trust, p293, Values, p298, Victim, p300

Do you hold back parts of yourself?

Boundaries, p94, Connection, p110, Control, p111, Fear, p141, Trust, p293

Are you so afraid of being left that you leave the relationship first?

Confidence, p107, Control, p111, Defensiveness, p125, Failure, p140, Fear, p141, Inner Child, p168, Loneliness, p186, Patterns, p212, Trust, p293

Commitment

Are you scared of commitment?

Assumptions, p67, Beliefs, p79, Big Picture, p83, Comfort Zone, p105, Confidence, p107, Connection, p110, Failure, p140, Fear, p141, Perfectionism, p216, Personality Typing, p219, Trust, p293

Should you get involved with this person?

Boundaries, p94, Connection, p110, Fear, p141, Laughter, p174, Listening, p181, Patterns, p212, Stress, p273, Values, p298, Victim, p300

Do you know how to cement a relationship?

Body/Heart/Mind Types, p85, Compromise, p106, Connection, p110, Creativity, p114, Curiosity, p117, Forgiveness, p148, Gratitude, p157, Listening, p181, Planning, p225, Play, p232, Relaxation, p251, Time Management, p290, Values, p298

Do you know how to get out of relationships?

Action, p61, Boundaries, p94, Change, p99, Comfort Zone, p105, Confidence, p107, De-cluttering, p122, Fear, p141, Feedback, p144, Goals, p153, Letting Go, p176, Outcome, p209, Saying 'No', p262, Worrying, p307

Do you want a divorce?

Big Picture, p83, Change, p99, Comfort Zone, p105, Confidence, p107, De-cluttering, p122, Depression, p128, Failure, p140, Fear, p141, Forgiveness, p148, Guilt, p159, Letting Go, p176, Loneliness, p186, Stress, p273, Trust, p293

Do you have time for yourself within the relationship?

Balance, p75, Compromise, p106, De-cluttering, p122, Goals, p153, Planning, p225, Play, p232, Prioritise, p234, Routines, p259, Time Management, p290, Work/Life Balance, p305

Communication

Do you know how to listen to your partner?

Body Language, p91, Connection, p110, Emotions, p131, Intuition, p170, Language, p173, Laughter, p174, Listening, p181, Non-judgemental, p204

Do you feel that you're not listened to?

Anger, p66, Assumptions, p67, Blame, p83, Bottom Line, p94, Boundaries, p94, Feedback, p144, Forgiveness, p148, Listening, p181, Loneliness, p186, Mirroring, p194, Negotiation, p203, Victim, p300

Are you arguing too much?

Anger, p66, Blame, p83, Boundaries, p94, Breathing, p97, Compromise, p106, Control, p111, Defensiveness, p125, Forgiveness, p148, Laughter, p174, Listening, p181, Negotiation, p203, Perspectives, p222, Problem Solving, p235, Questions, p246, Stress, p273, Trust, p293

Compatibility

Do you enjoy doing things together?

Creativity, p114, Happiness, p164, Laughter, p174, Personality Typing, p219, Play, p232, Relaxation, p251, Synchronicity, p283, Values, p298

Do you value the same things?

Body/Heart/Mind Types, p85, Compromise, p106, Curiosity, p117, Giving, p152, Intuition, p170, Listening, p181, Negotiation, p203, Non-judgemental, p204, Personality Typing, p219, Perspectives, p222, Values, p298

Expectations: Love

Do you expect love to be like a Hollywood romance?

Acceptance, p54, Advantages, p62, Assumptions, p67, Beliefs, p79, Compromise, p106, Non-judgemental, p204, Optimism, p208, Perfectionism, p216, Stories, p271, Synchronicity, p283, Values, p298, Victim, p300

Do you think finding love will change everything?

Assumptions, p67, Balance, p75, Beliefs, p79, Belonging, p82, Change, p99, Confidence, p107, Connection, p110, Envy, p133, Happiness, p164, Inner Child, p168, Loneliness, p186, Stories, p271

Friends & Family

Does your partner like your friends/family?

Acceptance, p54, Compromise, p106, Control, p111, Defensiveness, p125, Envy, p133, Feedback, p144, Guilt, p159, Letting Go, p176, Listening, p181, Negotiation, p203, Perfectionism, p216, Saying 'No', p262, Values, p298

Do you choose partners because your friends/family will like them?

Assumptions, p67, Boundaries, p94, Choices, p102, Compromise, p106, Confidence, p107, Fear, p141, Inner Child, p168, Intent, p169, Letting Go, p176, Loneliness, p186, Prioritise, p234, Regret, p249, Saying 'No', p262, Trust, p293, Values, p298

Do your other loyalties get in the way of your relationships?

Big Picture, p83, Blame, p83, Boundaries, p94, Choices, p102, Compromise, p106, Decisions, p121, Excess, p135, Forgiveness, p148, Letting Go, p176, Patterns, p212, Prioritise, p234, Saying 'No', p262, Values, p298, Victim, p300

Jealousy

Do you trust your partner?

Acceptance, p54, Advantages, p62, Anger, p66, Assumptions, p67, Blame, p83, Boundaries, p94, Confidence, p107, Control, p111, Fear, p141, Feedback, p144, Forgiveness, p148, Intuition, p170, Mirroring, p194, Personality Typing, p219, Trust, p293, Victim, p300, Worrying, p307

Are you jealous of other people's relationships?

Acceptance, p54, Anger, p66, Assumptions, p67, Beliefs, p79, Confidence, p107, Envy, p133, Failure, p140, Fear, p141, Forgiveness, p148, Gratitude, p157, Loneliness, p186, Perfectionism, p216, Perspectives, p222, Regret, p249, Role Models, p256, Success, p279, Trust, p293, Values, p298

Can you forgive yourself/your partner for past infidelities?

Accountability, p56, Anger, p66, Choices, p102, Envy, p133, Fear, p141, Forgiveness, p148, Guilt, p159, Letting Go, p176, Patterns, p212, Regret, p249, Trust, p293

Living Together

Are you scared of marrying/moving in with your partner?

Acceptance, p54, Assumptions, p67, Boundaries, p94, Change, p99, Choices, p102, Compromise, p106, Confidence, p107, Control, p111, Fear, p141, Happiness, p164, Laughter, p174, Letting Go, p176, Loneliness, p186, Procrastination, p239, Relaxation, p251, Trust, p293, Values, p298

Is your home conducive to a relationship?

Compromise, p106, De-cluttering, p122, Feedback, p144, Letting Go, p176, Listening, p181, Style, p277, Values, p298

Do you have different taste from your partner?

Acceptance, p54, Big Picture, p83, Compromise, p106, Feedback, p144, Letting Go, p176, Negotiation, p203, Perfectionism, p216, Style, p277, Values, p298

Does your partner have habits that annoy you?

Acceptance, p54, Big Picture, p83, Body/Heart/Mind Types, p85, Compromise, p106, Control, p111, Feedback, p144, Habits, p162, Listening, p181, Non-judgemental, p204, Perfectionism, p216, Personality Typing, p219, Perspectives, p222

Patterns

Do you date the same type of person over and over again?

Assumptions, p67, Belonging, p82, Comfort Zone, p105, Confidence, p107, Curiosity, p117, Fear, p141, Forgiveness, p148, Habits, p162, Intuition, p170, Lightbulb Moment, p180, Patterns, p212, Regret, p249, Values, p298

Do you compare every new relationship to your ex?

Acceptance, p54, Anger, p66, Belonging, p82, Choices, p102, Confidence, p107, Depression, p128, Failure, p140, Forgiveness, p148, Guilt, p159, Letting Go, p176, Non-judgemental, p204, Patterns, p212, Personality Typing, p219, Regret, p249, Values, p298

Do you remind each other of one of your parents?

Belonging, p82, Comfort Zone, p105, Fear, p141, Inner Child, p168, Lightbulb Moment, p180, Mirroring, p194, Non-judgemental, p204, Patterns, p212, Saying 'No', p262, Trust, p293, Values, p298

Do you constantly sabotage relationships?

Acceptance, p54, Belonging, p82, Change, p99, Choices, p102, Confidence, p107, Connection, p110, Control, p111, Failure, p140, Fear, p141, Loneliness, p186, Patterns, p212, Regret, p249, Trust, p293

Sex

Do you make time for sex?

Balance, p75, Excess, p135, Habits, p162, Outcome, p209, Planning, p225, Play, p232, Prioritise, p234, Relaxation, p251, Routines, p259, Time Management, p290

Do you enjoy sex?

Affirmations, p63, Assumptions, p67, Body Image, p88, Body Language, p91, Comfort Zone, p105, Confidence, p107, Creativity, p114, Fear, p141, Intuition, p170, Laughter, p174, Listening, p181, Optimism, p208, Play, p232, Relaxation, p251, Success, p279, Trust, p293

Do you use sex as a way of making things better?

Authentic, p72, Confidence, p107, Depression, p128, Fear, p141, Forgiveness, p148, Guilt, p159, Inner Child, p168, Listening, p181, Loneliness, p186, Negotiation, p203, Outcome, p209, Patterns, p212, Problem Solving, p235, Saying 'No', p262, Stress, p273, Trust, p293

Do you confuse sex with love?

Assumptions, p67, Belonging, p82, Confidence, p107, Connection, p110, Inner Child, p168, Intent, p169, Intuition, p170, Language, p173, Loneliness, p186, Outcome, p209, Patterns, p212, Trust, p293

Does your partner want more or less sex than you want?

Balance, p75, Belonging, p82, Blame, p83, Boundaries, p94, Compromise, p106, Connection, p110, Excess, p135, Failure, p140, Fear, p141, Feedback, p144, Forgiveness, p148, Guilt, p159, Listening, p181, Negotiation, p203, Perspectives, p222, Problem Solving, p235, Saying 'No', p262, Trust, p293, Values, p298

Are you aware of your own sexuality?

Acceptance, p54, Accountability, p56, Authentic, p72, Belonging, p82, Boundaries, p94, Confidence, p107, Connection, p110, Creativity, p114, Curiosity, p117, Emotions, p131, Forgiveness, p148, Guilt, p159, Happiness, p164, Intuition, p170, Letting Go, p176, Non-judgemental, p204, Play, p232, Role Models, p256, Trust, p293

A-Z
of Topics

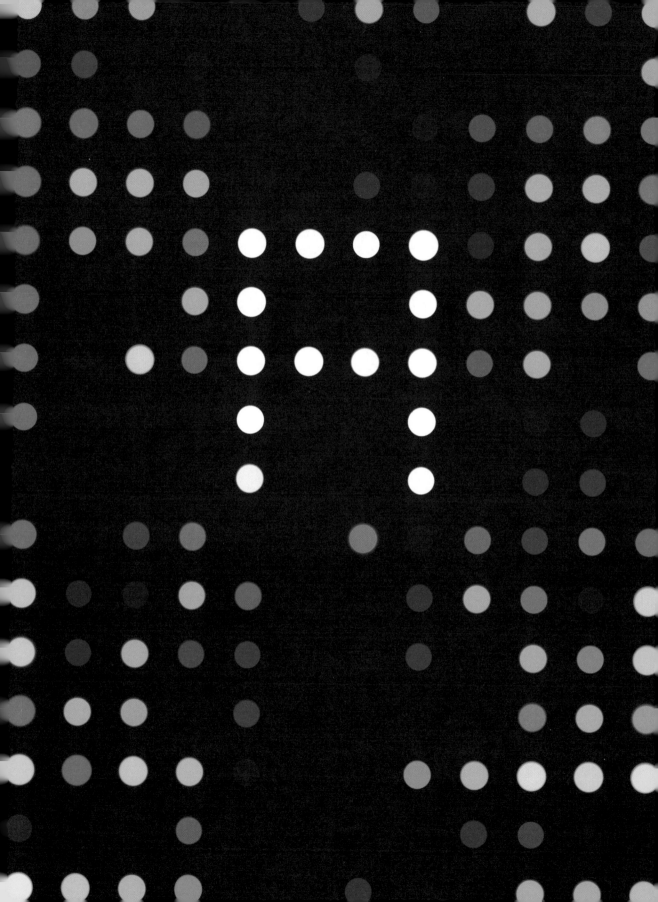

Absorption ● ● ● ● ●

I'm lucky because I can get absorbed very easily. I get absorbed when I'm drawing, designing or making something, then I forget any troubles in my life. It makes me a calmer person. My big revelation was that I can get absorbed with gardening too – I never knew I was an outdoors person. Whilst gardening, I noticed that when I focused on the ground, life felt suspended. I also felt a connection between myself and everyone who had gardened there before – even more than this, a connection with nature as I dug into the soil. It felt good to have a self-assumption challenged, opening up new future possibilities for me.

Absorption or 'flow' happens when you're entirely engrossed (absorbed) in whatever you are doing. All your focus is directed onto the activity. It's as if time has stood still and you're 'at one' with the moment. Nothing else matters.
'I got so absorbed in my accounts yesterday I couldn't believe it. I'm not normally a numbers person, but I completely forgot to eat lunch.'

The key to what you love
There may be some moments that stand out from your childhood – times when you were absorbed and totally engrossed in what you were doing. Once you bring that feeling of childhood involvement, of intuitively knowing what you loved back into your life, your confidence will soar. Remembering a love of reading could take you into a book club, remembering building tree houses could take you to a carpentry class, while remembering how much you loved dressing up could lead you into fashion. Once you've found something you can get absorbed in, you'll begin to enjoy your spare 'alone' time. It may at first take confidence to play the violin for a few hours simply because you want to – you may well feel you're being selfish – but you'll find it gives you an enormous boost. It takes confidence to play netball all evening just because you want to. It takes confidence to go to bed and write a diary, rather than go to the pub, but if you want to do it, why not? Take that time to rediscover the creative child in you. Start noticing what you want to do and allowing yourself to do it. You'll be happier with everyone and everything afterwards.

Total immersion
Throwing yourself into anything wholeheartedly will make you absorbed. You may enjoy lots of things about it:

- **The knowledge you amass (eg if your absorption comes from reading or watching films)**
- **Getting out of yourself and into the present moment (eg if your absorption comes from playing the violin, fishing or playing hockey)**
- **Discovering new things (eg if your absorption comes from swimming in waterfalls, mountain walks or photography)**
- **The intensity (eg if your absorption comes from drumming circles, bungee jumping or putting together a massive project)**
- **The calmness of it (eg if your absorption comes from meditating, drawing or tightrope walking).**

When you stretch yourself, even previously uninteresting things become interesting and what you might have seen as a chore becomes pleasurable.

Instant absorption

One way of getting absorbed instantly is to stare intently at this red page and repeat 'red… red… red…' in your mind over and over again.

Forget about everything

Using each of your senses can also absorb you. Smelling a new perfume or a familiar scent can give you a split second of absorption. Focusing on what your friend, child or partner is saying to you or listening to music and discovering the joys of hearing each individual instrument can absorb you too. Feeling can also make time stand still – go for a swim or a walk or run and focus on your body and exactly how it's moving or sit stroking a dog. Come into the present moment and you'll be amazed at how you forget about anything else.

Balance

Because being absorbed in something is so compelling, you can forget about life in the 'real' world. As usual, keep a balance so you make sure you manage to feed and care for yourself and anyone else who is dependent on you.

Project: Make a list of times you've been absorbed in the past and notice what absorbs you now – it could be hill walking, sharpening a knife or playing the trumpet. It's a way to discovering the things you love. Do more of what absorbs you.

(See Body/Heart/Mind Types, Connection, Creativity, Intuition, Play, Talents)

Acceptance ● ● ● ● ● ● ● ●

I spent years never feeling accepted by my parents. I used to imagine a dramatic and emotional situation in which they gave me the love and acceptance I craved. Ironically, it was only when I accepted who they were and what they could give to me that I finally felt the little bits of love and acceptance in between my own clutter.

Acceptance is when you're willing to accept a difficult or unpleasant situation. By accepting the situation, you are acknowledging that you know the difference between what you can and can't change and saving your energy.
'I've finally accepted that I'm jealous and I want to do something about it.'
'I know my step-father has been difficult, but I've accepted it and forgive him.'

Acceptance of the past

Many of us live our lives clinging on to a story about our difficult past. We are the victim in our story and much of us still wants to change that past. When you accept that the past is what it is and give up the hope of ever changing it you become free to live fully in the moment.

Acceptance of ourselves

We are often very critical about ourselves in the hope that this negativity will motivate us to change – 'I'm so fat, I look horrible, I have to diet.' This approach may motivate you, but only for a short period of time. What will really change you is accepting who you are. 'I'm gorgeous and look great as I am.' Once you love yourself – or even feel you're 'OK' as you are, you'll be on the first step to change.

Acceptance of reality

If you don't accept your life as it is, or you as who you are, it's as if you have difficulties in coping with reality. But reality is about life as it actually exists as opposed to an idealistic idea. It's only once you live in reality and can accept the situation as it is and see it clearly for what it is, that you can either decide to change it or to accept it.

Acceptance from others

Often when we don't accept others or feel accepted by them, it's because we feel fearful. We imagine them being critical of us (maybe mirroring our criticism of them). When you accept yourself and everything that's 'wrong' with you, you'll find you accept others too and fear will have lost its power over you.

Project: Start noticing what you're not accepting about yourself and your life. Are there things you can or can't change? How could you accept or change them? Where are you not being honest about what's really going on?

(See Assumptions, Blame, Forgiveness, Letting Go, Mirroring, Non-judgemental, Stories, Victim)

Accountability ● ● ● ● ● ● ● ●

It always comes back to balance. If I'm exercising I'm being accountable to my body, but not my mind. If I'm working, I'm being accountable to my mind (and bank balance) but I'm not being a mother. If I'm being a mother and accountable to my children, I'm not being a wife to my husband. If I'm being a wife and accountable to my husband, I'm not exercising and so on. I now know the balance I want in my life and am, overall accountable to this. Knowing the balance I want, and being accountable to it, means I can move forward with my life and feel in control.

As a concept **accountability** is similar in meaning to answerability, responsibility, liability – you can be called upon to account for your behaviour.
'This week at work I was accountable to Jack for organising the filing system.'

Put your accountability where you want it

The problem is that we don't always put our accountability where we want to put it and so we can lose confidence in ourselves. For example, we may forget to send our best friend a birthday card and get annoyed with ourselves. But instead of blaming yourself, look at the bigger picture of your life rather than nit picking about the small, individual things. You may sometimes forget to send a birthday card, but you go to the gym regularly and you haven't missed a day of work. Discover what is making you so effortlessly accountable in one area of your life but not in others. Start by looking at where you are responsible – those are the areas that have something in them that naturally works well for you.

Sunita worked in middle management and had been in the same position for a long time. Sunita knew she could do better and thought she should be aiming for a promotion. Every day she meant to work harder, but after a morning of checking emails and chatting to colleagues, she had often fallen behind – the afternoon always became catching-up time rather than an opportunity to be more proactive. Sunita did not feel accountable at work. In other areas though, Sunita was a model of accountability – she ate well, she went jogging five times a week after work and she took great care of her spirituality too, making time to meditate and working for charities at the weekends.

Sunita wondered what stopped her being as accountable at work. She worked out that all the things she was accountable for all had fairly instant results. When she exercised, she instantly felt good. When she helped others, again there was an instant buzz. When she ate well, she felt energised and, even better, in control. Sunita could see that it was easy for her to be accountable when she could see instant results and feel in charge of the situation. At work Sunita wasn't seeing any short-term results and she couldn't control her rise within the company. Becoming aware of this meant Sunita could see she needed to do things at work that would give her instant results and help her feel in control. Sunita had a word with her boss and they arranged that Sunita would start mentoring someone in the team and would be given some short-term jobs where she could see more immediate results.

Once you work out what makes it easy for you to be accountable, you can find ways of weaving these prompts into those parts of your life that you are stuck in. Sunita also realised that to give herself more of a feeling of control, she could make a list at the beginning of the day and cross off each thing when it was done. And that, although Sunita can't control whether she gets promoted or not, she can control her own goals and make a five-year plan about where she wants to be.

Five questions to ask yourself:

1 In which areas of my life do I find it easy to be accountable to myself?

2 What makes it easy for me to be accountable in those areas?

3 In which areas of my life don't I find it easy to be accountable to myself?

4 What makes it difficult for me to be accountable in those areas?

5 How could I use my answers to Q2 to help me with those areas Q4?

Project: Write a letter to someone (could be yourself) who you feel you are letting down and let them know that you'll be getting it together. Discover what will make it easier for you to become accountable in that area. There's no need to send the letter, just writing it will start you changing.

(See Big Picture, Blame, Confidence, Forgiveness, Motivation)

‘The wise don't strive to arrive.'

Zen proverb

Achievement ● ○ ● ●

I never used to think about achievements. I'd just 'do' things if I wanted to and didn't do them if I didn't. But since running regular workshops, where every week we notice what we've achieved for ourselves that week, I notice everything I achieve, big or small, and it feels good. My thoughts through the day can go a little bit like this: 'I'm replying to that email – boring, but I've done it… I've eaten a healthy lunch – well done for looking after myself… I've written another page of my book – and it reads quite well (yeah!)… I've just made a phone call I was dreading (broken through a comfort zone there)…' These thoughts make me feel good and are a great contrast to those other all too familiar thoughts which go: 'You always eat too much… That was a rubbish email… You've got to plan your phone calls better…' and on and on.

Some of us are very **achievement** focused and believe we are valued for what we accomplish. Others of us go to the opposite extreme and ignore all the things we achieve instead of using our achievements to boost our self-confidence. In our multi-tasking society, when we do one thing after another or even at the same time as another, it is essential to notice your achievements – and to keep noticing them – as doing this is key to growing your confidence.

'I had a great day today, I went to the gym, created an agenda for a meeting we're having tomorrow and had lunch sitting in the sun. I achieved loads and felt really good.'

High achievers

Just as it's essential to notice your achievements, it's also essential for some of us not to notice them too much. If you're a high achiever, you'll be interested in doing, succeeding, achieving. You'll set goals, work hard, fast and efficiently. The downside is that you can be impatient and pay no attention to your own – or anyone else's – feelings or indeed to the meaning of what you're doing. Since a child you've felt that the only way you will achieve acceptance and love is through your accomplishments. Your constant refrain is 'Was I good enough? Was I the best?' and in order to win this approval, you continually adapt yourself to everyone you meet and every new situation and lose touch with who you are. Relaxation can be a frightening place.

As a high achiever

As a high achiever, it's important for you to realise that you can be loved even if you aren't achieving anything. Set routines, take days off work, eat healthily and leave some time to just 'be' so you can realise that the universe will take care of itself even if you're having a day off.

Less can be more

Even non-achievers can want to keep achieving more and more. Ironically often when we feel exhausted, pressurised, even panicked, we work against our better instinct and begin to take on even more commitments and responsibilities in the hope that we'll feel happier with ourselves the more we achieve. But we don't get anywhere – except more stressed. There always seems to be things to do, so you keep going, ignoring the fact that you're tired or in pain. Before taking on new commitments, think about whether you have enough time. It's easy to fall into the habit of agreeing to everything, because you want to feel that rush of being busy and in demand and you don't want to disappoint anyone.

Leave time for achievements

Sometimes you set goals, but get distracted by other people's agendas and swayed from what you wanted to achieve. We are forever checking to see if we have texts or emails – how many of us can't even turn our phones off for a meeting or at home? Once you know your Life Ambition – or even your focus for the week – rather than filling up your diary start managing your time. Leave at least 50 per cent of time free for the things you want to achieve and, during that time, put your phone on answer phone, ignore your emails and cut yourself off as much as you possibly can. Wherever you can delegate, do so, always just work on the things that only you can do. It's only when your head feels clear, and you've given yourself some space, that you're allowing your creative thoughts to emerge and you to achieve.

Clear your mind

Sometimes our plans and goals can keep us awake. Last thing at night, before sleep, clear your head of the day that you've just had by writing about it and then making a list of the things you want to achieve the next day. Put a line underneath the list and then forget about it until you wake.

Project: My Achievement Log. Create an achievement log, or use a part of your diary every day to record your achievements. Make sure most of them are achievements for you, rather than for work or family. They don't have to be big achievements or they can be. If you're a high achiever, have some 'be-ing' achievements in there. Write down:

The achievement

....

Why it was important to you

....

How it made you feel

....

 **Your Lightbulb Moment:**
What do achievements mean to you?

(See Balance, Confidence, Focus, Goals, Life Ambition, Relaxation, Time Management, Trust)

Action ● ● ● ● ●

I think action is the way through most things – fear, negative beliefs, procrastination, under-confidence, worry etc. – and yet it can be so difficult to get going. I find a lot depends on the time of day. I used to love being active in the evenings, whether going out or working. Now I'm an early morning person (though not as early as the 4.00am starts I experienced in Canada) and feel compelled to start things the moment I get up. Whereas action after lunch is almost always impossible. If the action is intentional, I start feeling a real sense of control over my life and ultimately become much more confident.

Action is doing something, usually to achieve an aim.
'Today I'm taking action on getting some more clients. I've been saying I'm going to do it for ages.'

Feeling stuck

Sometimes action feels impossible. It's as if we're stuck in treacle, we have no energy and enthusiasm about doing anything. In those instances, just do something, no matter what it is. It could be getting out of bed or buying something to eat for supper. If that feels too big, then make your action smaller – buy a magazine and read it. Take small steps forwards.

Run to your future

Haruki Murakami's novel, *What I Talk About When I Talk About Running*[1], is an example of the power of action. When Murakami began running one day, almost instantly, things started slotting into place. Running gave him focus; it gave him direction. In this book, Murakami pays tribute to the power of action, of literally moving towards what you want.

Project: In order to achieve anything, you want to take action. Working with one area of your Balance Chart, think of one thing you'd like to do in that area. Put in your diary when you're going to do it and take action, even if it's the tiniest of tiny steps.

(See Beliefs, Control, Depression, Fear, Focus, Goals, Life Ambition, Procrastination)

---

[1] Murakami, H. (2009) *What I Talk About When I Talk About Running*, London: Vintage Books.

Advantages ● ● ○ ● ● ● ● ● ●

I always used to want to lose weight until I started thinking about all the advantages to being a little overweight. There are so many of them (from being invisible when I walk down the street, rather than at the mercy of every wolf-whistle going, to being able to eat what I want), that I've given up thinking about losing weight. I'm the weight I am because that's the weight I want to be right now. Once I decide that I want to get rid of those advantages, I will. It is only once you've worked out all the advantages you have to staying as you are that you can begin to make clear decisions about what you want to do. I remember vividly working with someone who claimed that she hated the way her feet looked. They were on the large side, and so it was difficult finding elegant shoes. When we thought about the advantages to her of not liking her feet, the Lightbulb Moment came. It turned out that she disliked going out and was using the fact that she 'hated her feet' as an excuse for staying in. Once she'd realised how she was using her feet, she could then decide what she wanted to do. Did she want to have her feet ruining her social life or was she going to get out of her comfort zone and go out despite them?

There are **advantages** (benefits) to everything we do or we wouldn't do them. Even when we can't immediately see the advantages to being something ('fat', 'scatty', 'under-confident' etc), there are always those advantages there.

'The great advantage to being so busy is that I never feel lonely.'

Find your advantages

Whenever something is to our advantage, we stand to benefit or profit in some way from it. These advantages are what keep us doing what we've always done. It's only when we can see each advantage clearly for what it is, that we can decide whether we want (or need) it any more. And, if we do want it – how we can change and still keep that advantage.

Project: Have a look at this exercise and see what you'd like to change. It could be something practical, like the time you go to bed or the food you eat or it could be something more intangible, like your under-confidence or your energy levels.

Is there something in your life you'd like to change?
(eg my temper)

....

Make a list of all the advantages to staying as you are (write as many as you can):
(eg it releases my tension; I like feeling everyone is scared of me, so I'm boss)

1 ....   6 ....
2 ....   7 ....
3 ....   8 ....
4 ....   9 ....
5 ....   10 ....

Think about why those advantages are important to you and whether you really want them any more:
(eg I do want to have my tension released, I do like feeling I'm boss)

....

How can you find those advantages somewhere else so you can change your habit whilst keeping the advantages?
(eg I could dance to release my tension, I could be calm to show I'm in charge)

....

(See Beliefs, Change, Comfort Zone, Lightbulb Moment)

Affirmations ● ● ●

Someone who used affirmations to great effect was Sara Crewe, heroine of A Little Princess, *one of my all-time favourite children's books*[2]. *As times got harder and harder for Sara, she kept on repeating 'I am a Princess' until, of course… no, I won't spoil it for you. I too have used a simple affirmation 'I am confident' in a couple of bleak periods of my life. I have no idea why affirmations really work, but they worked for me. They say it takes 21 days of saying positive statements over and over again to yourself for them automatically to replace the negative statements. All I can say is that it's worth experimenting with.*

[2] Hodgson Burnett, F. (2008) *A Little Princess,* London: Puffin Classics.

Affirmations are positive statements that can be used to boost your self-confidence and help you feel and achieve what you want. Usually our mind is filled with negative statements (our negative beliefs about ourselves), such as 'I'm no good at singing'… 'I can't make friends'… 'I'm bad at making money'. By repeating positive statements (affirmations) that you've created, to yourself over and over again, they will replace those negative statements, helping you to become more positive.

'The affirmation I use all the time is: "I am creative" and I'm now feeling so creative, that I'm ready to look for a new job, so I'm changing my affirmation to "I have a great job" and let's see what I find. I'm excited.'

Why affirmations?

You talk to yourself all the time, and it's usually negative disempowering thoughts that you hear, so it's your mind that stops you achieving what you want to. It's so full of 'I'll never be able to do that' and 'they don't like me' that you begin to believe these statements and imagine they're true. If instead of hearing those negative voices all the time, you could have positive voices saying 'I'm brilliant at that' and 'I'm great at meeting people', just think how different your life would be. Affirmations are about training your mind – they're a kind of mental acrobatics. The premise is that once you think these different thoughts, you will behave differently and your new behaviour will reinforce these new thoughts.

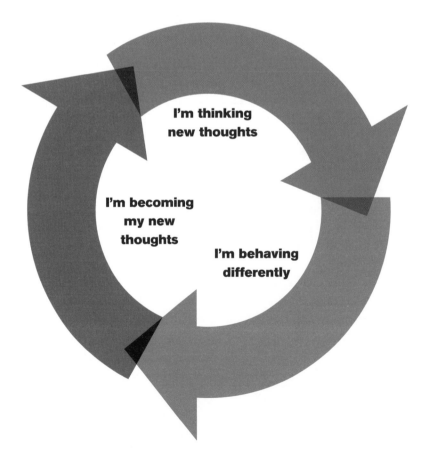

Deciding on an affirmation

Start by listening out for your thoughts. You'll probably find that there's one or more thoughts that always pop up and stop you doing what you want to do. These thoughts will almost certainly be in areas of your life that aren't working well, but they may also be in areas in which you are doing well and they just stop you getting up to the next level. Choose a thought that is stopping you the most to focus on changing first. After 21 days – by which time the first affirmation may well be working – you can then choose another thought to change.

Creating affirmations

Once you've chosen an area you want to work on and had a vague idea for an affirmation, check first that your affirmation is:

- **In the present tense**
- **Personal (about you and no one else)**
- **Positive**
- **Specific**
- **Short**
- **Realistic**
- **What you want.**

Ideas for affirmations

- **I enjoy my own company**
- **I make friends easily**
- **I have a great memory**
- **I have all the money I want**
- **I'm in the right place at the right time**
- **I belong here**
- **My body is healthy**
- **I go to sleep the moment my head touches the pillow**
- **I am always on time**
- **I trust in the universe.**

Push yourself. Choose an affirmation that sounds a bit far-fetched – something you think you could never believe. Or, if that feels too ludicrous to take seriously, start small and, every 21 days, make the affirmation bigger and bigger.

Project: Once you've chosen your affirmation, repeat it with conviction as often as you can (possibly every time you see a mirror or every time you wash your hands so it becomes a habit), over and over again in your mind, really focusing on it positively as you repeat it to yourself.

Project Two: Imagine going through your day and filling it with affirmations. This is a start: In the bathroom you look in the mirror and notice how beautiful you look – 'I am beautiful'

you say to your reflection. That makes you stand up straighter and smile. At breakfast with your bowl of fresh fruit you are eating healthily – 'I eat well and listen to my body' you affirm. Walking to work you breathe deeply and walk briskly – 'my body is supple and supports me brilliantly…'

(See Achievement, Beliefs, Change, Comfort Zone, Focus)

Anger ● ● ● ●

In our family we all get angry in different ways. Two of us claim never to feel angry and cross their arms and growl. Two of us are instant shouters and then, just as everyone is reeling from the assault, it's all been forgotten and they can't even remember what happened, and two just demand and if their demands aren't met they get louder and louder. It works fine because we all know how the others behave, so we just ignore them and wait until the storm blows over.

Anger is the blanket term for any emotion from mild irritation to extreme rage directed at yourself or someone else or at a situation.
'I was so angry with myself/the broken toaster today I shouted at my partner, which just made it worse.'

What happens
When you're angry, as well as emotional symptoms, you feel physical symptoms, such as increased blood pressure and heart rate. If you express your anger, you'll shout or physically lash out. If you don't express your anger you may become passively aggressive or constantly cynical and sarcastic. Either way, you're experiencing a loss of self-control.

What causes anger?
Anger, like all negative emotions, comes from pain – from having been hurt. Instead of embracing the pain and seeing that there's a lesson in it, you block what you were feeling and carry on. The outlet for that ignored pain has become anger and the way forward is to find out what caused that pain and what you could learn from it, so you can stop the suffering and the need to be angry can go away.

What causes pain?
Pain can start with anything. It could be your dog dying, your partner leaving you, someone being rude to you or your parents divorcing. Pain is part of life, but when it becomes a main part of your 'poor little me' story it becomes suffering, and then turns you into a victim, and then makes you angry or frightened – then you're blaming your anger on someone else and getting distracted from your own life.

What if someone else is angry?

If someone else is being angry, remember that it may not be you they're being angry with – even if it may appear so. They may be hurting because of their suffering and the only way they can be helped is for them to come to terms with what gave them their pain in the first place.

What can calm you down:
- Breathing deeply from your stomach, rather than your chest, repeating the word 'relax' over and over again in your mind
- Focusing on the now. Is the anger in the now?
- Avoiding dramatising the situation
- Thinking logically rather than emotionally – see if you can solve the problem
- Discovering if you can see the anger from a different perspective and find humour in the situation
- Talking about your feelings
- Imagining a relaxing experience you've had
- Going outside or into another room.

Things to do:
- Notice when you're feeling angry and work out why
- Can you see patterns in when you're angry?
- Understand what stops you being angry
- Work out how to turn your anger into positive energy. If you feel so angry about something, can you use that anger to motivate you to do something, such as working hard, going for a run etc?
- Find the pain underneath the anger and work with it to resolve it (you may want professional help to do this)
- Check if you need professional help with your anger – is it frequent?

(See Breathing, Emotions, Listening, Patterns, Perspectives, Stress, Victim, Visualisation)

Assumptions ● ● ○ ● ● ● ● ● ● ●

One of the first times I consciously thought about assumptions was when I was playing an assumptions game at a workshop I attended. We all sat in a circle and each of us decided what we thought the person to our left would have as their favourite hobby. Next to me was this young, good-looking, smartly turned-out man and I suggested that his favourite hobby was clothes shopping. He looked at me, contemptuously, 'I hate shopping. No, my favourite hobby is boxing.' That was my Lightbulb Moment about assumptions. Boxing is so off my radar, that I would never have assumed that anyone could like boxing – and that's how assumptions work. We assume what we know. And that's the problem – because we don't know very much.

Our **assumptions** are beliefs that we think of as if they were true. These assumptions are then what create our worldview. You can have assumptions about yourself, about other people, about situations and about life without having any proof that the assumptions are correct.

'I assumed you'd like Japanese food because I do.'

'I assumed I'd be no good at relationships because my parents weren't.'

Open your mind

We often assume that there is only one way to do things. One way to play music, one way to paint, one way to write and one way to cook, because that's all we've ever come across. These assumptions about ourselves and life are like a lens through which we look at the world, but it's essential to keep that lens open and flexible, looking through it from different angles, and using it in different ways. If you imagine everything to be one way, you're already blocking people and things off, so instead, make it your mission to find out everything about them and about yourself. Imagine you're a private detective and ask yourself:

- **What are you assuming about yourself and life?**
- **Where have those answers got you so far?**
- **And what are the facts of the case?**

So many assumptions

We assume things about everything and everyone all the time. We assume things about money and illness and work and ourselves and we can also assume things about relationships. We can assume our brother is happy and doesn't need us when he isn't and does need us and vice versa. We can assume our children would rather they weren't with us when they want to be and vice versa. We can assume our lover thinks we're no good at sex when they think we're great and vice versa. These assumptions slip easily, and often unnoticed, into all parts of the way we see each other.

Assuming you know all about people

We are often trapped by our ignorance, assuming something about someone that just isn't right. People have an uncanny ability to defy judgement – we are all endlessly surprising and original. When you meet people, be open-minded and assume as little as you can about them – ask them questions, be curious and listen.

At a London gallery opening, Chris, who worked in fashion, met Richard and instantly did a little character assessment based on what Richard was wearing. Chris considered himself an expert in the field and lived by the motto: 'you are what you wear'. Richard had black, thick rimmed, square glasses, spiky hair, and was wearing an olive corduroy jacket, and smart jeans. Before they had even said 'Hello', Chris automatically assumed that Richard was an architect or designer, probably living in London. When Chris discovered that Richard was actually a priest from Suffolk, he did a double take. He didn't know anyone from the church, and had always assumed that they wore dog collars all the time. He also thought it was odd to find a priest at a gallery opening, as he assumed a priest wouldn't be creative and so on and on... From then on, Chris's theory that 'you are what you wear' was under observation.

'A blind person who sees is better than a seeing person who is blind.'

Iranian proverb

Assuming you know about old friends

Even in long-term friendships and relationships, assumptions get in the way. How often have you assumed that someone you know really well won't be interested in something you want to do, or will have forgotten your birthday (when they're actually throwing a surprise party for you), or won't want to talk to you about a specific problem you have? Keep an open mind. No matter how long you've known someone, you won't know everything about them. Try them out and see whether you were right or not.

What if...?

A great way to unlock assumptions is to use a 'what if...?' question. For example, you're having friends round and you don't know what to cook for them. Instead of assuming you know what they'll be expecting and assuming you aren't a good enough cook, ask yourself:

- *'What if* they weren't coming round for a meal, what would I eat then?' or
- *'What if* they weren't hungry, how would we spend the evening?' or
- *'What if* they brought their own food, what would I contribute?' or
- *'What if* they didn't know what to expect?' or
- *'What if* I was a good cook?' or
- *'What if* I was going to them, what would I expect?' or
- *'What if* I was going to them, what would I enjoy?'

How would that free your thinking?

Challenging your assumptions

Keep questioning if that lens you're seeing the world through is open enough. Challenge each assumption as you become aware of it. Draw grids, as below, and challenge your assumptions, as in the example, as and when you notice them. If your new assumption is about you, you might think about using it as an affirmation.

My current assumption is: (eg I'm no good at getting a job)

Three facts supporting this assumption	Three facts opposing this assumption
eg I've been unemployed for six months	eg until now I've always held a job
eg I don't really know what I want to do	eg I've even been asked if I wanted to apply for jobs in the past
eg No one has suggested they give me work	eg I have been asked to submit my CV by someone I met recently

I'd like my new assumption to be: (eg I am great at getting jobs)

ASSUMPTIONS

When we assume things we're trapped
and can't move forwards.

Project: Become aware of every assumption you're making and challenge it: what are the facts supporting it; what are the facts opposing it? Then re-write any assumptions that aren't helping you – or anyone else – and use your new assumptions as affirmations (if they're relevant).

Project Two: Every time you notice you're making an assumption, see how many 'what if...?' questions you can come up with.

(See Beliefs, Boundaries, Lightbulb Moment, Non-judgemental)

Authentic ● ● ● ● ●

The other day I was on a walk with my 10-year-old son when we stopped to ask someone the way. Within 30 seconds he had started to tell us his life story. As we walked away from him, my son turned to me and said 'Mum, he told you everything about himself.' For me, that wasn't unusual. I've always had that in my life as did my mother (and brother) and you may well have too – that others stop and chat and tell you all about themselves. I love it – I love hearing about other people's lives, about their secret (or not so secret) worlds. I suppose if people want to stop in the street and talk to you it's because they feel you're 'authentic'. Authentic in its 'self-development' context is one of those 'more than' words. People always used to be 'nice' or 'open' or 'friendly' or 'warm' or 'understanding'. Now 'authentic' is more than that – it's all of them put together plus a little something.

When something is **authentic**, it is genuine, reliable – of undisputed origin.
'He is so authentic, I really feel he's telling the truth about himself and about everything. I know I can trust him.'

Nice vs authentic
You could say to a child (or an adult), 'be nice to him', meaning 'kind' and 'polite', but you couldn't say 'be authentic to him'. Authenticity comes from the heart. When you're authentic you're in touch with your feelings and know they have value – you've accepted who you are.

Nice	Authentic
Being pleasant	Genuine
Being agreeable	Knowing what you're feeling
Being polite	Operating from your feelings
Being good-natured	Able to discuss your feelings
Being kind	Able to share your feelings
Socially acceptable	Communicating honestly
Path of least resistance	Communicating openly
Wanting to win approval	Being considerate and tactful

If you're authentic...

- you know how you feel, what your expectations are and whether they're being met
- you share your feelings with someone in a way that gives them room to respond appropriately (to be authentic).

Project: Notice when you're thinking 'No, I shouldn't feel this way', silence that voice and allow yourself to feel whatever way you want. Be in touch with your feelings.

Project Two: Is there someone you'd like to get closer to? If there is, share your feelings with them and, in turn, listen to their feelings. Notice whether or not you understand each other better after your conversation.

(See Acceptance, Emotions, Listening, Trust)

Balance ● ○ ● ● ● ● ● ● ●

I think the balance that I haven't yet got right in my life is the amount of time I spend alone with my husband as opposed to the two of us being with the whole of the family. We seem to have snatched moments in cars on our way to a party or a groan in the morning as we pass in the bathroom. I have a feeling that it's an imbalance that will persist until the children all leave home.

Balance in life can be about the amount of time you spend at work versus the amount of time you spend at home or it can be about how you want to balance everything in your life.
'When I've had a day on my own writing, I like to balance it out by talking to friends or family in the evening.'

We are all different

There is no single 'correct' balance. What is right for you depends on your age and sex, your priorities, goals and character. The balance that suits you now will probably not suit you later in life and might not have suited you in the past. What's important is that it suits you now. Once you know the balance you want, you can control your time accordingly.

Balance everything

Think of your life as a whole, made up of the various activities that you devote your time and energy to. If we were to use a metaphor, we could compare our life to a garden, which needs variation, and constant work plus sun, rain and food to make sure everything is healthy. The same concept can be applied to your life. If, for example, you work outdoors all the time you will want to balance that with something that requires more mental concentration, such as learning German or playing bridge. If on the other hand, you come home with your brain whirring from a challenging, cerebral day, you'll want to do something calming and physical and intellectually undemanding, like knitting or yoga. Simple things have to be balanced too. If you're a plasterer and have been carrying heavy loads around all day, after work you'll want to stretch the tense muscles you've been using.

What will stop you achieving balance

- ● **Other people and distractions – set boundaries**
- ● **Not having a routine – book time in your diary for what you want to happen, even if it feels 'silly'. It's a great idea to put 'read novel' or even 'date with partner' in your diary or they'll get forgotten.**

Things to do:

Become aware of the balance in your life. A rigorous way of doing this would be by filling in a time sheet or diary and seeing where you were putting your time. Otherwise, simply by becoming conscious of balance, you will have a good idea. How do you balance:

- **the food you eat**
- **caffeine/water**
- **awake/asleep time**
- **alone/with others time**
- **being active/inactive**
- **inputting (reading etc)/outputting (talking etc)**
- **brainwork/intellectually undemanding work**
- **young people/old people friendships**
- **giving/receiving**
- **comfort/excitement**
- **laughter/tears?**

Project: Imagine time-travelling 10 or 20 years into the future and looking back at your life as you are living it now. Is it how you would like it to be? Or will you be saying 'Goodness, I was working too hard' or 'I was really wasting my time' or even 'I was so much in love I thought nothing else mattered'. Write down what you see from this perspective.

(See Accountability, Balance Chart, Boundaries, Goals, Life Ambition, Time Management)

Balance Chart ● ● ●

I remember the first Balance Chart I designed. It had over 20 areas to it; I wanted to cram so much into life. When my brilliant designer, Lucy Sisman, looked at it, she said 'Ten areas maximum' and so, with a sinking heart, I got rid of area after area. Of course she was right. It's difficult enough to find the balance you want in your life with 10 areas, let alone with over 20.

The **Balance Chart** is a great tool to use to determine whether you're balancing your life the way you want to. It will enable you to see immediately where you are unbalanced. Filling in a Balance Chart is like taking a snapshot of your life. It will help you understand what areas of your life you're happy with and what areas you want to give more focus to. All you do is think carefully about each area of your life and then give yourself a score for how satisfied you are about each area of the Balance Chart (with '10' being the most satisfied). It will help you see instantly what area of your life you want to focus on in order to 'up' your score. When you fill in the Balance Chart, use your intuition rather than over-thinking each area (see page xiv).

'Filling in my Balance Chart made me realise that I'm not seeing my family enough and that's making me sad and unable to focus on work, so both areas of my life are suffering.'

You're in control

If you use your Balance Chart weekly it will help to show you how in control of your life and goals you are, because when you work on an area, your score goes up and, when you don't, your score goes down. And, when you do nothing different in your life, your score stays the same.

Life Clubs Balance Chart:

In this Balance Chart, there are 10 areas of life to give you a holistic overview of life.

- Home
- Creativity
- Health & Fitness
- Rest & Relaxation
- Friends & Social Life
- Work
- Family
- Money
- Spirituality
- Love & Romance

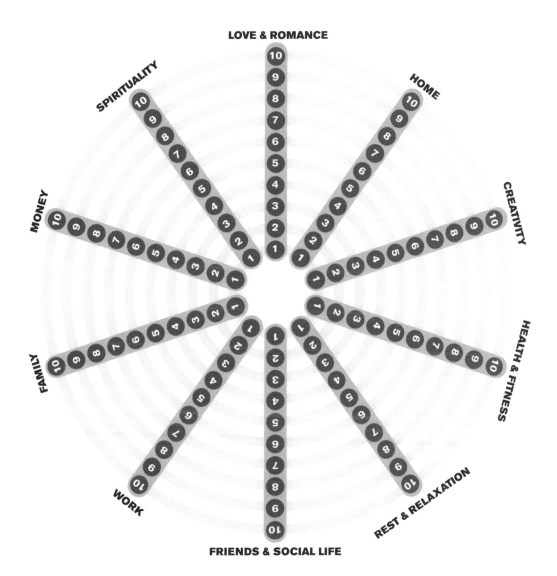

Your Balance Chart

You can also make up your own areas of life so you can track your progress in the aspects of life that are important to you. These are a few examples of possible areas. Score them in the same way.

- Confidence
- Fun/Holidays
- Finances
- Research
- Work

- Self-discovery
- Companionship
- Family
- Sleep
- Tennis

Project: Draw a Balance Chart with the headings you want on it and fill it in.

(See Accountability, Balance, Focus, Goals, Happiness, Life Ambition, Time Management)

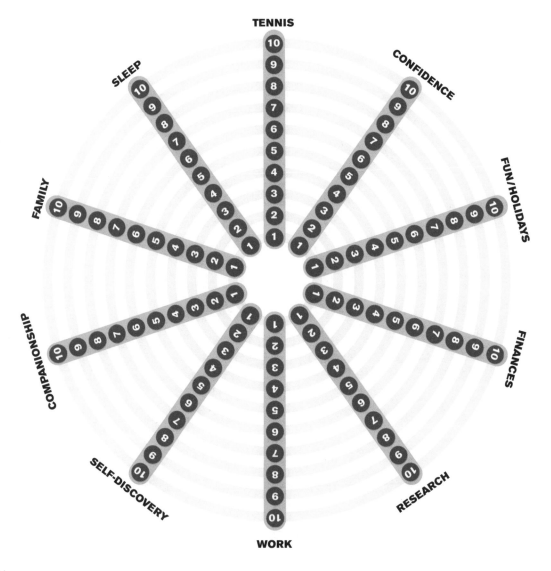

Beliefs ● ● ● ● ● ● ● ● ●

I think that one of the most difficult things for me, as a mother, has been watching my children slowly accumulate their limiting beliefs. To see your gorgeous six-year-old come home from school one day going 'I'm no good at maths' is difficult.

When we have a **belief**, we have accepted an opinion with confidence and conviction. We are so certain that this opinion is the truth that we believe it without having to have it proved. We have many beliefs about ourselves, some of which limit us, and some of which allow us to grow and be free, and each of these thoughts (beliefs) determines our actions. Most of these beliefs are created by the time we're seven, which is why they're often in such child-like language:

- **'I can …'/'I can't…'**
- **'I'm good at…'/'I'm no good at…'**
- **'I know…'/'I don't know…'**
- **'I like…'/'I don't like…'**
- **'They like me…'/'They don't like me…'**

'My belief always used to be that I was frightened of water, but this summer I learnt how to dive and I now love swimming.'

Our beliefs can block us

Whether you were categorised as a child as 'bright' or 'not very intelligent' might have some bearing on how you use your brain today. These thoughts that we have about our abilities can become so firmly embedded in us that we begin to assume they are the absolute truth; facts about us that we have to live with. In reality, they are not facts at all, but rather personal and often misguided beliefs.

- **We might block off earning money because we believe we're no good at it**
- **We might block off creativity because we believe only artists are creative**
- **We might block off new relationships because of our belief that we're too old to be starting new adventures.**

Ignore your beliefs and act the opposite

It can be difficult to change your mindset, instead change the way you act. For example, if you think 'I'm bad at relationships', make a list of all the relationships you've been good at and then stop thinking about that belief. Ignore it – push it away. Instead start acting as if you were good at relationships – rather than questioning your skills. You'll become your own role model, because you are good at relationships.

True or false?

Create a table and start writing a list of your beliefs – you may well have over one hundred. Focus on the negative beliefs. Can you prove they're true? Can you prove that they're made up? What are the advantages to keeping those negative beliefs? And finally, think of what you'd like to think

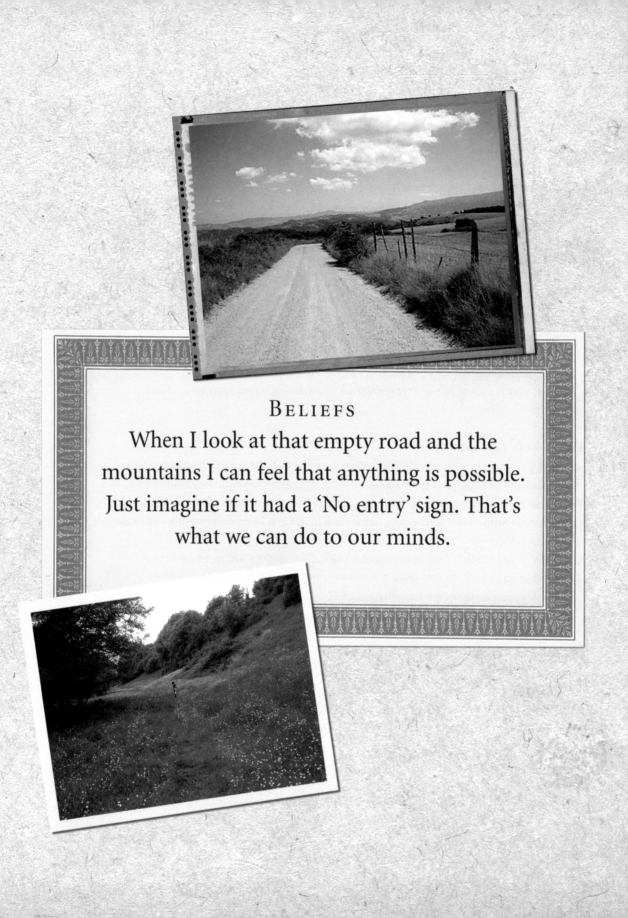

BELIEFS

When I look at that empty road and the mountains I can feel that anything is possible. Just imagine if it had a 'No entry' sign. That's what we can do to our minds.

instead of that negative belief. Make sure it really feels like a belief you want and think about using it as an affirmation.

List of my beliefs (negative and positive)

....

Proof that belief is true

....

Proof that belief is made up

....

Advantages to keeping that belief

....

What I'd really like to think instead of that negative belief

....

Project: Take a good look at your beliefs and see what's there. All the positive beliefs you find are worth holding on to. You want to think of yourself as 'artistic', 'innovative', 'sporty', 'sensitive', 'original', 'scientific', 'imaginative' and so on, but negative beliefs, such as 'stupid', 'forgetful', 'ugly' and so on, can be got rid of and seen for what they are – beliefs to be challenged.

Belief loops

Whatever you believe about yourself is what will change your performance – and therefore your future. If you believe you're good, you will work differently, successfully. You'll then get good results and you'll start raising the bar and aiming higher. Your future will start looking different. This belief circle can be limiting or enabling depending on your attitude towards yourself. Your only limitations are those of your own making.

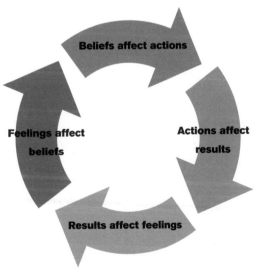

Project Two: Follow that belief loop round with one of your limiting beliefs and then with a belief you'd like to have. Just notice the difference.

(See Advantages, Affirmations, Assumptions, Comfort Zone, Confidence, Non-judgemental)

Belonging ● ● ● ● ● ● ●

My parents were German refugees and I grew up first generation British. I've never felt I belonged in the UK or in Germany or anywhere really. I used to mind always feeling an outsider, but I've now created communities that I feel a part of and definitely know I belong to. I don't know which came first – feeling happy that I belong, or feeling happy so I don't need to belong.

Belonging is when you take for granted that you are naturally part of something, that you are linked to something that is bigger than yourself. This belonging could be to do with your social identity or more intimate groupings.
'I really feel as if we belong together.'

Belonging in life

Sometimes we just don't feel we're making the best use of our time. Maybe we're fearful about doing something or don't know where to begin or maybe we just don't enjoy a certain part of our life. It's as if we didn't belong in it. It may be that you don't know what spirituality is all about and you don't feel any connection or sense of belonging to it. Similarly you might not feel you ever want to rest and relax and that it's a real waste of time, so you feel left out when others are talking about their holidays or afternoons in the hot tub.

Belonging to others

It may be that sometimes you're with a group of people and you just don't feel you belong there. They might all be talking about how they enjoy going to pubs, for example, and you don't or they may all have children and you don't. When you're in that situation, you can have fun with perspective. You can imagine that everyone there really liked you and how that would feel or even that just one person really liked you. You could also imagine what it would feel like if you did really belong to that group. How would your life be different? What would belonging to that group bring to you?

Things to do:
- Make a list of the groups you feel you belong to at present. How does it make you feel – are there more than you thought, or less?
- Think about any groups you would like to belong to – what would make you feel as if you belonged to them?
- Check whether others think you belong to groups you don't feel you belong to
- Go through your Balance Chart (Life Clubs version) and see where you feel you belong and where you don't
- What could you do to feel you belong in areas where you feel an outsider at present? (eg I don't belong in the Health & Fitness area because I don't like sport. I could belong by drinking more water and going on more long walks.)

(See Connection, Perspectives, Values)

Big Picture ● ● ○ ● ● ● ● ●

I remember working with someone once who was feeling very despondent about the amount of jobs she was going through. She kept on applying for new jobs, getting the job and then getting bored and leaving. It was only when she stopped focusing on the detail of the situation and started thinking about the Big Picture that she realised that with each of these jobs she was getting the experience she needed in order to be able to start up her own business, which was what she ultimately wanted to do.

You create your '**Big Picture**' by coming out of detail thinking and developing a bigger vision. It's looking at the same situation with a different perspective. Once you've found your Big Picture, you can then get more detailed again, by breaking down your Big Picture into smaller and smaller achievable targets.

'I'm redesigning the filing system and have started with the Big Picture. I know what I want it to be like and I'm now going to fill in the detail.'

Walk backwards

We can feel so caught up in the detail of the situation and what we're doing that it's good just to stop and look at the broader picture. What do we ultimately want? It's almost as if you're walking away from the situation and seeing it through a pair of binoculars used the wrong way round. It's another view, another version of your life.

Your Lightbulb Moment:
Where in your life are you getting bogged down by detail and could use some Big Picture thinking? How would it help you?

(See Goals, Life Ambition, Perspectives, Spider Diagrams, Visualisation)

Blame ● ● ● ● ● ● ● ●

I feel terrible writing this, but I've heard my family play an almost identical Blame Game to the one below – in the best humour, of course.

Blame is when you attribute fault to someone else – or they attribute it to you. Something has gone wrong and someone is being held accountable for the mistake. Blame is a way of avoiding personal responsibility.

'I was late for the meeting and I'm blaming you for not driving me to the station like you said you would last night.'

Do you ever blame others?

If you answer 'Yes' to most of these questions, you may not be being accountable for your life.

- **You rarely say 'Sorry' to others**
- **You think more about the past than the present or future**
- **You would say that the things that have gone wrong in your life are out of your control**
- **You feel life has been unfair to you**
- **You copy others when they're doing something wrong, using their irrational behaviour to excuse your own ('They're not stopping for that woman to cross the road, so why should I?')**
- **You often feel sorry for yourself.**

Instead of blaming others:

- **Apologise when you've made a mistake (accept that you're not always right)**
- **Focus on the present and future and what you want from your life**
- **Understand that you are responsible for your life**
- **Decide what you don't like about your life and change those things**
- **Forgive others and yourself and decide what you want to do next.**

Blaming parents

No matter what our parents did when we were younger, they inevitably did something 'wrong' and that's often what we focus on, rather than all the things they've done 'right'. We can usually remember the times we made our pillow wet from crying far easier than the times we bonded either as a family or with one particular member of our family. But rather than blame your parents, see if you can embrace anything good that came out of the relationship and remember that and forgive them for everything else.

A typical family 'Blame Game'

Where everyone blames someone else so no one takes responsibility.

Father to son: **You came home last, you should have locked the front door.**
Father to daughter: **You never lock the front door either.**
Husband to wife: **You've never taught them about being responsible.**
Brother to sister: **I didn't come home last night, you were out.**
Son to father: **Don't blame me, I thought you were going out.**
Son to mother: **He always blames me, why don't you protect me?**
Daughter to mother: **You told me you were going to be out late, mum.**
Sister to brother: **You didn't tell me you were going out – I wanted to come with you.**
Daughter to father: **I'm never the last one in, you always blame me.**
Mother to daughter: **Darling, you didn't listen. I never said we were going out.**
Mother to son: **Darling, you don't take responsibility for locking up.**
Wife to husband: **Yes, I know, it's all my fault. You always blame me.**

Things to do:
- Notice when you feel like blaming someone else and stop
- Observe how it feels when someone blames you
- Discover what could stop you blaming and start accepting responsibility
- Think about where in your life you keep on using blame.

(See Accountability, Big Picture, Control, Defensiveness, Failure, Forgiveness, Victim)

Body/Heart/Mind Types ● ● ● ● ● ● ●

I first came across this way of thinking of people as body, heart, mind types when I discovered the Enneagram (a system which can be used in personality typing) many years ago. I think if I had to give one single thing credit for helping me both in work and play, I'd give it to the Enneagram. I am constantly reading Enneagram books by David Daniels, Russ Hudson, Helen Palmer and Don Riso[3] and learn something new every time. Here (and in Personality Typing, page 219) I am literally just scratching the surface of this amazing study.

In our lives, each of us engages with the world using either our '**body**', our '**mind**' or our '**heart**'. And although we are all a combination of each, one will be dominant. You may notice these three areas within you when you have a decision to take, and you feel yourself pulled in three directions – or you may notice other people have different ways of dealing with the decision to you.
'*At this course I was on, the lady who ran it was a heart type – she was very dramatic and wanted to connect with everyone on a deep level. Her assistant was a body type and wanted to keep things moving along nicely and I'm a mind type so I was in my head constantly thinking of ideas. It was exciting and buzzy, but also quite scary because I never know which idea to go with.*'

The three types:
If you're a body (gut) type: you'll feel the world through physical sensations, intuition and gut instincts. You're open and aware of what your body is communicating to you. It's important to you to be comfortable – to know that life is the way it 'should be'.

If you're a heart (or soul) type: you'll be attuned to feelings, moods and emotions. You'll notice what you're feeling first which will help you connect to others, gain approval or acceptance or feel special. Your desire is to have meaningful interaction with those around you.

If you're a mind (or head) type: you'll see the world through analysis, imagination and planning. All this logic will help you become less anxious and fearful. You'll remain objective – observing and then deciding.

---

[3] Daniels, D. (2000) *The Essential Enneagram*, New York: HarperCollins Publishing; Palmer, H. (1991) *The Enneagram*, New York: HarperCollins Publishing; Richard Riso, D. and Hudson, R. (1999) *The Wisdom of the Enneagram*, New York: Bantam Books.

Which one am I?

Imagine you're at a conference and don't know anyone – how would you react?

If you're a body (gut) type: you're very open and in the present. You'll use your intuition and just be as you are. You're straightforward, uncomplicated and you'll take things as they come.

If you're a heart (or soul) type: you'll want everyone in the room to love you and connect with you straight away. You want emotional closeness with them all, now and forever.

If you're a mind (or head) type: your mind will start whirring and you'll want to work out what is the best thing to do. Rather than leaping in, you'll quickly assess the situation and then decide.

We are all different

When you know which type is dominant it will help you become aware of the way you behave, the way you think and the way you feel. Knowing your type can also help you relax. Each of us has our own individual style of relaxing, which is why when, for example, you're relaxing with a partner or a group of friends, you may find yourself wondering why you're not feeling refreshed. Each of us is different and we usually relax by using the part of ourselves that we have the most emotional attachment to in order to unwind. You can discover which type you are by seeing what really relaxes you.

Ben, Laura and Dan were on a walk together. Ben (a body type) threw himself into the countryside, enjoying the walking, noticing the different textures under his feet, spotting the changing weather with its shifting clouds, picking the blackberries, looking for mushrooms and listening to the birdsong. Ben wanted to walk for ages – he felt at one with nature and was aware all the time of his physical being in nature and his feet on the ground. Laura (a heart type), wanted to take things more slowly and get in touch with her feelings about the beautiful environment and her friends. She wanted to study the flowers carefully, noticing the difference in each one of them, smelling them, delighted that she was lucky enough to benefit from them. Laura was happy holding hands with her friends. Dan (a head type) didn't notice much of what was going on as he was thinking about something that interested him. When he did look round, he thought about the history of the fields and how they'd been like that for centuries. He wondered about what type of trees they were and how they were maintained, if at all. And, sometimes, when they were going down gravel paths, he felt worried about whether he'd slip or not. Dan was happy observing and analysing everything that was going on around and inside him.

Body type relaxation

If you're a Body type, the way into relaxing can start with your body. You may find a meditative walk or going rowing on the river in the early morning very calming, or even doing a 'dangerous' sport, like skiing, which relies on quick-witted intuition. Body types often want an energy-packed holiday – rushing around visiting ancient ruins or going shopping or trekking. Another Body way of clearing your mind quickly – maybe before an important phone call or to get to sleep – is to stretch your face – pretend you're shaving or pulling ugly faces or sticking your tongue out. In the same way you can stretch the rest of your body too.

BODY/HEART/MIND
We can all relax staring at
a beautiful sky.

Heart type relaxation

Heart types will find it calming to do something creative, or even spiritual, like meditating. You'll want time on your own, maybe watching an intense film or making one of your own. It may help you to find a quiet place to acknowledge your stress and then focus on being grateful. Gratitude is the Heart person's healing balm. You can meditate on your gratitude by thinking of something you are really grateful for. A simple exercise for a Heart type would be to trace the provenance of whatever you are doing. If, for example, you are ironing a shirt, you can think about how grateful you are to have been able to afford that shirt; you can then think about where the shirt came from and be grateful for the shop that sold you the shirt. Then you can be grateful for the people who made the shirt so it could be sold; and then be grateful for the people that wove the spun cotton into fabric so the shirt could be made; and be grateful for the spinners that spun the cotton and the pickers of the cotton and the planters of the cotton that was grown so you could have that shirt. If you focus on these thoughts as you iron your shirt and really imagine the history of that shirt, you will be amazed at how connected you feel to the shirt and the world and how calm you are.

Mind type relaxation

It can be very difficult to still the mind of a Mind type. One way is to fight thought with thought, by reading or talking or using a calm thought to get rid of the stressful ones. You can start by creating a storage file in your head of calm, happy thoughts or images that you can pull out when wanted. These thoughts could be of the day you earned your degree, or swimming in a lake or giving birth. If you want inspiration, look through magazines and cut out pictures that make you feel peaceful. Keep these substitute thoughts very clear and concise and, whenever a niggling thought won't let go, very adamantly focus on the relaxing thought, holding it in your head and breathing deeply. Use all your senses (vision, smell, sound, touch, taste) until that thought takes over everything else and calms you down.

Your Lightbulb Moment:
How would your life be different if you were a Mind, Body or Heart type (work with the two that aren't your dominant type)?

(See Absorption, Gratitude, Intuition, Meditation, Personality Typing, Relaxation)

Body Image ● ● ●

Age 16 I was at a charity fair in Belgravia, where Patrick Lichfield, a renowned photographer, was taking photos for £5. It remains one of my few regrets that at that age I didn't have enough money to ask him to take my photo. I watched him at work for a long time and remember clearly this quite plain lady coming up to have her photo taken by him. To my sophisticated teenage eyes, she hadn't put her make-up on very well and looked a little nervous as she made her way into the makeshift photographic studio, but as Patrick Lichfield rearranged the lighting and told her how gorgeous she looked, she turned from an ugly duckling into a beautiful swan and positively glowed from within. Her body image had taken on a new lease of life.

'A pearl is worthless as long as it is still in its shell.'

Indian proverb

Body image is how you feel about your physical appearance based on your self-observation and the way others react to you. Including what you imagine others might think of your body.
'I must have a really distorted body image as I always pick up all the size 12 clothes in the shop only to go back and find they are all too big and I am really a size 10.'

Believing what we see

Our self-image is a bit like having an imaginary pocket mirror that automatically flashes up throughout the day, either boosting our esteem or keeping us in check. This reflection is changeable and tricky, based on our deep-rooted insecurities and memories, as well as how we looked that morning or a recent compliment someone gave us. The way we see ourselves can dominate us and interfere with most aspects of our lives.

Think beautiful

You may consider certain people to be beautiful or handsome, but then discover that they clearly don't think so – they slink into the room at parties almost apologising for their presence. Conversely, those people you might overlook in terms of physical beauty, may emanate self-confidence. They seem to glow from top to toe – their body image is very positive, they don't worry about what others think of them; they know they're beautiful – and they're right.

Body image affects...

- Our relationships
  - if you're feeling unattractive you may not want to be touched by a partner or you might feel inhibited sexually
- Our personality and sense of self-worth
  - you might hold yourself back, repress ideas or decide not to tell that story you wanted to share, because you're distracted by this negative image of yourself
- Anything to do with health and fitness
  - you're frightened or intimidated by the idea of facing and exposing your body.

...and our behaviour too

Each of us allows our self-image to determine the way we behave.

- If we see ourselves as overweight, we eat too much and don't exercise, creating a vicious cycle as we continue to put on more weight. Eventually others will begin to see us in this way and treat us as if we have an eating problem, which, in turn, will encourage us to play into that role more and more
- If we see ourselves as handsome or beautiful, we will pay close attention to our physical self and appearance, and we will intuitively know we're attractive. Others will see us as attractive too, which again means we will play into that role, building an even greater positive self-image. So one good place to start increasing your self-image is simply to act attractive.

Your body strengths

Our body critique is ruthless and unfair – just imagine if we only loved our partners, children and friends for what they looked like, instead of all the wonderful things they do and give. Instead of looking at your body, pay attention to how strong and resilient it is, and all the things it can do. Once you feel your body from the inside rather than criticise it from the outside your perspective on it will change.

Project: Do a drawing of your body and look lovingly at your body as you draw it. You may like to say as you draw each area, 'What a stunning smile. It's so open and welcoming… what a beautiful neck. It's so supple and flexible… what strong arms, they're so long and mobile…'

(See Affirmations, Change, Excess, Perspectives)

Believe you're beautiful

Others will think you are beautiful

You'll feel more beautiful

Others will think you are more beautiful

Body Language ● ● ● ●

I often feel like letting people know what their body language is telling me about what they're thinking, or what I'm telling them with mine. The other day the builder surprised me by coming early and I was still in bed. As I answered the front door – looking perfectly decent, but in my nightie, I noticed that without thinking I'd put my hands crossed in front of me in a 'keep out' position.

Body language is the way we communicate without words. It's about our facial expressions, our posture, our gestures and our eyes. Over half our communication is non-verbal and has a significant input into what is communicated. We are interpreting and giving body language signals all the time, whether we are conscious of it or not. Body language varies from country to country, so never assume you understand someone's body language when abroad.
'She was looking all round the room and tapping her toes. Her body language really gave me the message that she was feeling restless and bored with my company.'

Some of the more obvious body language meanings

Arms crossed	I want to keep my distance (protecting body)
Legs crossed	Closed off to the person you're talking to
Hands in pockets	I can't help (I've got no hands available)
Shrugged shoulders	I really don't know
Leaning towards	I'm interested in what/who I'm leaning towards

Work backwards with body language

You can use your own body to work out how you're feeling too:

- **If you've got your arms crossed, ask yourself why you want to keep your distance**
- **If you've got your legs crossed, think why you're closing off to the person you're talking to**
- **If you've got your hands in your pockets, discover why you don't want to help them**
- **If you shrug your shoulders, think what could help you know**
- **If you're leaning towards someone, question what you like about them.**

What are your strengths?

You will have a body language strength, whether it's a great smile or a strong presence. Discover your strength and work with it. If you've got a good smile, for example, the next step is to relax your face and smile with your eyes. If you've got a strong presence, for example, don't contradict it by crossing your arms.

Body language in relationships

Often you can tell how intimate your relationship with someone is by how your bodies are working together. You may notice how they're standing or sitting next to you or opposite you in exactly the same pose. It wasn't planned, but it's an indication of how in tune with each other you are. Similarly, if they're sitting close to you on the edge of their chairs with their arms open, you know they're responsive and interested in knowing more about you. Conversely, if friends sit or stand with closed arms and crossed legs or lie far back in their chairs you may feel as if they're pushing you away and if they avoid your eyes, you'll know they don't want to get too close to you.

Look at the whole person rather than just one part of them. Their eyes might be saying 'talk to me' whereas their body is turned away. Are they friendly, nervous, pushing you away, or quite simply, have they got backache? The more comfortable you feel in your body, the more your friend will relax and start echoing what you're doing. When you start relaxing your face, smiling, uncrossing your arms, looking into their eyes and generally showing that you are open to what others say it will open the way to deeper conversations and more intimate friendships.

Did you know?

Body language affects your emotions, so if you 'look' and act happy, it's a good way to start changing your emotional state.

Things to do:

- **Ask friends and family what their first impression on meeting you would be**
- **Ask friends and family what your strongest body feature is and how you could capitalise on it**
- **Enjoy your body – stretch it, curl it up, hug it.**

(See Assumptions, Emotions, Feedback, Listening, Relaxation)

BODY IMAGE

Neither cows nor babies think twice
about their body image.

Bottom Line ●

The expression bottom line can be used to focus both your own thoughts and those of others. Often when you've asked someone what's wrong, you can hear when they're telling you the same story (sometimes, it feels, word for word) as they've told everyone else. It's only when you ask them to bottom line that you get to what's really important.

By **bottom-lining** you are delivering a short sentence (reply or question), which gets to the heart of the subject matter. You are focusing your thoughts and/or those of others.
'Can I bottom line you? Rather than telling me about your dishwasher and the flood, please tell me what you'd like me to do.'
'Let me bottom line. I had a messed-up childhood.'

Project: Bottom line everything you say for an hour and see what happens and how you feel.

Project Two: Think of any problems you have and see if you can write them down in one sentence. What's at the heart of each of them?

(See Focus, Listening, Victim)

Boundaries ● ○ ● ● ● ● ● ●

I learnt my lesson about looking after myself when I was very tired one afternoon. I'd been working all day and my colleagues were about to go home – we'd had a long day. When I opened the door it was pouring with rain and I imagined none of them would have umbrellas as it had been sunny that morning. I was the only one with a car. I was about to say 'Would you like me to drive you to the station?' when I stopped and thought about how I was feeling. I was shattered and possibly too tired even to be a safe driver. I let them leave on their own and collapsed into exhausted tears. That was the first time I consciously put myself first. I put a boundary around my generosity and by doing so protected myself.

We set **boundaries** to protect and take care of ourselves. We put them in place to make us feel comfortable, although sometimes we put boundaries in our mind that stop us achieving our potential.
'My mum keeps on asking me to come and see her, so I've set a boundary in place and told her I can only come and see her once a week or I've got no time to finish decorating my place.'

Boundaries that restrict

You may have put imaginary boundaries up in your head that stop you living the life you could. It's often difficult to see these as removable, but just as you put them there, you can take them away. They may be:

- Beliefs that limit you
- Assumptions that limit you
- Fears that blocks you.

Boundaries that liberate

Sometimes you have to put barricades up between yourself and others to give you some space and freedom. But sometimes what was put up as a barricade to give you a bit of space can end up trapping you. These are some boundaries you may want to put up to give you some space:

- Saying 'No'
- Deciding what you will and will not do for others – what you're prepared to give (eg time, but only Sunday nights; eg help, but only in an emergency)
- Knowing what you want and don't want in a relationship (eg want an equal partnership; don't want the role of cleaner)
- Being busy so you're not available
- Keeping things to yourself.

After a relationship had finished painfully, Louis felt as if he'd built a brick wall around his heart. Rather than risk getting hurt, Louis hid away, putting his emotions and feelings in a safe place – surrounded by these bricks. After a year or so, Louis got brave again and one by one he decided to take those bricks away. His first steps were tentative, but slowly he grew in confidence. Louis started by saying 'Hello' to his neighbour and went on to sitting with colleagues in the canteen instead of on his own. He started talking to his friends more about his thoughts and gradually he began to make new friends and feel happier and more open within his existing relationships. Louis noticed how he was able to talk to people about things he'd never been able to mention before and was amazed that they didn't walk away from him, but instead seemed even more interested than before. Brick by brick, they were all removed and Louis knew he was just beginning to live.

Boundaries between friends

If you have friends or acquaintances you don't want to see as often it can be difficult to tell them that (and you may not want to say something that blunt). Instead invite them round as part of a crowd, rather than alone, or see them for short meetings only. Practise saying 'I want more time for myself these days'. Make it about you.

 Your Lightbulb Moment:
What boundary will you set up (or take down) first?

(See Assumptions, Beliefs, Fear, Letting Go, Loneliness, Negotiation, Saying 'No')

Brainstorming ● ● ● ● ●

I love brainstorming, whether on my own or with others. It's a connecting process if you do it with others and a fun mind game if you do it on your own. Genevieve Hawes and I (and anyone else who's working with us at the time), use it a lot, thinking of ideas for websites or workshops.

Brainstorming is when you take a word or concept and think of as many ideas as you can that spring from that word or concept. You brainstorm when you're stuck for ideas. The goal of brainstorming is to break out of habitual ways of thinking and give us more ideas to choose from which can be especially useful if you have a problem to solve. Brainstorming in a group means you can bounce ideas around, but you can equally brainstorm alone. And you can write down your thoughts or say them aloud or both – whatever works for you.

'We brainstormed what we should call our new cat and came up with "Amata". It sounded loving.'

How brainstorming works

For example, think about a 'ham sandwich' for two minutes brainstorming anything that comes to mind:

Bacon... Pig... Farm... Pink... Picnic... Bread... Sun... Rain... Wellington boots... Caravan... Camping... Mud... Festivals... Music... Happiness...

Or you could go off on another tack:

Egg & cress... Cucumber... Jam... Scones... Cricket... Summer lawns... Croquet... Pimm's... Flowery dresses... White linen... Hats... Picnic rugs... Stately homes... Vintage cars... Hampers...

The next level

If you want to, you can throw in a random 'seed' (a silly word), any word will do.

Harry didn't know where or when to go on holiday. He chose as his random 'seed' a canary. By brainstorming around a canary he came up with lots of ideas – the first, and most obvious, was the Canary Islands, then somewhere yellow – fields with buttercups – so spring would be a good time to go on holiday. He thought about where birds fly freely, so the Scilly Isles or a jungle or maybe he could have a trip to London Zoo to see the aviary.

Project: Brainstorm what you want to do this weekend, using 'paper' as your random seed.

(See Connection, Creativity, Laughter, Metaphor, Spider Diagrams)

Breathing ● ● ● ● ●

I remember when I was first shown how to breathe properly. I was absolutely amazed – I had been doing it all wrong – almost backwards. That night as I was lying down and relaxed, I was intuitively breathing how my body intended me to, but when I was standing up and running around, I'd just forgotten how.

Breathing is the act of taking air into and out of the lungs to supply the body with oxygen. We breathe deeply or shallowly, quickly or slowly depending on what we're doing and how fit we are. Breathing properly will alleviate stress, calm you down, make you think more clearly. Controlled breathing is used in many forms of meditation and yoga.

'I never know how to breathe when I'm swimming.'

Breathe properly

When you were a child you automatically breathed properly. Now, as an adult, when you are lying down you will automatically breathe correctly too. Just in case you've forgotten, this is how to do it.

1 Lie on your back with your knees bent and your feet flat on the floor – you can do this sitting or standing, but you'll find it easier if you do it lying down at first
2 Put your hands on your abdomen (stomach)
3 Breath in through your nose to the count of four
4 Imagine a balloon in your tummy that you're inflating with the air that you're inhaling – your hands should rise as your tummy does
5 Hold the air in for a few seconds
6 Then exhale slowly through your mouth to a count of four. Imagine letting the air out of the balloon in your tummy. Your hands should fall as your tummy does.

Project: Practise proper breathing at least three times a day for a minimum of five minutes at a time.

(See Meditation)

Change ● ● ● ● ● ● ● ● ● ●

I tend to think in massive visions – 10, 20, 30 years ahead – and it can scare me. The amount of changes I'm going to have to go through to get to that 30-year-ahead "me" can seem overwhelming. If, instead of living in the future, I break those massive changes down into something small and tangible I'm going to do today to move me in the right direction, everything feels manageable. It's thinking and doing that one step at a time that works.

There are two kinds of **change**: change that you want to make and change that is thrust upon you. Even when you don't make a decision to change, things change. Choosing to change is a conscious, rational decision as is choosing not to.

'There's so much change going on – we're moving house, Max has got a new job and I'm pregnant. I'm not sure I can take much more.'

'I'm getting older and can see how I'm changing physically. I wish I wasn't getting older and I wish I could change myself so I didn't care.'

Life changes

There are changes that are thrust on us and changes that are self-imposed. Some of us thrive on change and are constantly putting ourselves through new experiences, but some of us dread change and are filled with worry in case things should go wrong.

Change within families

There is a potential for so much change in a family, whether it's a baby being born, a parent leaving to get divorced, children leaving the parents' home after their education has finished or a family member dying. We also change and sometimes it's not noticed or appreciated. Has your family allowed you to grow and develop and have they noticed the changes in you or are they still treating you the way they used to? Have you been observing what your brothers and sisters are really like now as adults and how they treat you? Are you aware of how they've changed and grown?

Things to do:

- Work out all the things that you'd like to change. Use the Balance Chart (Life Clubs version, page 77) for inspiration
- Notice the difference between your Life Ambition and your life now. Use a Spider Diagram to work out what changes you'll want to make to get from here to there
- Think about all the things that have changed in your life even though you didn't want them to and who or what helped you cope with those changes.

The change circle

Happiness, leads to **Loss**, leads to **Suffering**, leads to **Hope**, leads to **Happiness**. In our lives we go through many changes at any one time and are in different places on the circle with each change. These cycles are often not synchronised, so you may be in loss in

'He who has health has hope, and he who has hope has everything.'

Arabian proverb

one area of your life, whereas in another you are regaining hope. No matter how small the change, we go through these four emotions each time.

Sarah woke up and smiled. It was a stunning day, the sun was shining and she didn't have to get into work as early as usual. She felt happy. Sarah had a lovely long shower and put on a new shirt she had bought, but when she came down for breakfast she realised there was no fruit (and not much else to eat). From happiness, Sarah felt in loss. Leaving for work with an empty stomach, she saw in the distance the bus she had to take to work pulling away from the bus stop. From loss she went into suffering. It was a long wait until the next bus, but after a while one of Sarah's neighbours joined her at the bus stop, so from suffering, Sarah went into hope. At work, Sarah was complimented on her new top and found herself back in happiness.

That was a fairly quick change circle. This is a slightly longer one.

After 10 years of smoking, Luke decided to give up. He was really happy about his decision and felt good about himself and his addiction free future. By midday Luke was in loss. He was nervous, worried and uneasy. He was beginning to recognise how badly he wanted a cigarette. Luke felt as if his life had fallen apart. What had happened to his comfy routine of a mid-morning cigarette walking round the block? By the end of the day, Luke was really suffering. He was super tense, stressed, sad and depressed with a raging headache and a mega temper. His suffering lasted a few weeks and then along one day came hope. Luke realised he didn't crave that cigarette so badly. He could feel that giving up smoking could be a reality. Luke had given up and could return to happiness.

As you can see, sometimes we can be in each emotion – each part of the circle for years, sometimes seconds. Like happiness, suffering is a part of life and, until you experience the lows you cannot experience the highs.

Use change

If you change the perspective you are viewing a problem from, you will get a new answer. You can do this by asking someone their perspective on your problem or you can use your imagination to think how fictitious characters or those you know would respond to your situation. Having a perspective that isn't yours, literally can help you to 'put things in perspective.'

You can only change yourself

You may be able to influence and inspire and motivate others, but ultimately you can only change yourself. If there's something about someone else that's annoying you, see how you can change so that it no longer upsets you. For example, you can't make your partner pay you more attention, but you can change the way you experience this. Get your attention from someone else? Give it to yourself?

Confidence and change

When change is thrust on you it can take a while in suffering to recover. Building your confidence up is difficult in those situations, but essential, so that you don't become depressed. Your confidence will help you either tackle the situation or accept it – or both. Change yourself by believing you can. If you see yourself differently, others will too.

Coral had been lying low for a while and avoiding parties and seeing people. Ever since she had gone grey (the first out of all her friends) she had completely lost her confidence along with her natural ability to choose clothes that suited her. Coral had wanted to dye her hair, but her hairdresser had told her it was too dry, but that she looked gorgeous. Coral knew she was lying. She felt she looked years older and that the clothes she used to wear suddenly appeared ghoulish on her. However, she couldn't ignore her best friend's hen night. For weeks she dreaded the event – it was in a fashionable bar, followed by a celebrity guest-list style restaurant and she knew exactly who else would be invited – they were all incredibly elegant and intimidating. However, it didn't quite turn out as she expected. As soon as she arrived she met someone she had never met before, who worked in fashion and also had grey hair, but it was dyed grey. She immediately asked Coral who did hers – it turned out that having grey hair was the height of fashion. Coral's confidence began to grow from here, as she regained her sense of proportion about the fickle and ridiculous world of fashion and beauty. That night she learned to appreciate how much fun it is to be different.

Coral acted differently because of the way she was spoken to and the people around her then saw her differently and encouraged even more change, which impacted on Coral's behaviour and, ultimately, improved her self-image. It was a positive circle with a positive outcome.

Things to do:
- Think about the changes you've been through that you didn't want to go through and find one good thing that came out of each of them
- Take one small step towards your Life Ambition or any goal you want to achieve.

(See Acceptance, Affirmations, Beliefs, Comfort Zone, Letting Go, Life Ambition, Perspectives, Procrastination, Role Models, Spider Diagrams)

Choices ● ● ● ● ● ●

I find it difficult to make speedy choices. What works best is when I stop and think about what I really want, giving my intuition a chance to be heard. Otherwise I get confused by all the exciting options.

In life we always have **choices** and, usually, we have the freedom to choose. What can be very difficult is deciding which option we want.
'I don't know what I want to eat – it's such a long menu.'
'Which advertising campaign do we want to go with? They've all got merits.'

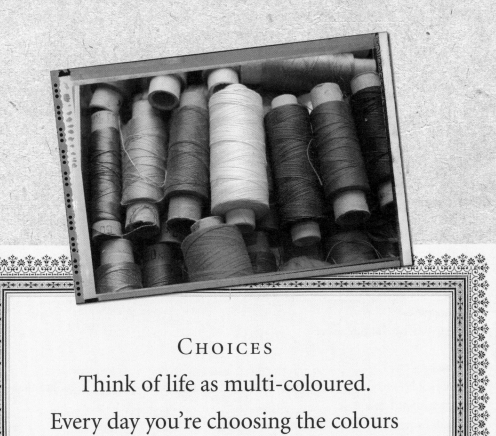

CHOICES

Think of life as multi-coloured.
Every day you're choosing the colours
to create the day you want.

No idea…?

Many of us find the idea of choice exciting. Having all these choices is like having lots and lots of different options floating out there in front of us and tantalising us. Life looks like one of those ice-cream vans with lots of different flavours to choose from and no idea what flavour to choose. We don't want to get rid of any of our options in case we regret it. Just losing one would give us a loss of freedom. Ironically, our happiness can only start when we do get rid of all the options and focus. Holding that ice cream in our hand and consciously focusing on licking and enjoying it will bring us more contentment than having all those options out there.

Why not…?

What can make it so difficult for us to choose is either that we're worried we're going to make the wrong choice or that there are so many choices that we feel overwhelmed. The crucial thing is just to pick one – if it doesn't work, you can resort to Plan B.

Can your decision be made:
- Rationally?
- Intuitively?
- Combination of the above?

Rationally

1 Know exactly what the decision is. Sometimes decisions seem linked, separate them out and answer one at a time
2 Work out what's important to you
3 Make a list of pros and cons
4 Think whether your values could help you make the decision
5 Notice any assumptions you're making
6 Ask friends, colleagues, experts, others for their views.

Intuitively

1 Trust your initial instincts
2 Use visualisation to help you imagine various scenarios
3 Toss a coin to get your intuition going
4 Meditate.

Combination of the above

1 Remember your Life Ambition goal. Which decision most closely aligns with that?
2 Choose different options to visualise and imagine them one after the other.

Delegate

Because making decisions can be so difficult, it is often easier to delegate or just ask someone you trust and do what they suggest. There are two books, *The Dice Man* by Luke Rhinehart and *Yes Man* by Danny Wallace which have taken this to extremes. In both books, the authors/heroes get rid of all their choices[4]. In *The Dice Man*, every decision is taken by a roll of the dice and in *Yes Man*, the author meets someone on a bus who suggests he 'says "Yes" more' and from that moment on, 'Yes' is his answer to all choice.

Your Lightbulb Moment:
What worries you about taking decisions – is it that they have to be perfect or that you feel overwhelmed by them?

(See Decisions, Focus, Intuition, Problem Solving, Procrastination, Regret, Values)

Comfort Zone

I was mentioning to someone that I was running a Life Club for hundreds of people. I clearly appeared a little nervous because she looked at me and said 'You're right out of your comfort zone, aren't you?' My emotions always give me away and she was right – I was scared. I needn't have worried as it went brilliantly and I broke out of one comfort zone and… into another. Now I'll be worried about talking to thousands of people.

Our **comfort zone** is that risk-free place where we know what we're doing and feel settled and comfortable; we're doing what we've always done. In order to achieve what we want to, we have to step out of our comfort zone – changing our behaviour and experiencing different reactions – and that can feel frightening and dangerous.

'The only way for my business to grow is if I step out of my comfort zone and become a sales person, but that feels so scary.'

'I want to meet a partner, but it would mean so many changes to my lifestyle, I'm not sure I'm ready to step out of my comfort zone. I know what life as a single person is like.'

Project: The Comfort Zone Circles

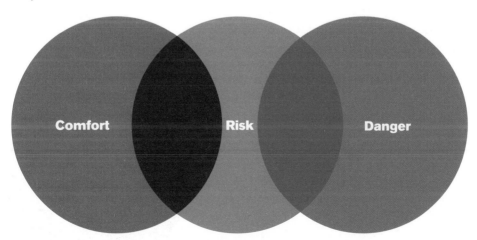

---

[4] Rhinehart, L. (1971) *The Dice Man*, Talmy,Franklin Ltd; Wallace, D. (2005) *Yes Man*, London: Ebury Press.

1 **Decide on an area you'd like to change (eg you'd like a new job)**

2 **Draw a circle, 'The Comfort Zone Circle' and in the circle write down everything that feels comfortable about your job – all the advantages to staying there (eg I like my colleagues, it's an easy commute, I know the ropes etc)**

3 **Then draw another circle a few centimetres to the right of it, 'The Danger Circle' and in it write down everything that feels dangerous about leaving your job – all your assumptions about what might happen (eg I might not get another job, I might not like my new job, I might not be able to see my kids as much)**

4 **Overlapping the two circles, draw 'The Risk Circle'. There will be some things you have to do that feel risky but more comfortable, write them in the section where 'The Risk Circle' overlaps 'The Comfort Zone Circle'. There are other things you have to do that feel quite scary, write them in 'The Risk Circle'. There are some things which will feel both risky and dangerous, write them where 'The Risk Circle' overlaps 'The Danger Circle'**

5 **Do one thing that you have written in the section where 'The Risk Circle' overlaps 'The Comfort Zone Circle'. In order to experience change, you have to take that first risk. Think about how it feels doing it.**

(See Advantages, Assumptions, Beliefs, Change, Confidence, Emotions, Fear, Procrastination)

Compromise ● ● ● ○ ● ● ● ● ● ● ●

They say that the secret of being happily married is compromise, but I think that if you are happily married, you don't always see it as compromise – you just want to make the other person happy.

Compromise can feel like a limitation, but it's when two parties settle on a mutual agreement which benefits both of them rather than one or the other. Usually the compromise is reached by both of the conflicting parties giving way.
'We can't afford two holidays a year and I like going somewhere hot in the winter, but Peter likes going away in the summer. I think we'll have to compromise by taking it in turns to choose each year.'
'I really want to go to a party tonight, but it's my rock-climbing club. I might have to compromise and miss a bit of both.'

Compromise circles

If you find you can't agree with someone, each of you draw this diagram and write in the middle what you can't compromise on. Once you understand exactly what you're dealing with, you'll know where the boundaries are. Then put your negotiations in the outside circle and see where you can compromise.

Life can be a compromise

So many of us sit at home at the weekends waiting for our partners (or others) to return from whatever they've planned, wondering why we didn't organise our weekend so we too had something to do. Others of us go out with friends and find ourselves again compromising – they all want to go to the pub whereas we'd rather watch a film (or vice versa). Holidays too can be a compromise – trying to please everyone and leaving no one feeling truly relaxed or satisfied. Compromising with others may mean that at the weekend you each get two hours to do exactly what you want or that you decide together what plans you're going to make.

Nick and Felicity had compromised on many holidays. They both relaxed in different ways and yet they wanted to go on holiday together. One holiday they had flown all the way to New York for a week's break. Neither of them had ever been before. Nick spent the entire time lying on his bed, reading. He had never felt better. Felicity, in the meantime, went shopping, visited museums and socialised. It was just what she needed. They met for breakfast and supper and then had the day to themselves. When they finally got together they were both replenished, recharged and excited to share their news and thoughts with each other.

Project: Go through the Life Clubs Balance Chart, page 77, and notice where in your life you're compromising when you'd rather not. How could you change those situations?

(See Body/Heart/Mind Types, Boundaries, Personality Typing, Saying 'No')

Confidence ● ● ● ● ● ● ● ● ●

I've been under-confident in many areas, but the one that stands out is my under-confidence about my looks, especially as a teenager. My teens were spent with my mother putting my mass of wild, frizzy hair in curlers in an attempt to straighten it, smiling a lot to hide my long, serious face and wearing fake tan to cover my alabaster white skin. Needless to say, all those things I then hated have become the things I now like most about myself. They make me different and memorable. If only I'd known.

Confidence is having a trust or belief in a person or thing or oneself (self-confidence).
'*I learnt French last year and now am confident that I can learn Spanish too.*'

Confidence is learnt

Confidence can be built with practice and, once built, will keep growing. This confidence will enable you to step out of your comfort zone and have a go at more and more complicated things. For example, you now feel so confident about tying your shoelaces (remember as a child when you couldn't?) that you're prepared to have a go at doing a double knot. We often succeed at things because of our confidence rather than because of any special abilities.

Ten things to help your confidence

1 Instead of doing things you 'should/need to/have to/must', do things you 'want' to do – notice your language

2 Being loved is not about achieving. Be pleased with everything you do, whether it works or doesn't – you've done something and you can learn from your mistakes

3 Don't let small things you do 'wrong' (like failing a test) put you off feeling good

4 Forget about seeking the approval of others. Be you

5 Just because you feel 'ugly', 'stupid', 'boring' (etc) doesn't mean it's true

6 Avoid using words like 'failure', 'loser', 'twit' about yourself

7 Ask those you love what they appreciate about you – write down what they say

8 Trust your intuition rather than other people

9 Enjoy things you have enjoyed before

10 Realise the advantages to staying under-confident.

Toby had been thinking about learning to drive for years. He had once attempted to learn and had failed his test, which had shaken his confidence – he decided at the time to leave it and come back to it later when he could afford more lessons. Years passed and Toby was now earning enough money to pay for the lessons, but he still put it off – even though he knew that getting his driving licence would help his career. Part of him knew that he was afraid of failing again – as a grown man, failing his test would be even more humiliating. There was also a secret advantage to not driving – Toby didn't have to become a chauffeur to friends and family. Through a mixture of affirmations ('I am a brilliant driver'), focusing on the freedom that driving would give him and breathing slowly and calmly during the test, Toby passed. As you would expect, his life and confidence changed.

There are always advantages to keeping under-confident – whether it's being able to call up a friend to help you hang those bookshelves or ensure your boss never asks you to deliver a presentation because you're 'not very good at it'. Step out of your comfort zone and boost your confidence.

 Your Lightbulb Moment:
What are all the advantages to you to staying under-confident?

Project: Set yourself a small goal every day and achieve it. Do it for a few months or until your confidence has grown.

(See Achievement, Advantages, Authentic, Beliefs, Change, Comfort Zone, Goals, Language, Role Models, Success, Values)

'Confidence is
half of victory.'

Yiddish proverb

Connection (Feeling connected) ● ● ● ● ● ● ●

Connection has always been a word I've felt uneasy with. Probably because it seemed too spiritual a concept for me and not grounded enough. And yet, just by starting to become aware of the idea of being connected, I've realised that I too feel connection. I was sitting with my arm round my youngest on the Tube the other day and suddenly felt as if we were totally linked. It wasn't one of those 'I love him' moments, it was just a rush of heat that flowed between the two of us. It felt magical.

Feeling connected is when you really link with nature or animals or other people (individuals or groups) or yourself. It's finding where we are part of each other and part of a whole. You can feel connected to places and things and even to a Higher Being as well, although not everyone feels connected to everything.

'I feel so connected to this place – these trees. I know I've been here before. Something is touching me at a deep level.'

'As we were sitting together I felt we were just so connected that I could have talked all night.'

'Connection to me has a timelessness to it. When I cuddled the cat this morning I forgot the time and missed my run.'

Start small

Rather than focusing on your lack of connection, focus on the connections you make easily. If you can connect with nature or music or art, for example, enjoy that and watch as your connections with people grow. Connection doesn't have to be huge. It can be a small, but powerful thing. If you don't feel connected to someone, that's fine – a genuine handshake is better than a fake hug.

Connected?

Begin by noticing when you're feeling warm and open to others, because then you can recreate that feeling as often as you want to. It might be when you're on holiday that you have the space in your life for others. It might be that when you truly stop and listen to someone else, you can feel how much love you have for them. Sometimes when you're involved in an activity with another person you might notice a bond that you had both forgotten about. Being vulnerable and helped by another can also bring out your love for them. Or it could be that discovering more about the special, unique person you are, allows you to be there for others and to love them. Feeling emotionally tied in with others gives a wonderful feeling of wellbeing. It provides you with the strength to accomplish other things and gives you a warm glow of affection.

Project: To start becoming connected with other people, think about the things you have in common; maybe you're the same height, maybe you've both had a busy day, maybe they dance the same way you do, maybe they have children like you do, maybe their parents were both from the same place as yours were. Once you notice that there is a connection between you and another person, you could play this little game: look at them in as non-judgemental a way as you can, ignoring what they look like on the outside, but focusing, instead, on who they are on the inside – see what happens and prepare to be happily surprised.

Project Two: Notice how you feel connected outdoors. Is it that you feel connected to the seasons and the effortless cycle of nature or that you like to slow down and really notice all the details, closely observing, say, a flower, seeing how many petals it has, what it smells like, its texture and touch – how it moves, what it's like to play with? Or do you enjoy thinking about why those fields are used for that purpose or notice when nature resembles a drawing or painting you've seen?

(See Absorption, Belonging, Body/Heart/Mind Types, Non-judgemental, Personality Typing)

Control ●●○●●●●●●●

I definitely like being in control of some things and not others. Understanding which ones were which was key to working out the roles I wanted in the home and those I was happy to relinquish. Things like reading the children a bedtime story, I really love; whereas, looking after them when they've hurt themselves, I don't love. I remember my eldest, age four or five, saying to his father one day, 'Daddy, you make a really good Mummy.' No doubt Daddy was dealing with a grazed knee.

Having **control** is about having the power to direct or determine situations, emotions, actions, activities, the course of events, behaviour and other people's behaviour. Control means different things at different times. It can be as full on as commanding or governing (when you exercise power over someone) or used to limit intensity (such as reining in a temper). It can be used to manipulate or to show that you're the master of knowledge.
'I struggled to control my jealousy, but I couldn't control my anger.'

We like being in control
You are the only person in control of your life. Whatever you decide to do, you'll do and whatever you decide not to do, you won't. A large part of our satisfaction with our life is to do with how much control we have. Many of us have too much going on in our life for it to feel anything other than chaotic, let alone successful and controlled.

Harry and Tom were on holiday. It wasn't a long break – just six days, but they took their laptops with them to make sure they didn't miss anything. For the first two days they both checked emails regularly until the Internet connection crashed and they were out of contact with the world. At first they were a bit lost. They felt a little discombobulated, but after a while it was as if a weight had lifted off their shoulders; they relaxed, lazed around and enjoyed each other's company. They felt younger and lighter and vowed never to take their laptops away on holiday again. When the Internet connection was restored a few days later, Harry and Tom took control of how often they looked at their computers instead of feeling sucked into them.

'Today is the tomorrow we worried about yesterday.'

Proverb

Remove distractions

One day pretend you're stuck in the 1970s. You don't have a mobile or a computer or anything else electronic and you just do what you can do from where you are. You make appointments and keep to them because you can't tell anyone (at least not very easily) that you're running late. When you have a brainwave you write notes on pieces of paper and, if you've got time, you just sit calmly and think. Calmer days help you feel in control, as do setting goals and keeping to routines. Re-introduce technology slowly.

Control freak

To call someone a 'control freak' is a rude way of saying to someone that they're wanting to gain control over you and the situation. For example, a 'back-seat driver' who is constantly telling you not only which way to go, but when to change gear in your car might be a control freak. Control freaks don't realise that other people are capable of doing things. They are perfectionists gone wild.

Am I a 'control freak'? quiz

If you answer 'yes' to most of these questions, you may well want a bit too much control in your life. Think about what could help you relax and let go.

- **Are you always finding fault with others?**
- **Do you get really upset if friends are late?**
- **Do you always know that you have the 'right' answer?**
- **Do you make most of the decisions for friends and family?**
- **Do you get a knot in your stomach if plans are changed at the last minute?**
- **Do you want everyone to do things your way?**
- **Do you dislike your partner wanting to do things on his/her own?**
- **Do you lose your temper easily?**
- **Do you find it impossible to relax and be in the moment?**

Losing control

It can be very difficult being with someone who wants everything the way they want it, who loses their temper and who doesn't trust you. What's important is to remember that their behaviour is not personal. It has nothing to do with you, but stems from their own under-confidence and fear. Reassure them that you love them or respect them (if they're your boss), but that you are doing the best you can. If you find them becoming very manipulative and that this is affecting your happiness, leave the relationship or suggest you both seek professional help.

Leave room for being out of control

Sometimes everything in our lives can be so controlled and organised, it's good to leave room for a little randomness so you can stumble on something new or be taken out by a friend spontaneously, or just get lost.

Give up control

The keys to loosening a need to control are tapping into your sense of humour – i.e. not taking life so seriously – and finding ways to relax. Somewhere in your memory is something amusing that has happened to you in the past. Keep that memory as present as you can at all times and use it to help you see things differently when you feel yourself getting tense. Breathing deeply is another thing that can help you relax, think 'everything will be perfect as it is' as you breathe. And, finally, remember that there is something you can always control – yourself.

Project: Play the 'Left/Right' game. It's best with two or more people, but you can play it alone. Start walking, cycling (or even driving) and, every time you come to a junction or roundabout, one of you choose which way to go. The object of the game is to get lost – out of control – and see what you can discover.

Your Lightbulb Moment:
In what areas of your life could you renounce control?

(See Accountability, Balance Chart, Excess, Fear, Perfectionism, Stress, Values, Victim)

Creativity ● ● ○ ● ○ ○ ● ● ● ●

I was very flattered when a friend who's known me since she was five said she used to love going round to my childhood home because it was so creative. I loved going to her home because I felt it was creative. Creativity is everywhere, it just takes different forms.

Creativity is having the imagination and inventiveness to generate new ideas and concepts or to make new associations between already existing ideas and concepts. Some say we are born creative, others that we can teach creativity.
'When I'm feeling creative I pick up the phone and ask someone round.'
'My great creative achievement was digging a pond in my garden.'
'I find preparing assignments for my students very creative.'

Get re-creative

Our natural instinct is to be creative – it gives us pleasure, makes life surprising and fills us with a kind of inspired, buzzing energy, which is infectious and attractive. As we grow up it's easy to lose touch or fall out of love with our creative side – suddenly we become overly serious and decide that we haven't got time for messing around or dreaming up strange ideas. Making things, being original, doing something different, simply entertaining ourselves with the storm of our imaginations, memory and emotions, is a way of understanding life and coming to terms with whatever it throws at us. Reconnect with your talents and creativity.

CREATIVITY

There is nothing more creative
than looking at nature. And nature
can inspire us to be creative too.

Eight ways to be creative

1 Think of yourself as a creative person
  – creativity isn't about being original – it's about being relaxed, open and determined. Creativity is not just an ability, it is also an attitude

2 Keep looking at things as if you were seeing them for the first time
  – get curious about everything

3 Get responsive
  – start seeing, feeling, breathing and laughing

4 Find people who will support your creative endeavours
  – Picasso had his art teacher father, who can encourage you?

5 Watch how children don't censor their ideas
  – be happy with silly, outrageous, wild ideas

6 Discover a creative zone for you to be creative in
  – it may be a place in your head

7 Make time for creativity to percolate
  – creative moments come whenever there's space for them

8 Don't worry if you don't like what you produce
  – each work is a new layer of ideas that you're building on.

Find a creative home

You may only feel creative in an art class, an orchestra pit, or daydreaming in the bath, but discovering those places where you feel at your most creative is key. So many children are banned from doing 'messy' things at home that they begin to associate creativity with school. Maybe you're like that too. Make your first creative step to discover new places that make you feel creative or to find a space in your home – a creativity zone. It might be that you need a quiet area away from distraction, or you might find that you like to work with music or the radio on. Even without a special zone you can bring creativity into all areas of your life at any time of day or night, because maybe the creative zone is a place in your head?

Find creative role models

Spend time and share ideas with people who bring out the creative you. Getting out of an 'uncreative' box can be difficult – it's as if everyone you know is sitting on the lid and squashing you in. If you can, find people who fully embrace your imaginative side. You might have met them along the way, so get back in touch, or find new support by joining a choir or attending a class. Find teachers or mentors who believe in you and understand how to inspire adults rather than children. Allow yourself to be influenced by others and learn from them. They can give you the lift you need until you're ready to fly on your own.

Make space for creativity

It can feel deeply self-indulgent suddenly to study creative writing, for example, when there are so many other demands on your time. On top of this, you still may not be sure if you're going to be any good at it, but, if it's what your heart is longing to do, it's essential to follow your creative instincts. Cutting back on social time in order to strike out alone might seem awkward at first to explain but ultimately everyone will be glad that you're inspired by what you're doing, particularly when you treat them to a performance of a piece of music you've mastered or a beautiful knitted jumper you've made. Even if you're not physically producing something creative, but rather increasing your knowledge, for example attending philosophy classes, your friends will soon appreciate your newfound energy and excitement.

Make space for spontaneity

We want random, unexpected things to happen and new experiences to shake us out of our complacency. It sounds a contradiction, but it's essential to build spontaneity into our diaries because only when unexpected things happen can we feel truly alert, awake and creative again.

Enjoy the process

Even if you start off thinking that what you produce is no good, keep going – it's the process that counts and leads, ultimately, to your best creative work. Tchaikovsky hated *The Nutcracker* and the French composer, Paul Dukas, whom we know for *The Sorcerer's Apprentice*, destroyed almost all of his other work. Think of each project as new ideas that you are building on and learning from – they might be the start of brilliant things yet to come.

Things to do:
- Clear time in your diary in which to be creative and spontaneous
- Start using creativity in your work, your home life and your personal presentation.

(See Brainstorming, Curiosity, Laughter, Metaphor, Planning, Spider Diagrams, Stories, Talents)

Curiosity ● ○ ● ● ● ● ●

I'm phenomenally curious. I wish I wasn't as I know it can border on the nosy, but I'm just fascinated by anything and everyone – how do others live their lives, what do they think, what do their friends think? It's all so interesting. One of my favourite things as a child was going on holiday to Holland. We used to take the sleeper train and, when you got to Holland, everyone had their curtains open – unlike in England – and you could see everyone living their own lives in their homes. It was like looking at lots of different doll's houses next to each other and imagining what the lives were like of the people living in them and what my life would be like if I was them. Not only was I fascinated by their lives, but also by what made them keep their curtains open when they knew we could all look in.

Being **curious** is being eager to gain knowledge and understanding of something. Wanting to learn. Questioning what you know or are being told.

'I am curious to know what happened to our old neighbour. She vanished suddenly and I wonder what kind of life she's living now.'

'Doubt is the key to knowledge.'

Iranian proverb

Get curious about yourself

This book is about you and who you are, how you function and how to make the best out of yourself. Just by reading it, you've started being curious about yourself and what's possible for you in your life. Once you start getting curious life becomes so exciting. You can feel yourself becoming more confident and risking more – even if it's tiny increments at a time. You can start to feel in control of your life.

What starts curiosity?

Curiosity can start because you're feeling unsure about something that's going on in your life. No matter how happy you are or how successful, at some time (or maybe even regularly) you're going to have 'blips'. Those 'blips' may be triggered by change or they may be triggered by an absence of change. Either way, those doubts will be what get you thinking.

Get curious about others

Relationships are built on being interested in other people. If you have no interest or respect for someone else, there is little point in pursuing the relationship. Get curious when, for example, you go on an interview for a new job – study the company and the individual you're meeting as much as you can beforehand. Not only because people are flattered if you know things about them, but also because you'll feel prepared. Being curious about others is being curious about life.

Get curious about life

A curious mind never stops questioning – How can that be done better? Why is my answer not helping? Keep challenging yourself by solving puzzles, perhaps start with games such as crosswords or Sudoku, playing chess or draughts, Scrabble or Boggle. Never stop exposing yourself to new influences, whether it's travelling, even armchair travelling, or reading a book that people are always talking about. You might find something surprises you or delights you or shocks you and next time it comes up in conversation you'll have your own opinion. It doesn't have to be something intellectual, we can find inspiration in all sorts of places – Walt Disney revealed how he always used to get a burst of ideas from scouring *Reader's Digest*. Go to the cinema or on a walk, perhaps with the intention of spotting a bird or plant you've never seen before along the way. So long as you are actively opening your mind to everything new and suspending all judgement so that you take things in, you will start to get a stronger vision of possibilities and options ahead. Being curious is a chance to experiment, explore, evaluate and learn from others and everything around us.

Curiosity is about you

Distracting yourself on the Internet searching for more information about some Hollywood star or other is not getting curious. It might help you engage in a conversation at the pub, but really it's a form of procrastination. True curiosity is going to help you grow in the direction you want to grow in.

Your Lightbulb Moment:
What one thing (who/what) in your life could you get more curious about? What would you like the outcome to be?

(See Change, Creativity, Happiness, Listening, Questions, Play)

Decisions ● ● ● ●

My husband arrived in our relationship with an Oliver Wendell Holmes 'When in doubt, do it' quote that he'd inherited from his mother and it's made our lives so much easier. We've moved house, had children, changed career and done all sorts of things just using that simple saying.

When you make a **decision** you make up your mind and choose one thing out of several alternatives. You reach a conclusion, which can be an action or an opinion. Because decision making can be so difficult, some people use aids, such as the I Ching, astrology, tarot cards or Ouija boards to help them.
'I just can't make up my mind whether or not to get married. It's such a big decision.'

Work backwards
Sometimes it's easier to think about what you don't want and allow that to help you make your decision. If, for example, you're deciding whether to take a degree, you could think about what you don't want.

- **I don't want to do anything but study**
- **I don't want to write masses of essays**
- **I don't want to live in student halls**
- **I don't want to travel far**
- **I don't want to give up my job.**

You can see how you've started to refine your decisions so it'll be easier to make.

- **I want to keep my job, so a part-time degree in a non-essay writing subject would be good**
- **I want to keep living at home, so either a local university or a correspondence course would suit me.**

Just make that decision
Often we fear decision making. You may feel overwhelmed by the pressure of feeling you have to know everything about something before you can take action. You may worry about whether you have the ability to make the necessary decision. You may feel you want your decision to be 'right'. You may worry that by getting the decision 'wrong' you're going to start thinking you always make 'wrong' decisions. But the worst thing you can do is not make that decision. Doubt is shutdown. It freezes you and causes endless worry. Without a decision, you can't move forward.

Things to do:
- **Think about the worst that could happen if you got that decision wrong**
- **Think about the worst that could happen if you didn't make that decision.**

(See Choices, Intuition, Perfectionism, Planning, Problem Solving, Procrastination)

DE-CLUTTERING

I can never find time
to clear it up.

De-cluttering ● ● ○ ● ● ● ● ●

I get a thrill when I see my room all clear, spacious and tidy – and sadly it doesn't happen very often. But my desk is a different matter. When my desk is empty and bare with everything put away I feel a little lost and unsure of what I'm meant to be doing. It's only when it's got a few papers here and there that I can get on with what I'm doing.

De-cluttering is when you get rid of anything that you don't use or love or want. You can de-clutter anything from your sock drawer to your mind and body.
'I de-cluttered my diary and cleared some space for me today – it felt liberating.'

What do I have?

To feel confident of yourself and what you're doing, it's important to know the contents of your home and work place. We don't realise how much clutter stops us from moving forward until we've got rid of it and feel free. Our clutter is symbolic of our unfinished decisions, our disorganisation and our dragging along of our past. It takes up space that new things, like a new job or a new relationship or a new project or even a new family, could drop into.

The advantages of clutter

Yet still, many of us revel in chaos, filling our lives with as much clutter as possible. Somehow a messy desk, or a full inbox, or over-flowing diary, make us look busy and important, as if we're in demand. Only having a few emails in our inbox could make us feel unloved and empty. But it's much easier to get on with achieving what we have to do if our diary is empty.

At work Tracey's desk was never to be seen. It had layer upon layer of papers and files and books, old cups of coffee and letters on it. Tracey's clutter defined her as a person – busy, valued, lovable, a fountain of knowledge. One day her boss suggested that Tracey's desk was making her look bad to clients who had to walk past. She asked Tracey to tidy it. Days later, Tracey sat at her tidy desk. She felt empty, bare and exposed. She now had to think carefully about what would be a really good use of her time. It took her a while to work out how she was going to adapt to her new environment. She started by making a list online of all the projects that she needed to be getting on with. She began changing her outlook, and discovered that she could fill her desk with things that were beautiful rather than messy – a postcard of an inspiring image or a small bunch of flowers, and a neat pile of books to help her with her next project. Ultimately, Tracey found that she was able to tackle each project in a more clear and methodical way, rather than rushing about between tasks.

Discovering clutter

Go round the Life Clubs Balance Chart, page 77, and find out where you feel clear and where you feel cluttered. In Health & Fitness, for example, you may feel cluttered by being overweight or you may feel cluttered by ignorance – not knowing what would help you eat more healthily. Or you could feel cluttered by a family who only like stodgy food. Similarly in Friends & Social Life, for example, you might feel cluttered by friends you no longer want to spend as much time with or by having to help your mother when you'd rather be going out with friends or by having too much work, so you can't go out as often as you'd like to. Discover all the clutter in your life.

Stop making excuses

What excuses do you make for not tidying your home, your desk, your computer, your diary or any other part of your life or body that could do with a de-clutter? What could you do this week to ensure you started tackling that clutter? How are you going to get organised?

What makes de-cluttering difficult?

The difficulty of removing clutter from your life is that it forces you to come to terms with who you are and everything you've failed to do. Goals you scribbled on a piece of paper and never achieved, names of contacts you were going to get in touch with and never did, ideas for marketing that never happened. You have to face up to your past. De-cluttering is difficult.

- **You have to make decisions**
- **Your clutter reminds you of everything you failed to do**
- **It takes time**
- **You're worried you'll lose something**
- **You're worried you'll need something in the future**
- **You don't want to throw memories away**
- **It's tiring.**

Seven hints to make de-cluttering easier

1 Only do 10 minutes a day

2 Start with a contained task – a box or drawer

3 Throw away one item a day

4 Focus on one job at a time

5 If you haven't worn or used something in six months, get rid of it

6 Every time you buy something, throw something out

7 Ask a friend to help.

How might you de-clutter…your routine?
Get rid of…

- **Lying-in in the mornings?**
- **Watching television every night?**
- **Reading the papers every day?**
- **Checking your emails every 10 minutes?**

…your mind?
Get rid of…

- **Unfinished to-dos? (Write them down or forget about them)**
- **Procrastination?**

- **Phone calls you want to make? (Do them or make a note of them)**
- **Worries?**

...your body?
Get rid of...
- **The habit of eating anything once you've noticed your stomach is full**
- **Unhealthy food**
- **Alcohol, sugar, caffeine, nicotine.**

And once it's clear...

Once that clutter is removed from the top of your to-do list you are left with a wonderful blankness. Suddenly, you have to decide what to get on with and it could well be something more challenging. It may feel scary – it's so much easier just to hide behind a sea of clutter and yet you have cleared space for something far more exciting. The relief and clarity that will come when you finally have that space and freedom around you is empowering – you'll feel lighter, more positive and focused. Now get creative and think what the best use of your time could be.

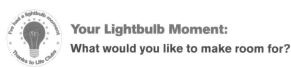 **Your Lightbulb Moment:**
What would you like to make room for?

(See Choices, Decisions, Excess, Intuition, Letting Go, Stories)

Defensiveness ● ● ● ● ● ●

When I get criticised it really hurts. I feel wounded and a failure and sink rapidly. My gut response is immediately to want to say something hurtful back. Recently I've got calmer and better at handling the situation. Instead of instantly feeling upset, I think about their criticism and imagine seeing the situation from their perspective.

Defensiveness is when you expect to be criticised or attacked and so your whole focus is looking out for criticism or attack so that you can defend yourself from it.
'All I asked was whether she'd seen my book. She was so defensive and shouted "No. Why?" back at me so quickly that I wondered if there was something going on.'

Imagine a game of chess

Defensive behaviour is used, like in a chess game, to protect you and prevent an opponent from attacking you and 'winning'. In life terms, defensiveness protects you from criticism, from having your 'faults' revealed and from your ego being threatened. By protecting you from situations in which you'd feel out of your depth, defensiveness allows you to stop worrying. The flip side is that it also stops you from being able to receive valuable feedback or being teased as you are too sensitive to the possibility of attack, and it can make it difficult to form close relationships with you.

'When you are in a hole, stop digging.'

Proverb

Are you defensive?

Do you think others:

- want to get at you?
- want to attack you?
- are accusing you all the time?

How do you respond:

- Do you snap at people a lot?
- Do you use sarcasm?
- Do you make excuses for not having done something?
- Do you withdraw into silence?
- Do you want to be 'right' all the time?
- Do you teach or preach?
- Do you find it difficult to forgive?
- Do you play the Blame Game?
- Do you lose your sense of humour?

Understanding defensiveness

Defensiveness can start because of your doubts and fears. You believe what your fear is telling you without finding any evidence for whether it's true or not. By focusing on this unexamined fear you become even more fearful. You act and feel as if these assumptions are the truth.

Working with defensiveness

Even if you feel like you're being attacked all the time, the reality is you're not. The way forward is to become as calm and rational as you can. If you're feeling under attack:

1 Notice your body – is your breathing faster, your heart racing? Do you feel hot or cold? Slow down and breathe deeply. If you can, go for a walk

2 Then go into your mind. Detach from the situation. Ask your 'attacker' a question to understand more clearly what they've said or just listen to what they're saying now

3 Check whether your fears are actually true – can you prove them to be true?

4 Check what the evidence is that your fears are false

5 See your fear as a belief, not a fact and get rid of it

6 Make an affirmation that states exactly the opposite to your fear.

Project: How could you start seeing things from their perspective?

(See Assumptions, Beliefs, Blame, Confidence, Perfectionism, Victim)

Depression ● ● ● ● ●

Thankfully I've never been clinically depressed, but I spent much of my childhood covering my pillow with tears. When you're in that state you can't ever imagine another way of living, so it's great when you realise that things have changed and you're feeling hopeful. In my case being in control of my life had a lot to do with my change of mood. Once I was free to leave home and start my own life, I started becoming more hopeful. Sadness as an adult has usually come about through feeling under-confident. I found not having a Life Ambition for so many years was difficult for me – I felt in a no-man's land for much of the time. Looking back has also often made me sad. I remember vividly sending my oldest child off to school for the first time and crying solidly for a week. I couldn't bear that he should have to go through something I hated so much. Of course, he loved school and it made me realise, not only how different we all are, but also that looking back and reliving past sadness is a total waste of time.

Depression is feeling severely despondent and dejected – usually over a period of time and accompanied by a feeling of hopelessness and inadequacy.
'I've been so depressed for quite a while that the doctor has put me on medication.'

Depression as a term is also sometimes used more flippantly in conversation.
'I'm so depressed that I've got so much homework. I didn't realise how much a degree was going to feel like school.'

Advice on low spirits
In 1820, Sydney Smith, the famous wit and clergyman, sent his friend, Lady Morpeth, this list of things to do when she was in 'low spirits'. Depression is a serious and sensitive condition and his musings can be seen as frivolous, but if you are feeling a little 'gloomy' you could do worse than follow his advice. In amongst the humour, there is compassion and common sense.

- 1st. **Live as well as you dare.**
- 2nd. **Go into the shower-bath with a small quantity of water at a temperature low enough to give you a slight sensation of cold, 75 or 80 degrees.**
- 3rd. **Amusing books.**
- 4th. **Short views of human life – not further than dinner or tea.**
- 5th. **Be as busy as you can.**
- 6th. **See as much as you can of those friends who respect and like you.**
- 7th. **And of those acquaintances who amuse you.**
- 8th. **Make no secret of low spirits to your friends, but talk of them freely – they are always worse for dignified concealment.**
- 9th. **Attend to the effects tea and coffee produce upon you.**
- 10th. **Compare your lot with that of other people.**
- 11th. **Don't expect too much from human life – a sorry business at the best.**

12th. Avoid poetry, dramatic representations (except comedy), music, serious novels, melancholy, sentimental people, and everything likely to excite feeling or emotion, not ending in active benevolence.

13th. Do good, and endeavour to please everybody of every degree.

14th. Be as much as you can in the open air without fatigue.

15th. Make the room where you commonly sit gay and pleasant.

16th. Struggle by little and little against idleness.

17th. Don't be too severe upon yourself, or underrate yourself, but do yourself justice.

18th. Keep good blazing fires.

19th. Be firm and constant in the exercise of rational religion.

20th. Believe me, dear Lady Georgiana.

Advice on Low Spirits, from Sydney Smith to Lady Morpeth, 1820 [5]

When I need you

Even though Sydney Smith stresses the importance of friends, it can be very scary to phone a friend when you're feeling low – especially if you haven't seen them for a while. If you're feeling gloomy, your instincts might be to clam up and hide away, rather than phone anyone, and yet you know that talking to a friend could help you. They could boost your confidence and let you know that you're not alone in the world and that they're there for you. If you don't feel like talking to anyone, but know it may help, pick up the phone and call anyone for some neutral, practical purpose, such as calling a theatre to see if they have tickets left for a show, or a shop you'd like to go to, to ask what time they close. This will help break the barrier between you and the outside world. Or go for a walk and let the space above you free you from your mood and then phone a friend.

Nothing is forever

Even depression doesn't usually last forever. It's often cyclical like the seasons, and after the rains, the sun shall surely come. There are many different forms of depression, from sadness to clinical depression. If you have 'low spirits', follow Sydney Smith's advice. If your depression is more serious, seek professional help.

Things to do:
- Pick anything from the above list that appeals to you and do it.

(See Action, Change, Confidence, Gratitude, Laughter, Life Ambition, Loneliness)

---

[5] Writings by Sydney Smith can be found in Auden, W.H. (ed) (2009) *The Selected Writings of Sydney Smith*, London: Faber Finds.

Emotions ● ○ ● ● ● ● ●

Our emotions can take us from high to low in seconds and they can last for years. Some of us can suppress our emotions, but I can't, and find my emotions affect me greatly. I can go from envy to anger or boredom to fear very quickly. Luckily my personality type means that I'm a bit of a ping-pong ball and bounce into the positive emotions of joy and surprise quite quickly, but not always – sometimes the sadness can last.

Emotion is a state of mind formed by your circumstances, mood or relationship with others. Any of the feelings that characterise that state of mind (anger, fear etc) are also emotions.
'I'm so over-emotional right now. I'm not even sure if I'm crying because I feel happy or sad.'

Recognising emotions
Our emotions are our feelings, are a part of the 'mood' we're in. If you can put 'I feel…' in front of a word, that word is probably an emotion. Some of us have very intense emotions, others are less aware of what our emotions are. Sometimes emotions last for a few seconds and sometimes they last for years. We can literally feel these emotions in our body – we get goose pimples or our heart seems to stop or we may go tingly. These emotions will be telling us to do something, or nothing.

The basic emotions
Anger, Fear, Joy, Love, Sadness, Surprise

A few other emotions

Amazed (Surprised)	Envy (Anger)
Annoyance (Anger)	Frightened (Fear)
Anxiety (Fear)	Guilt (Sadness)
Boredom (Fear)	Happiness (Joy)
Contempt (Anger)	Hope (Joy)
Depression (Sadness)	Hostile (Anger)
Desire (Love)	Jealousy (Anger)
Disappointment (Sadness)	Pity (Sadness)
Disgust (Anger)	Pride (Joy)
Ecstasy (Joy)	Rage (Anger)

Balancing emotions
Our emotions make our life vibrant – or sometimes dull. They can vary in terms of intensity – anywhere between complacent to annoyed, through to rage or from accepting to admiration. Generally we want to establish balance of emotions in our lives – both happy balanced with sad, but also intensity balanced with moderation.

Feeling emotions

Sometimes your emotions are so clear that others can tell what you're feeling before you even can, and sometimes they're not so clear. For example, you may feel that you're envious of someone having something, let's say a promotion. You know that you wouldn't want the job they're getting, but you imagine you're feeling envious that they've got it. However, thinking about it, feeling that emotion within you, you realise that it's really anger you're experiencing (all emotions link into the six basic emotions, so you know that you'll find one of them underpinning whatever it is you're feeling). Maybe you're angry with yourself that you're not 'good' enough to get a promotion. Once you've discovered that it's anger, you can then use that anger – to step up your work flow so that you too get promoted or to get energised into looking for a new job. Or perhaps you can turn it around completely and think about not beating yourself up so much.

Using emotions as a health check

As well as checking how your body is physically, check in with your emotions – what are you *really* feeling? Emotions left unattended can begin to manifest as pain or illness. It is no coincidence that unhappy people are ill more often than happy people. Emotions left to fester can cause weight gain, poor sleeping habits, incessant colds or flu and very low energy levels. Emotions can appear to manifest in the body physically, which you can read metaphorically to reveal what the real problem may be.

- **If you have a sore throat, are there things in your life you are not speaking up about?**
- **If you are having feet problems, are you moving in a direction in life you don't like?**
- **If you've got an earache, is there someone who might not be listening to you or vice versa?**

See if you can find a metaphor behind your illness that might connect to your emotions.

Masking emotions

Often we ignore our negative emotions (variations of anger, fear and sadness) by doing more of what we know brings us positive emotions (variations of joy, love and surprise), be it eating or shopping or sleeping or smoking or drinking. This excess can be stopped by working on the emotions that have caused it. Notice what your emotions are doing when you overdo things by noting them down in a diary. Just do it for a week – no more.

Things to do:

- **Whenever you feel an emotion, work out what the emotion is (look at the six basic emotions, page 131), how it's making you feel right at that moment and whether you want to be feeling it**
- **Notice how you can change your emotional state through your face. Once you start smiling and relaxing your face, you'll find you'll feel lighter and more positive. And vice versa. Walk around with a sad, droopy face and you'll feel melancholy**
- **Observe yourself and what makes you feel good emotionally. Once you know, you can keep repeating it.**

Project: What do you have time for? Do you make time in your life for laughter? For tears? For anger? When you feel something, acknowledge it, accept it. Rather than rushing on to the next task, allow time for your emotions. Discovering those emotions will make you feel more alive.

(See Anger, Balance, Change, Depression, Envy, Fear, Guilt, Happiness, Stress)

Envy ● ● ● ● ● ● ● ●

Do you ever get that 'They're so much more successful than I am' feeling? I don't have it often, but sometimes I do, and whenever I think about what it is that I'm envious of, I realise it's usually that they're so much more focused and determined than I am. Now, focus and determination I can do something about, so I immediately do a little bit of work and forget about the lack of success that was niggling me. Who cares about that kind of success anyway?

Envy is the resentment and pain you feel when another has something that you want. You may feel very strongly that you want that thing (possession or quality) yourself, or you may instead feel that you just wish they didn't have it. Envy is classically associated with the colour green.
'I really envy your new jacket - you look so great in it and I think it would suit me too.'

Success or failure?
Although envy can be used to spur you on to success, it can also leave you so panicked and fearful that you can't act at all.

Rosie and Will went to Istanbul to celebrate their anniversary. A quiet, intellectual couple, they spent most of their time exploring the city, keeping themselves to themselves. At the same hotel, there was also an incredibly loud and sociable couple, who spent a lot of time at the pool and seemed to know everyone. Although Rosie and Will didn't much like the look of them from afar, they also felt slightly envious and excluded from the party atmosphere. They hadn't met anyone and after a couple of days felt it was too late suddenly to introduce themselves out of the blue. Rosie and Will sat far away from the noisy crowd at the pool and muttered to themselves that no one at the hotel looked very interesting anyway. At the end of the holiday, Rosie and Will bumped into the popular couple at the airport. They weren't at all intimidating, as they had appeared from afar, but incredibly friendly. It turned out they were catching the same flight home and by sheer coincidence lived in the same area back home – they spent the next few hours laughing and chatting together, sharing a bottle of wine. If only Rosie and Will hadn't been so paralysed by their envy, they too could have been included in the social whirl.

'A dog with a bone knows no friend.'

Dutch proverb

Things to do:

- Next time you feel envy, make sure you've understood what you're actually envious of – are you envious of what they're achieving or the skills and talents they have or are you angry with yourself for not being like them?
- Notice your envy instead of feeling embarrassed about it. What can it tell you about yourself?

(See Confidence, Emotions, Excess, Success)

Excess ● ● ● ● ● ● ●

We can take our excessive habits and make a joke out of them. 'Oh, I love eating', I always say, or 'I'm a workaholic', and I make light of the situation. But visiting one of my best friends who was in an intensive care unit after a lifetime of excess alcohol and work, made me stop short and think about how important balance really is.

Whether you're doing too much eating, drinking, exercising, working, sleeping, surfing the net, worrying or anything else, you're using **excess** to remove yourself from the stress of living and to avoid facing up to your real needs. Excess is a learned habit and so can be unlearned.
'I know it's excessive, but if I don't get to the gym every day for at least an hour I can't cope with the day. I become irritable and a nightmare to be with.'

'Are you doing something to excess?' quiz

If you answer 'Yes' to five or more of the following questions, you may well be doing something to excess. Think how you can cut down or exclude this habit altogether.

- Does this habit make you lose time?
- Does this habit make you lose energy?
- Does this habit make you feel low afterwards?
- Does this habit waste your money?
- Does this habit make you feel guilty?
- Does this habit deprive you of love?
- Does this habit make you cross with yourself?
- Does this habit make you feel out of control?
- Does this habit make you lie to others?
- Do you take this habit with you when you go on holiday?

The more you listen, the more you'll hear

The more you listen to your body and learn to be in tune with what it's telling you, the more you'll understand how to use it. Understand how it works:

- Halfway through eating a meal, stop eating and think about whether or not you are full

- **If you are sitting with friends or working and start feeling restless, go for a walk or do some other physical exercise**
- **If you have a pain, become aware of it and then do something about it.**

There's no need to obsess over your body or talk endlessly about it – just let your body know you've heard it and are going to deal with it. Your body listens to you even if you don't listen to it.

What are you hiding?

Check out what your over-indulging is hiding. Start getting honest with yourself and instead of focusing on the habit, think about whether you aren't living your life the way you 'should' live it, rather than the way you 'want' to live it. Then consider what you can do to get that 'should' out of your life, because if you can, you might find yourself losing interest in the habit of excess.

Jack was always staying on late at work. He felt much happier there than at home where he knew his partner, Maya, would put pressure on him to do the housework and help put the children to bed. Somehow work was a refuge, a respite from Maya and all the things he was expected to do. He'd sit at his computer and make more work for himself, as all his colleagues gradually filtered out of the office, waving goodnight to him. Jack, alone in the office late at night, was lying low so that he wouldn't have to face up to his relationship. Then when he knew things would be winding down at home, he'd slink back and find Maya and the children asleep. Instead of being honest with Maya and suggesting they changed (or even ended) their relationship, he hid away hoping it would all vanish like a bad dream. In work, Jack was doing things he 'wanted' to do. At home it felt like a long list of 'shoulds'. One day Maya confronted Jack and they had an open, honest discussion. It took a while, but together Jack and Maya made a list of all the things that were 'shoulds' at home and all the things that were 'wants'. Jack soon felt happier at home and started coming home earlier.

Nobody wants a partner who is always hard at work or hung over or lolling on the sofa with indigestion. And, even more importantly, you know how you beat yourself up after the 'binge'. But don't judge yourself. Remember you are not your habit. You are a happy/confident/organised person (use whatever positive adjective you feel suits you best) and you're fine with or without this habit. Rearrange your life in a way that breaks the pattern and know that right now you are not indulging.

How to get through excess:

- **Ask yourself what the excess is a substitute for**
- **Next time you want to excess, take three deep breaths to become aware of what you're about to do – or, better still, wait 10 minutes, then, if you still want to, indulge consciously**
- **Notice who – when you indulge are you alone or with the same people as usual?**
- **Notice where – is it the same place you always indulge in?**

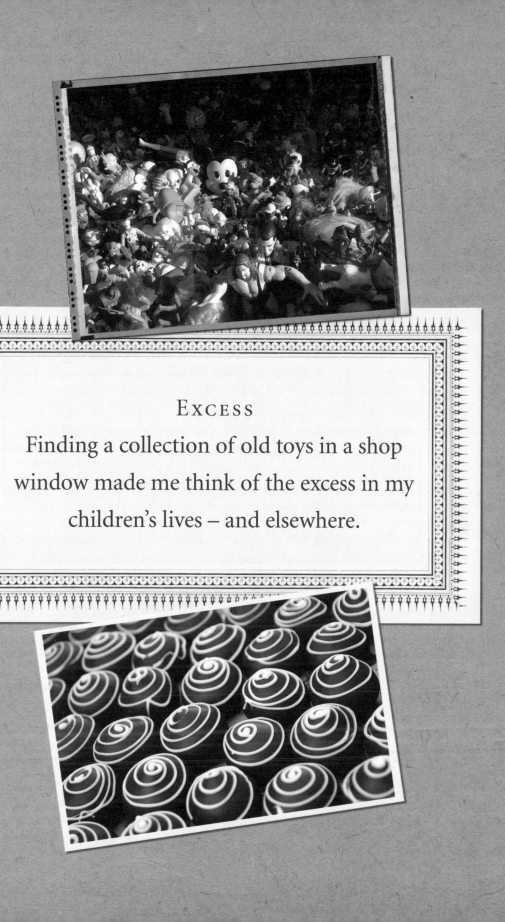

Excess

Finding a collection of old toys in a shop window made me think of the excess in my children's lives – and elsewhere.

- Notice what – what's your physical and emotional response, both as you indulge and later?
    - How does your body react?
    - Does your mouth salivate?
    - Does your heart beat?
    - Do you feel all your muscles relax?
    - Do you enter a strong emotional state, such as excitement?
    - Or do you just feel numb?
- Find replacements you really enjoy (healthy food for junk food etc)
- Remember how great you are.

My diary

Keeping a diary can be extremely useful to help you monitor your habits.

Anna worked at home and found she snacked whenever she went into the kitchen for a drink. It was just the sheer boredom as she waited for the kettle to boil and there was that minute or two in which to raid the biscuits. As Anna was putting on weight she decided to write a food diary for a week. What Anna discovered was that about half-an-hour after eating a biscuit (or two) she always had a dip in energy and felt tired and unable to concentrate. Anna knew she had to take action. She couldn't stop buying biscuits as her family all loved them, but she could do something else instead. Anna knew that the one thing that perked her up and energised her was to sit and read, so she decided to leave a newspaper on the kitchen table. Now, after filling the kettle, Anna sits and has a couple of minutes' reading time. Not only does Anna feel re-energised, she's stopped putting on weight.

Project: Keep a diary for one week only and then study it to see if there's a pattern to your indulging – do you always indulge at the same times, in the same places? Then you can decide how you want to change that pattern. If worried, seek professional help.

My habits diary	M	T	W	T	F	S	S
What time is it?							
How am I indulging?							
Who am I with?							
Where am I?							
What am I feeling now?							
What am I feeling one hour later?							

(See Balance, Beliefs, Boundaries, Emotions, Forgiveness, Guilt, Habits, Inner Child, Patterns, Planning, Saying 'No', Work/Life Balance)

Failure ●●●●●●●●●

A failure proverb that's become a catchphrase in our family came to us from Sri Lanka. Soon after I first met Ira Perera, who looked after my children for 20 years (and still does on occasion), a publisher rejected a book proposal of mine and I felt downhearted. Ira calmly said to me 'Every cloud has a silver lining' and she was right. I got a much better offer from another publisher and everything was fine again. From that moment on, every time something goes wrong – whether it's something I've done wrong or something that's happened that's been awful – I look for the silver lining. Sometimes it can take a while to find, but there are other times when the lining is instantly visible.

Failure is the opposite to success. Yet what success is to one person might be failure to another, so we each have a different benchmark for failure, unless the action is judged externally, as in an exam.

'I feel such a failure. I've got this recipe wrong again.'

Fear of failure

We have all experienced some degree of failure – failure and rejection are things everyone has to go through. Yet, even so, sometimes we don't want to experience new things because we're afraid of failing or being rejected. We aim so high and success is so stressed, that we would rather not try than fail. But the failure lies not in failing, but in not doing anything, because often when we do try things and they don't at first work out, it can bring out the best in us. The more we do, the more experience and wisdom we gain, which will in turn make us more rounded, bold and confident individuals. And, ultimately, what we want to happen will.

Ignore 'failure'

Just as 'right' and 'wrong' are in the eye of the beholder, so 'failure' and 'success' are too. You decide what 'failure' is and how much you want to berate yourself for having 'failed'. Accept that failure is essential as part of the learning process and just have a go at whatever it is you want to do. Think of failure as necessary for success.

Finding the success within the failure

In the chart below, the first column is for you to write down something in your life that you see as a failure – no matter how big or how small (eg failed my driving test). In the second column, think about the success in that failure. This could be a learning or a practical benefit (eg by failing the driving test you practised more and became a more confident driver). The third column is to write down how this failure and success has or will move you forward (eg I have become a better driver and I will not attempt exams again before I am really prepared and ready).

My 'failure'	The 'success' that came out of it	How my learning has helped me move forward
eg Had too much to drink and dropped off to sleep on the last bus, missed my stop and went all the way to the terminal	eg I walked home and felt how lucky I was to live in such a beautiful place	eg I'll appreciate where I live more and won't drink as much when I go out

Think small

If you imagine whatever you want to achieve as a massive mountain to climb, or whatever metaphor you wish to use, you will probably start feeling that there's a possibility of failure ahead. If, however, you imagine that mountain smashed into lots of tiny rocks that you have to walk over, you can probably see how that would be quite easy to do. Plan and use Spider Diagrams, page 269, to break your goals down and make them less fearful.

Your Lightbulb Moment:
When was the last time you allowed yourself to succeed and when will you allow yourself again?

(See Comfort Zone, Confidence, Emotions, Fear, Goals, Optimism, Perfectionism, Planning, Procrastination)

Fear ● ● ○ ● ○ ● ● ● ● ●

Even as a child I was frightened of masks. As a 'grown-up' the fear continued. Once my children had to rescue me from the circus I was going to take them to and my husband has had to remove me from fancy dress parties where I just couldn't move I was so frightened of what/who I was going to bump into. At a workshop I was on, I was talking about this fear to another of the participants. A moment later, he lifted up the sheet of paper he was holding until it was in front of his face and I was petrified. The session stopped and I went to lunch wondering what could make me so scared of a piece of paper held up in front of a face. My Lightbulb Moment happened that lunch break inside Debenhams. I suddenly understood that the person behind the mask (or paper) was no longer there for me. I could no longer see them. To all intents and purposes they had vanished. My father had left home (he hadn't vanished, but it felt like it), when I was six and there was the connection. I wasn't really afraid of masks, I was afraid of being left again. Once I'd realised that, there was no longer any need to fear a mask.

Fear is an emotion that comes about when you believe that someone or something is dangerous, may cause you pain and is likely to cause you harm.

'I'm so frightened of flying. I've been to a few hypnotists, but I'm still terrified. It makes it really difficult to travel.'

What is fear?

Fear can feel like anything from mild worry or anxiety to apprehension or disquiet through to dread or terror. You feel it when you're in the presence of danger or when danger is imminent. It's a basic survival mechanism, but sometimes we fear things too much – if you feel you do, seek help. Fear can be used as a motivator and as an excuse for procrastinating. It can paralyse us and stop us taking risks. Notice if your fear is real or whether there is nothing to fear except your imagination. Fear starts with some scary stimulus, real or imagined. This stimulus triggers off a release of chemicals that give you the flight-or-fight response of fast breathing, racing heart and active muscles. We don't consciously start it and often don't realise what's happening until it's over.

Some of the most common fears are:

- Spiders
- Snakes
- Heights
- Water
- Enclosed spaces
- Tunnels and bridges
- Pain
- Death
- Failure
- Public speaking
- Fear of success/failure
- Social rejection

Daniella had been working in the same place for years, but she had never made any real friends there and only ever went to organised work social events. On lunch breaks, she always ended up eating a sandwich while walking around, so that she didn't have to stop and sit on her own. She disliked the idea of feeling a social outcast and thought that if only she had a friend at work who she could have lunch with it would make the day so much better. There was someone else working there who Daniella had occasionally smiled at, but even though they'd never had anything else to do with each other Daniella realised she'd really like to get to know her colleague better. One day Daniella bravely suggested they have lunch together. Daniella hadn't asked her before for fear of being rejected, but, once she'd thought about it, she knew that the worst that could happen was that her 'new' friend would say 'No'. Daniella took the risk and was rewarded.

The worst could have happened

What if Daniella had been rejected? She would have coped. Hopefully she would have realised that this was not a pattern, she was not a victim and made no assumptions about the rejection apart from that her colleague was genuinely busy.

'He who fears something gives it power over him.'

Proverb

Five steps to overcoming fear:

1 Be aware that you feel frightened

2 Identify what you are really afraid of

3 Discover the advantages to being scared

4 Develop a sense of control over fear (write down how you're feeling, tackle your fear as soon as you can, just take small practical steps forward)

5 Think how you would approach your fear differently if you felt excited rather than frightened.

Things to do:

- Work out which fear is holding you back most in your life
- Decide what you're going to do about overcoming it – and start.

(See Advantages, Assumptions, Emotions, Failure, Motivation, Procrastination, Goals, Stress, Victim)

Feedback ● ● ● ● ● ●

One of my daughters always greets people with a huge hug and a compliment and I love the way she does it. I find it difficult to give such natural positive feedback. I often admire the way someone has got his or herself together that day and am enjoying looking at them but, even though I am thinking wonderful thoughts about them, I find that I consciously have to push myself to say something nice. It's always good when I do as they feel appreciated and I feel happy as I wanted them to.

Feedback is when you 'feed back' information about a person's performance to that person and it can be good or bad feedback. At work it's usually employed as a basis for improvement.
'You're so good at handling people. When you'd finished giving John his feedback, even though you pointed out some pretty serious issues, he felt pleased with his progress and knew what he had to do in the future.'

Uses of feedback

Feedback is used to help the person to whom you are giving feedback to assess how well they have done so they can learn from their success as well as from their mistakes. If you're giving negative feedback, always check with yourself first what your reason is for giving it. If it's just to get something off your chest or to attempt to change someone's character so they no longer annoy you, don't do it. If it's to help the other person develop, feedback can be very effective. We also repeatedly give feedback to ourselves, though these beliefs and assumptions are not always accurate or helpful.

Receiving feedback

- Be open and receptive – listen to what they say, rather than talk over them
- Use body language which shows you're listening, not closed
- If you're receiving negative feedback, ask them for facts rather than opinions – for positive feedback, opinions are fine
- Keep focused on the issue
- Let them know you've heard them – in your own words repeat back what they said to you
- Take on board the positive as well as the negative feedback.

Giving positive feedback

- Give positive feedback in the second person 'Your presentation was inspirational.' Focus on them
- Don't expect a compliment back.

Giving negative feedback

Giving negative feedback in this order makes it more palatable

1 Say something positive ('I love working with you')
2 Ask them a question ('Is there anything you'd like to change?')
3 Give the negative feedback in first person ('I find it difficult...')
4 Make them important – ask for their advice ('I always value your input. What do you think...?)

PS: Know the outcome you want, stick to the facts, avoid accusations and the use of 'never' and 'always' with negative feedback. They exaggerate.

The Feedback Sandwich

Negative feedback has to be handled very delicately and for that reason it has rules around it. The bottom line is that you want to make sure the person you are giving feedback to feels that they are important and their opinion is being sought too.

Negative feedback is sometimes called the 'Feedback Sandwich' because you're giving the negative feedback inside two bits of praise.

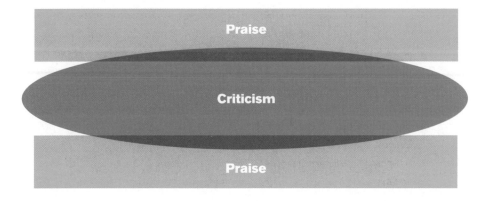

Julia and Karen shared a job, a desk and a file into which they both put their case histories of previous clients. Although they got on extremely well in most parts of their working relationship, Julia was never very thorough about writing down her client's histories, which Karen found difficult. One day, when Karen had found Julia had left a client's entry blank, Karen decided she had to say something – Julia's sloppiness was really getting her down. Karen started with a compliment: 'Julia, I just wanted to let you know how much our clients rate you – they're always singing your praises and it makes me proud to work with you.' Then, Karen asked Julia a question: 'Are you happy with our job share or is there something you'd like to change?' This question made Julia gather her thoughts and focus on the job share. Karen listened to Julia's ideas and they talked about them for a while. Then Karen moved onto the reason for their chat. 'Julia, I find it difficult to visit a client when I've got no notes for them – I feel unprepared.' Karen made it clear that this didn't happen often, but when it did, she felt embarrassed and awkward. She then asked Julia what she felt the best way of dealing with this situation would be. Julia realised that she could make sure she left more time to write up the case histories and, from then on, that was what she did. By her clear and careful feedback, Karen had helped Julia solve a situation that Karen had found frustrating.

Things to do:

- **Make a list of who you'd like to give feedback to and check your motives for wanting to give feedback – are they honourable or controlling?**
- **Practise giving positive feedback. Every time you think something positive, say it.**

(See Assumptions, Body Language, Change, Control, Emotions, Listening, Mirroring, Outcome)

Focus ● ● ● ● ●

I have what is called a 'butterfly mind'. I love ideas, connections and thoughts. I get bored quickly, change topics of conversation and don't always know what my focus for the day is. However, it's when I focus that I'm happiest. For example, lying on my sofa, writing this now is making me feel peaceful and contented. I'm totally focused on what I'm doing. What we focus on is important too. I remember when Harriet Griffey, a great freelance journalist and friend, once came to one of my workshops. She decided that, as it was her birthday, she'd like to have 'celebration' as her focus for the week. She wrote out a long 'to do' list with everything from food shopping to article writing, yet when she looked closely at her list it began the same way as all her lists begin, with work commitments at the top and herself at the bottom. Harriet laughed at her Lightbulb Moment, 'I wrote it without thinking.' Harriet rewrote her list as a celebratory week with parties and pampering treats at the top and everything else underneath. It now had the focus she wanted. You can focus your life whichever way you want to.

Just as when you **focus** a telescope on a star or focus the lens of your camera on a blade of grass, you can focus your mind on something. That something can be yourself, another person, a task, your energy or what you want from a conversation, your day or your week.
'When I really focused on what the lecturer was saying, it was riveting. I don't think I've got so much out of the lectures before.'

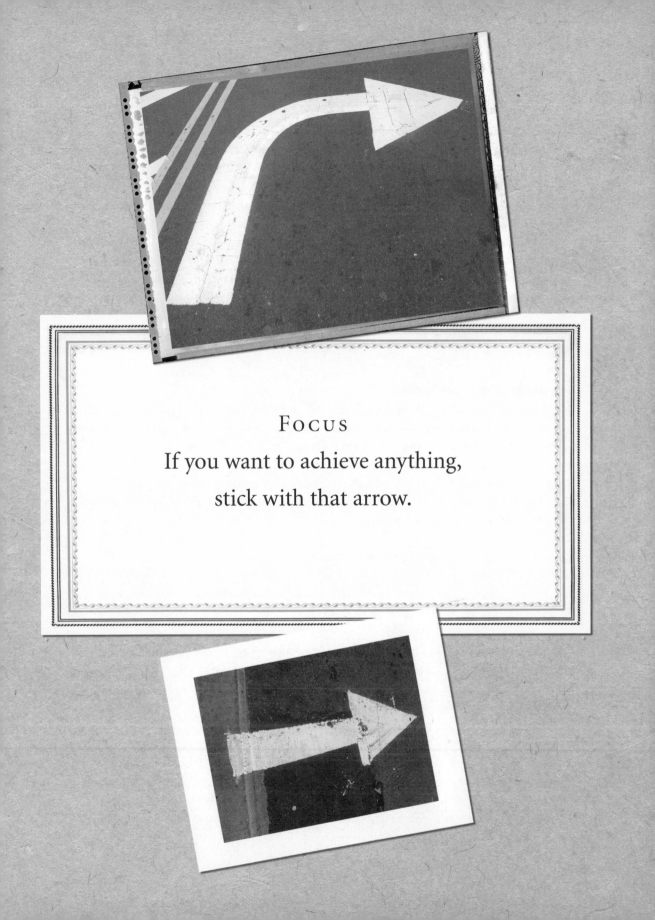

Focus

If you want to achieve anything,
stick with that arrow.

'If I focus on completing one thing at a time and don't get distracted, I can do so much more and feel satisfied with what I'm achieving.'

Microfocus

Choose a goal and work on it. Usually it doesn't matter which goal you choose, so long as you focus on one and just go for it. Then choose your next goal – once you've reached the first – and focus on that. If you have too many goals your energy is dissipated. Once you've decided where to start, focus on the job you're doing instead of worrying about what else you might be doing. Focus can bring drive and energy and a feeling of success.

Macrofocus

Making a list of what you want to do (or have to do) for the week ahead will focus you. Write down everything – from buying a new battery for your watch to running a half-marathon. Then, if you'd like to, think about a focus you want for the week. If, for example, you want a creative week, prioritise your 'to do' list so creativity can emerge. Your 'to do' list can reflect the focus you want from the week.

Focusing after interruptions

No matter how focused we are, we'll usually be interrupted by 'stuff' – other people, emails, phone calls etc. When that happens, look at a collage of your Life Ambition – it will re-focus you. Or, take a deep breath and calmly ask yourself what the best use of your time would be at this moment.

Project: This week decide on a theme you'd like for your week – look at your Life Clubs Balance Chart, page 77, for inspiration. Would it be a 'get fit' week or a 'Brazilian' week or a 'laughter' week? Plan your week to build in your focus.

(See Control, Decisions, Goals, Intent, Life Ambition, Planning, Visualisation)

Forgiveness ● ● ○ ○ ● ● ● ● ● ○

My great friend and mentor, Jane Whistler, taught me that forgiving someone is only half of the loop and that, in order to complete the loop, you want to ask for forgiveness from them too. This has helped me enormously and, although I still find it slightly incredible, you can even close wounds with those who have died. Jane introduced me to the two visualisations below. I hope you will find them as useful as I have.

Forgiveness is when you forgive someone or yourself and stop being angry or resentful towards them (or yourself) for something they (or you) have done.
'I've forgiven myself for eating so much and I've stopped focusing on food.'
'I forgave my mum for my childhood and I feel so much happier. Carrying around hate was making me a bitter person.'

Let go

We often feel that forgiveness is what the person who has 'done us wrong' should ask of us, but for us to be set free of that destructive thought we must forgive them. It's a clear way of releasing yourself from the negative thoughts that you may be having about that person and allowing yourself mental freedom again. Forgiveness has little or nothing to do with 'them', it's about you. You can also forgive yourself for the things that annoy you about you.

Forgiveness is circular

Letting go of your resentment is not as easy as simply saying 'I'm going to let go'. In order to let go, you have to forgive that person for all the things that, until now, you have blamed them for and, in order to complete the forgiveness process, you have to ask them to forgive you for any unhappiness and grief that you caused them.

Forgiving them

This visualisation can help you to forgive anyone (including yourself) that you feel anger, resentment or sadness towards. Find a quiet time when you can be alone for as long as you want because you may want to allow at least half-an-hour to do this visualisation and the one below. Start by remembering everything you know about the childhood of the person you want to forgive. If it's a parent, you'll find you're amazed at how much you know. If it's a teacher or a friend of your parents or a friend or colleague of yours, you may not know as much, so use your imagination – you may intuitively know more than you think. If it's you, you'll know yourself well. When you're ready, close your eyes and…

Imagine yourself as a child, around 12 years old. It's a lovely sunny day and you're in a beautiful, open landscape. You decide to sit under a tree for shade and, as you sit down, you notice another child (this is your father or mother or whoever you are doing the visualisation about), around the same age, coming towards you. As he or she approaches, you know who they are (really imagine them as a child). Watch as they move, how they smile, how openly they look at you. As they sit next to you, you ask them some questions. You want to ask them about their childhood, so you might start with 'What was your childhood like?' Then, listen very closely as he/she answers you. They will answer amazingly accurately because intuitively you will know what they would say. When they have answered, you can then ask another question, such as 'How did your parents treat you?' or 'Were you frightened of your parents or were they warm and supportive?' Just keep asking questions and waiting to listen to their answers. Your resentment will help you with the questions you want to ask. For example, 'Did your parents put you down a lot and prefer another of your siblings?' or 'Were you ever praised?' Just take your time. Ask him/her very slowly and listen very carefully to each answer. There is no hurry. You can ask him/her anything you want to, especially specific questions about things that are relevant to your past, such as 'Who was so critical to you?' or 'Did you feel secure?' – whatever it is that you want to find out about. Finally, thank him/her and tell them that you'll come and visit them again.

Although you know everything the person you want to forgive will say intellectually already, when doing this visualisation you will be amazed at what you hear. It will help you forgive them and let go. Seeing that adult as the vulnerable 12-year-old they once were will make it easier to move on from their hold over you and to forgive them.

Forgiving you

This visualisation will allow you to be forgiven for any 'wrongs' you may have done to the person you want to forgive. Once you have done the visualisation above, you are ready to do this visualisation. Prepare yourself by thinking of everything you might have done that made their life more difficult. You can even do this visualisation with yourself. When you're ready, close your eyes and…

Imagine yourself as you are now. The person you want to ask forgiveness from can be any age you like. You see them sitting down comfortably in a comfortable chair and you approach them. When you are ready, just start slowly asking for their forgiveness using very specific memories. You can ask things like 'Will you forgive me for that time I stayed out late without telling you?' or 'Will you forgive me for having deliberately been a truant to spite you?' or 'Will you forgive me for leaving home as soon as I could?' or 'Will you forgive me for taking the client you liked away from you?' – whatever it is you'd like forgiveness for. You can even ask them what you could be asking forgiveness for. Then, just wait for them to say that they forgive you. Ask for as much forgiveness as you want, then thank them and, again, let them know you may be coming to see them in the future.

Moving on

You may feel that you've behaved impeccably and 'shouldn't have to do this', but it's you who wants your mind cleared of bitterness and the only way for that to happen is for you to forgive the person who caused it. You can never change anyone else, you can only always change yourself. Often our parents are the ones we want most to be able to forgive so that we can move on.

Trish's parents had always idolised her older brother, Steve. Now, even though her father had died, Trish's mother could never talk enough about what Steve was doing, how successful he was, how happy he was, how settled he was. In her forties, Trish could now understand that her entire life had been spent trying to make her parents proud of her and that, even though she was the most successful research doctor in her field, it still hadn't worked. Instead of staying the victim of the situation, Trish decided that she had enough life left to live and that she would leave the hospital and her life of research and do what she'd always wanted to do – go and live in Italy and write. Trish worked on forgiving her parents for having put her into a 'not good enough' box and constantly comparing her to her brother and, in her mind, asked for forgiveness from her parents for having let them down by never really enjoying what she was doing. With her savings, Trish helped pay for her mother to have help when she needed it and, with a calm heart, Trish moved to Italy.

Your Lightbulb Moment:
Do you find it easier to forgive yourself or others?

(See Acceptance, Accountability, Blame, Change, Failure, Guilt, Letting Go, Perfectionism)

Giving ● ● ● ● ● ● ●

Some people are naturally good at giving. They have a wonderful insight into what that other person actually wants. One of my daughters is just like that. She once chose a t-shirt to give a friend of ours for her birthday and on the birthday the friend unwrapped two presents – one from us (chosen by my daughter) and one from her parents (that she had chosen for herself). They were identical.

Giving is to transfer freely a possession or bestow love or help to another.
'He gave his son so much encouragement, it was great to watch the child blossom.'

Types of givers
- **Those who have much and give sparingly, mainly for recognition, which makes their gifts unwholesome**
- **Those who have little and give it all – they believe that there is plenty for them in life and their funds never run dry**
- **Those who give with joy, and their joy is their reward**
- **Those who give with pain, and that pain is their experience**
- **And those who give without pain or looking for joy or without thinking of being virtuous, they just give naturally 'as in yonder valley the myrtle breathes its fragrance into space'.**

('Types of givers' was adapted from Kahlil Gibran's The Prophet *(1991, Pan Books))*

Over-giving
Some of us ignore our own feelings in order to get love. It may mean that we give more attention to others than ourselves, imagining that we have to give in order to get. There are a few downsides to this behaviour:
- **Over-givers can burn themselves out by ignoring their needs**
- **Over-givers can start manipulating, or even controlling, others to get their needs met, rather than asking for help directly. For example, they may buy something for you so that they have an excuse for seeing you, rather than just ask if they could come round**
- **Over-givers can become rescuers, finding victims to look after, not realising that they would be happier if they put themselves first.**

Giving to ourselves
There are four parts of you that need equal nurturing – the physical, the emotional, the mental and the spiritual. Consciously spend an hour or two on one or more of these parts a day.

- **The physical: eating nutritious food, exercising regularly and relaxing**
- **The emotional: meeting friends who refresh and stimulate you and being of service to your family, friends and the community**
- **The mental: giving your brain sustenance by going on courses, applying yourself to problem solving, doing crosswords and quizzes and playing cards**
- **The spiritual: meditating, praying, listening to beautiful music, reading a poem or spending time alone somewhere you love.**

Giving Circles

Giving Circles are a philanthropic trend started in America. Small groups of people get together informally, raise money and give it all to charity, usually a charity in their own community. More information can be found at www.givingcircles.org.

Project: For a few hours every day, give yourself the nurturing you usually give others, it's not being selfish – it's essential. See yourself in the third person if it helps, as that inner child. Remember what you enjoy doing and do it.

(See Control, Inner Child, Mirroring)

Goals ● ● ● ○ ○ ● ● ● ●

I never really saw the point of goal-setting. I had 'ideas' and 'things I wanted to do', but the point of goals fell into place when I read the line 'without having a goal it's difficult to score' in the late Paul Arden's incredible book It's Not How Good You Are, It's How Good You Want To Be[6]. *Paul was right, unless you know what you really want to do and focus on it you'll never know if you're succeeding and your life may feel aimless.*

A **goal** is the object of your ambition – the destination. It's the result you want to achieve. It's your target. Goals can be short or long term, so you can complete them in a few minutes or they may take an entire lifetime. They are your priorities in life. Goals give you a feeling of aspiration.
'My goal for today is to go and see my best friend who is in hospital recovering from an operation.'

Why set goals?

Setting a goal is a proactive step towards achieving more, it gives you a sense of control, plus it's a wonderful boost of accomplishment when you finally reach your target. The goal you set might simply be to make time in which to do nothing at all, so that creative thoughts can come into your head or so that you can relax – not all goals have to be about 'doing'.

Five rules for motivational goals

In order for a goal to really fulfil and motivate you, follow these five rules:

1 Listen to your language. Make sure you really 'want' to achieve your goal, rather than that you feel you 'ought' to

2 Express your goal positively ('I want to eat healthily' rather than 'I want to lose weight')

3 Be clear that you can achieve the goal on your own

4 Write your goal in the present or future tense depending on which inspires you more

5 Check your goal is SMART (Specific, Measurable, Achievable, Realistic, Timely).

[6] Arden, P. (2003) *It's Not How Good You Are, It's How Good You Want To Be*, London: Phaidon Press Ltd.

How does SMART work?

SMART makes sure that your goal works for you. If your goal answers all the SMART criteria, it might say 'I want to have six friends round for a meal in the next two weeks.' That way you can tell if you've achieved it, rather than 'My goal is to see some friends' which is too vague.

Is your goal SMART?

Use this flow chart (opposite) to see if your goal is the right one for you. When you answer 'No' to a question, rewrite your goal and then start again at the top of the flow chart.

A weekly goal

Setting and achieving a simple weekly goal for yourself (rather than family, friends or work) will show you the control you have on your life. Both your Balance Chart and your confidence will expand. If you don't achieve your goal you'll learn something – that it was the wrong goal for you.

Don't know what goal to set?

There are several questions you can ask yourself if you don't know what goal you want to set. Often it helps to start with a smaller, weekly goal – you'll soon find your goals get bigger and bigger. Use the questions below to help you set your goals:

- When you complete a Balance Chart (see page 77), is there an area you score lower in than others? Would you like to set a goal in that area?
- Is there anything you've been putting off or that's keeping you awake at night worrying that you'd like to achieve?
- Do you have something that's frustrating you?
- What could you achieve that would make the biggest difference to your life?

Is it a 'should' or a 'want' goal?

Sometimes goal-setting is about the language we use. We set goals for ourselves that we think we 'ought' to do. But who says you 'ought' to? Where did you learn you 'ought' to? If there's no passion the goal won't feel worthwhile and may not be completed. Use these questions:

- Are you looking forward to completing the goal you've just set?
- Who are you doing the goal for?
- What would be the benefits to you of achieving that goal?
- What value of yours is that goal engaging?

Is the goal too big?

You may choose a goal that's too big to be done in the allocated period of time. It's then important to restructure the goal so that it can be divided into many smaller goals. A simple way of doing this is using a Spider Diagram. You can ask yourself these questions if you're not sure you're going to be able to achieve your goal:

- What does your goal represent? What's the first step?
- Can you break your goal down? (eg don't write a book in a day, write 500 words)
- What could make you more confident and more committed about achieving your goal?
- What qualities do you need to access in order to achieve your goal?

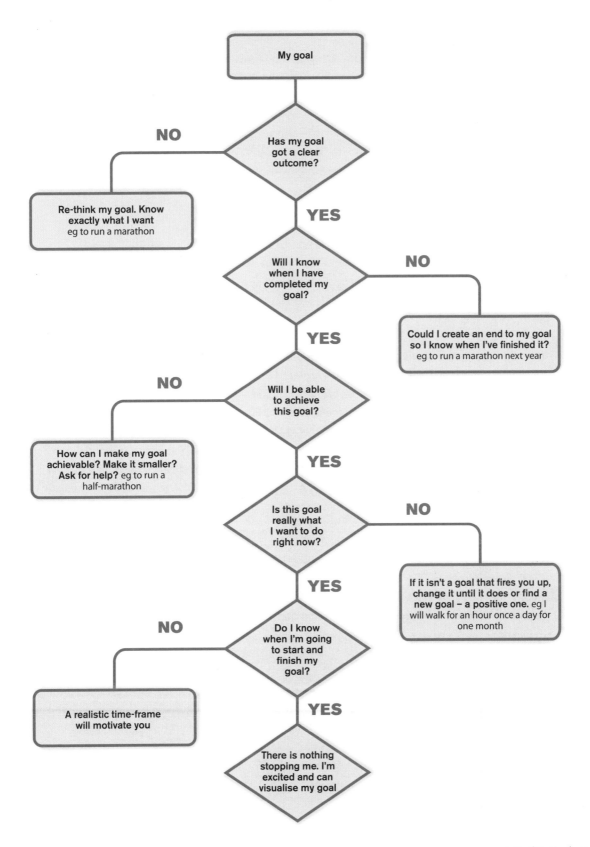

My goal

Has my goal got a clear outcome?

NO → Re-think my goal. Know exactly what I want eg to run a marathon

YES

Will I know when I have completed my goal?

NO → Could I create an end to my goal so I know when I've finished it? eg to run a marathon next year

YES

Will I be able to achieve this goal?

NO → How can I make my goal achievable? Make it smaller? Ask for help? eg to run a half-marathon

YES

Is this goal really what I want to do right now?

NO → If it isn't a goal that fires you up, change it until it does or find a new goal – a positive one. eg I will walk for an hour once a day for one month

YES

Do I know when I'm going to start and finish my goal?

NO → A realistic time-frame will motivate you

YES

There is nothing stopping me. I'm excited and can visualise my goal

Longer-term goals

If you're a Big Picture person and know what your long-term goal (your Life Ambition) is, break it down, depending on just how big it is and how far into the future you can plan it. Divide it into five-year or one-year goals and then into a three-monthly plan and then divide that up week by week and finally day by day. You'll always have your 'to do' list, but prioritise three goals you want to achieve every day towards your goal. Make those priorities both the things you're not naturally adept at doing and may have a tendency to put off – everything from financial management to organising a repair job – as well as all those things you're more inclined towards such as creative work, or networking (or vice versa).

How do you see life?

When you set a longer-term goal, perhaps it might be finding a new job or getting a degree, remember that we all work in different ways. Some of us like thinking about what we are going to do today and approach each new challenge as it comes day by day, while others start in the future with an ideal image of what we want to create and work our way back in order to discover the process of getting there.

Anna and Larry were planning the colour scheme of their bedroom. Anna had found some lovely pillow cases and wanted to buy them. They were pale blue and white and she thought they would be a good start to changing the room. However, Larry clearly had a problem with her choice and it annoyed him that she had just simply plunged in without planning how the room would fit together. He had a strong vision of how he would like their design project to turn out. In his mind he could see the finished room and it was now a matter of finding out where to get the things to fill it. Similarly when they were planning a meal, Anna would check what was in the fridge and start from there, whereas Larry would envision the entire meal in front of him and then go out and buy the ingredients. Once they learnt how differently they each approached the future they could see things from the other's perspective.

Claire wanted to learn jewellery making. She had her heart set on creating her own Russian wedding ring, with three bands of different coloured metals. When Claire went to enrol for the jewellery class, the teacher almost laughed in her face. 'That's the most difficult ring to make' he said 'aim a little lower.' Claire was so despondent that she didn't join the jewellery class and ended up never making her ring. What the teacher hadn't understood was that Claire liked aiming high and working backwards, whereas the teacher saw things step by step, one at a time.

Things to do:
- **Look at your Balance Chart, page 77, and work out what goals you have for each area**
- **If you have a Life Ambition, use a Spider Diagram to break it down into weekly goals**
- **Set yourself one goal a week – something you can achieve for your benefit only.**

(See Beliefs, Big Picture, Language, Life Ambition, Motivation, Personality Typing, Planning, Problem Solving, Procrastination, Spider Diagrams, Time Management)

Gratitude ● ● ● ● ● ● ● ●

At the regular weekly workshops I run, I ask everyone to think of the best thing that has happened to them that day. It can be the most difficult part of the workshop because we're all used to noticing what's been bad about our day rather than what's been good. It also can feel almost impossible to notice any good things when we're going through bad patches, yet it's so important to find a balance between good and bad in our lives. When we start thinking about the best things in our life it can be a moment to express our gratitude for all the good things and how wonderful it is to have them.

Gratitude is another word for thankfulness and implies a readiness to show appreciation for kindness received or about to be received. As gratitude is an emotion, there is often a feeling connected with it. Each of us feels gratitude to different degrees and with differing amounts of frequency.

'I'm feeling so grateful that my family is healthy, that I live in a great country...'

Best thing that happened to me today

Start making a note in your diary of everything good that happens to you every day or that you've made happen. It can be small things (the sun was shining when I woke up, I got a text from a friend, someone smiled at me as I was walking to work) or large things (I got a job, she loves me, we're buying a flat).

The power of gratitude

If you're having a bad day and hate everyone and everything, if you can convince yourself to be grateful for something – anything – it can turn the day around. Even on days where you feel nothing is worthwhile, if you just start saying to yourself 'I'm so grateful I'm not ill' or 'I'm so grateful the sun is shining', within a short space of time you'll start noticing more good things and within another hour you may well be out of your bad mood.

Things to do:
- Show your gratitude to anyone who is kind to you
- Notice everything there is to feel grateful for.

(See Balance, Body/Heart/Mind Types, Success)

'Gratitude is the heart's memory.'

French proverb

Guilt ● ● ● ● ● ● ●

I can feel guilty over almost anything. Taking a few days out from writing this book to go on a course made me feel very guilty. I was deliberately trying to push my 'Protestant' work ethic away and pretend it doesn't exist. How successful do you think I was?

Guilt is doing wrong or having a feeling of doing wrong to another person – whether in thoughts or actions. Sometimes you can feel you've done wrong for imagined offences from a sense of inadequacy. Guilt is a learned concept and therefore can be unlearned.
'I still feel guilty that my parents split up.'
'I feel guilty – and sick – after eating all that cake.'

Guilt is about standards
When we feel guilty it's showing us that we have morals and values that we're upsetting. We've fallen short of a standard that we have set ourselves. What we have to question is whether that standard is ours or not and, even if it is our standard, whether it's a standard we want to keep.

Guilty about anything
Being 'selfish', for example, can make you feel guilty, so you end up doing something you don't want to do and then blaming someone else for making you feel guilty and yourself for doing what you didn't want to do. It's a negative loop.

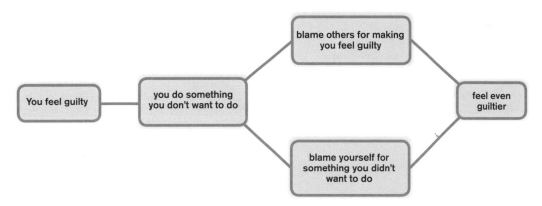

You can feel guilty about anything – not wanting to see friends, wanting to see too much of them, not doing something 'productive' with your time, not seeing your parents enough, not helping others more – the list is endless. Guilt mainly manifests itself around not being 'good enough' for others or not being good enough for yourself.

Others can make you feel guilty

As if you couldn't make yourself feel guilty enough, others can make you feel guilty too. Emotional blackmail ('Please make me a cup of tea and I'll love you forever' or 'If you don't make me a cup of tea, I won't talk to you for the rest of the day') is a weapon to make you feel guilty and all sorts of threats – from divorce to death – can be invoked.

What can guilt do?

Guilt can rule your life. From 'I don't deserve happiness' to 'Everything is my fault', guilt is a strong emotion. When you feel guilty you want to make life for yourself and everyone else 'right' and 'happy'; you worry about all the possible negative consequences of actions and sometimes you are unable to sort out your feelings.

Guilt as an advantage

Feeling guilty can be an advantage too. You can act the victim, wallow in guilt, or use guilt as an excuse for not moving forwards. Feeling guilty can be a pattern that keeps you safe in your comfort zone. Once you've worked out the advantages to you of feeling guilty, you can decide whether or not you want to unlearn these feelings and replace them with new ones.

> **Guilt I'm feeling**
> eg I didn't go to Jon's party
>
> **Why I'm feeling guilty about this**
> eg He wanted me to be there. I was being selfish plus my friends were expecting me and they'll feel let down
>
> **Advantages to feeling this guilt**
> eg I had some time to myself. I didn't get drunk. I enjoy beating myself up about letting Jon down. I can feel a 'bad' person
>
> **Action you'd like to take**
> eg Forgive myself and enjoy the rest of the weekend. Realise that it's OK for me not to socialise when I don't want to

Your Lightbulb Moment:
If you felt no guilt, what would your life feel like?

(See Accountability, Assumptions, Depression, Emotions, Forgiveness, Perfectionism, Perspectives, Regret, Stress)

Habits ● ○ ● ● ● ● ●

Since I gave up caffeine, I've been attempting to drink more water, rather than herb tea after herb tea. A habit that I've adopted is to drink a glass of water before getting out of bed in the morning. That gets me started with my water for the day.

Habits are regular practices of behaviour, which can be helpful or harmful.
'I wish I could get rid of my habit of having to have some chocolate after every meal.'

Develop healthy habits

It can be easy to excess on cigarettes, alcohol, worry and other habits, but making a conscious effort to develop healthy habits tells your subconscious that you intend to take care of yourself. Wear sunscreen, drink water, put on that seatbelt and cycling helmet. Make time to be alone and time to relax, eat well and use your body. Don't forget to make those yearly check-up and dentist appointments. Start becoming aware of the changes you're making – write down daily achievements and Lightbulb Moments. Creating healthy habits is extremely helpful and often simpler than meeting emotional and mental demands.

Ben was having a bad week. He'd been stuck in the car all week driving around the country on appointments for work, ignoring his body, which was telling him it was stiff and needed exercise. On top of all this, Ben was over-eating because he was rushing every meal and having to eat at motorway service stations and drinking all sorts of caffeine-filled drinks to keep himself awake. Because Ben was so down on himself, he was down on others too. He shouted at all the people he loved the most, ignored his best friend and didn't have time to visit his father. Then Ben got a cold.

Unless you put some good habits into your life, the bad ones will take over and that spiral of not loving yourself will affect your entire life. Let's have a look at that story again, but this time with Ben in control.

Ben was having a good week. Although he had lots of driving to do he'd planned ahead. Every morning Ben made himself healthy salads and wraps and, when he stopped at service stations, he bought bottles of water to drink. In the evening Ben went to the gym and then got to bed early – that meant missing a bit of television, but so what? Ben felt pretty relaxed – he was taking good care of himself.

Be patient

Habits take anywhere from three to six weeks to change and it's important just to focus on changing one habit at a time. As you start changing, use the time and money you save from energy draining activities to treat your body instead. Having a few less glasses of wine a month might seem more palatable when you enjoy a massage or a new shirt with your savings. Check out what your over-eating, for example, is masking. Are you unhappy at work or in your relationship? Do you find yourself in situations that you don't want to be in? Discover how you could make your life more the way you want it, because once you can do that you will find yourself losing interest in the habit of excess.

Joe was in a job he disliked and he smoked like a chimney. When he finally left the job he hated, he found that without even trying he stopped smoking. It might have been that he no longer needed the excuse to pop out of an office he wasn't happy in, but maybe it just wasn't necessary as a support any more.

The advantages of habits

There are usually enormous advantages to the habits we have. Through his smoking Joe could pop out of the office for a cigarette break and get some fresh air, and he no doubt formed bonds with the other smokers at work. Smoking may have made Joe feel 'cool' when he first started, it might have given him something to do with his hands in social situations, it might have relaxed or stimulated him, it might have given him an instant social circle. There are always enormous advantages to us in the things we do and, in order to get rid of a habit, those have to be thought about first, so you'll know how to create those advantages in other ways. For example:

- **Feeling cool – Joe could wear different clothes, listen to different music, join a gym**
- **Do something with his hands – Joe could hold his mobile, put his hands in his pockets**
- **Be relaxed – Joe could breathe deeply, listen to calming music**
- **Be stimulated – Joe could listen to invigorating music**
- **Have an instant social circle – Joe could join a club.**

Your Lightbulb Moment:
What would happen in your life if you replaced your bad habits with good ones?

(See Advantages, Affirmations, Beliefs, Change, Comfort Zone, Excess, Fear, Patterns, Routines)

Happiness ●○●○●○●○●●

I always thought happiness was simple (or not simple, depending on how you see it), but Positive Psychologist, Charlotte Style (see page ix), broke down happiness into:

- **Life satisfaction**
- **Pleasure**
- **Purpose in life**
- **Engagement**
- **Self-acceptance**
- **Personal growth**
- **Environmental mastery**
- **Hope**
- **and a few other things besides.**

Suddenly you can see why happiness sometimes seems so difficult to obtain.

Happiness is when you feel pleasure, contentment, satisfaction or joy. Researchers have found that 50 per cent of happiness is genetic, 10-15 per cent is due to measurable life circumstances, such as money, marital status, income, health etc. The remaining 35-40 per cent is to do with the actions individuals take to become happier.

'Being with you has made me feel so happy.'

Aiming for happiness

Happiness is a state of mind. It's an attitude and a perspective on life that some of us are more predisposed to than others. For example, for you, being happy in one aspect of your life might mean that you would feel happy about everything – the happiness would spread. Whereas for others, being happy in one aspect would mean that they were happy in that one aspect only and would remain despondent about the rest of their lives.

Characteristics of happy people

When you think about happy people, usually one of these characteristics will stick out for you. Notice which of these could describe you and build on it and on the others.

- **They enjoy themselves as much as they can**
- **They look at life creatively**
- **They look for the best in others and situations**
- **They avoid comparing themselves to others**
- **They live in the present as much as possible**
- **They avoid dwelling on the past**
- **They enjoy being with others**
- **They feel comfortable being alone**
- **They feel grateful for what they have**
- **They live life to the full.**

HAPPINESS
To me happiness is being by a
swimming pool in the sun.

Rules of happiness

In so far as there are 'rules' for happiness, these guidelines will give you an idea what to think about, and possibly pursue, if you want to find happiness:

- Happy people feel connected
    - Make time for being alone and with those you love and time for meeting new people or going for walks, or whatever else makes you feel connected
- Happy people feel in control of their lives
    - Control comes from knowing what you want in your life, from goal setting and being focused. It's an ability to live in the present whilst preparing for the future
- Happy people are able to get absorbed in what they are doing
    - Whether you can lose yourself in canoeing or crocheting, being actively involved is a key to happiness, rather than worrying about the past or the future
- Happy people have high self-confidence
    - Those who like themselves are more likely to be happier than those who don't. Celebrate what you can do and what you have done, even if today it's only that you ate a healthy lunch or didn't get angry with your pushy colleague
- Happy people are wise
    - Wisdom is about understanding the problems and challenges in our lives and resolving them. Wisdom is about staying objective rather than becoming emotional
- Happy people have a purpose to their lives
    - Whatever our Life Ambition is, having it gives us a deeper feeling of happiness.

Virtuous circle

The happier you are, the more you'll want to think of others and the more you think of others, the happier you become.

Project: Go through each of the rules of happiness and see where and whether you are living those rules in your life. Think about the changes you will make so you can increase your scores.

(See Absorption, Authentic, Change, Confidence, Connection, Control, Emotions, Focus, Goals, Life Ambition, Perspectives)

Inner Child ● ● ● ● ● ● ●

I find thinking about our 'inner child' can be very useful to help us look after ourselves. Sometimes, when we're not taking care of ourselves, if we can imagine the 'us' that was a child still there, we can look after that child without feeling selfish or guilty.

The **inner child** is your true and original self. It is still a part of you and may be waiting to be healed from an unhappy childhood – when it was wounded by abandonment, neglect, abuse etc. By learning to love yourself (this inner child) unconditionally, you will be able to create good relationships both with yourself and others.

'When I feel someone is making fun of me, it brings up all my childhood insecurities. My inner child just wants to hide.'

Find your inner child

Some of us find it enormously difficult to look after ourselves – we put everyone and everything else first and forget about our own needs. Last thing at night, no matter how exhausted we are, we still tidy up the mess in the kitchen, put away the clothes that have dried, close the curtains, pick up the clothes dropped on the floor, put out the cat and sort out the bathroom. We somehow can't put ourselves first. One of the ways round this is to imagine yourself as that child you once were and start looking after yourself.

Keith had always shelved his own needs for the needs of others – work, friends, family, lovers and even strangers. Even though he was now married, he could see he was still putting himself second. 'I always make the packed lunch for both Toni and me', he said 'and shop and cook for supper. I'm happy doing that. Some days I'd like to just be able to get out of bed and go off to work, but I always prioritise the needs of others above my own.' As Keith thought about himself over a period of weeks, he understood that looking after others, both Toni at home and those at work, meant that he was getting run down. But Keith didn't know what to do. He always put others before himself – he'd even dropped out of college so he could help his rugby team further their successes. Suddenly Keith had a Lightbulb Moment. He created a little mind game he could play where he thinks of himself as a vulnerable separate entity – his 'inner child' – who has basic needs that only Keith can fill. It worked. Keith became a soccer mum for himself ('Keith needs to go to the gym, Keith needs his lunches made for the week, Keith needs to swim') and found it so much easier to look after this 'inner child' because it didn't feel like him, but like someone else who was very important to him. By taking care of this part of himself, Keith found that he slowly found it much easier to say 'No' to others and to put himself first. Over time Keith felt as if the two parts of himself – adult and child – had become integrated and he was finally able to see himself as someone of value that needed to be cared for. Although Keith still enjoys giving to others, it is no longer an obligation.

Finding your inner child

Usually only as children do we have the luxury of just indulging ourselves in play or boredom. As we get older we start making compromises until we're no longer sure what it is we really want to do. Finding your inner child is about using your intuition until you know what it is you want. It's about noticing 'Am I enjoying this?', 'Do I want to go to sleep now?', 'Is this what I want to be doing?', 'Do I like being with this person?', 'Am I happy?', 'Am I sad?' until you know what it is you really feel and want. Then you've found your inner child and will know how to look after it.

Your Lightbulb Moment:
What would your inner child like best from you? Think about everything you could do to look after your inner child and write those things in the outer circle.

(See Boundaries, Emotions, Excess, Intuition, Language, Prioritise)

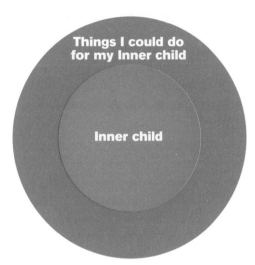

Intent ● ● ● ● ●

Sometimes I know I don't do things with the clearest of intentions. For example, when I tell my family I'm going to see my mother. Yes, my intention is to see my mother – and I will see my mother – but, when I'm honest with myself, I know my intention is to have a beautiful walk through the parks across London with my son. It's a chance to have some alone time with him without all the rest of the family, who might come along if we simply said we were going to the park for a walk.

Whenever we do something we do it because we have an intention, an aim or a plan. We often aren't completely honest with ourselves or with other people as to what that intention is. When we stop and work out what our real intention is, it can be very revealing.
'What's your real intention behind giving that present? Is it because you saw it and thought of them? Because you really like them? Because you want them to like you? Because you'll get something in return later? Or because you know they won't want it and will suggest that you keep it?'

Get clear

It doesn't necessarily matter why you're doing something, as long as you know why it is you're doing it. You don't have to tell anyone else what your intention is, but you want everything you do to have a clear aim to it or time can be wasted, the purpose muddied and outcome unclear. For example, rather than say 'I'm procrastinating on getting a job', recognise that you really want a break between jobs and delight in your period of relaxation. When you understand the intention behind the action, you can commit to it and achieve it in a focused way, taking full responsibility for it.

Project: Before you start doing anything – from making a phone call to going on holiday, just check what your intent is. Really check with your intuition what the reason you're doing it is or you may not get the outcome you want.

(See Authentic, Intuition, Outcome)

Intuition ● ● ● ● ● ● ● ● ● ●

A friend of mine was looking for someone to help her with her children. She interviewed about three people and none of them were right. Her husband was desperate that she found someone quickly, because she was so tired and needed help, so when the fourth person came along he suggested that they just take her. But my friend said 'No'. At the time she blamed her decision on the fact that this girl was wearing white stilettos and that wasn't appropriate footwear for anyone going to a childcare interview. But it wasn't really the shoes – it was my friend's intuition going 'Don't take her – there's something not right about her'. About six months later this same girl was all over the papers for having abused the children she was working with.

Intuition is when we sense or know or understand something instinctively without using conscious reasoning. It's like having brief but clear insights or feelings that appear to come from nowhere and will help you make decisions quickly. You're acquiring information without any logical input.
'My intuition told me to walk down the dark alleyway and that I would be all right. I was, and what's more, I found out later that there was an accident on the main road just when I would have been there had I gone the other way.'

Practise intuition
Use your intuition by asking questions of yourself. First decide what you want to know the answer to and then ask. For example, you might be standing in front of a counter of food and not know what you really feel like eating. Just ask yourself what it is you really want to eat and feel the answer. Similarly you have a free hour or afternoon, what do you really want to do with it? Just ask and wait for the answer. You can use your intuition with bigger questions too, for example 'Where do I want to live?' Just keep asking and don't worry if the answer doesn't come immediately. You'll soon start having flashes of intuition about certain places or a certain area. These flashes may well feel like Lightbulb Moments or like your head or heart or body talking, but they may occur regularly at moments of synchronicity so you feel surer that it is your intuition. For example, you're thinking of moving to a new area, but don't know which one. If one option is Chelsea and

that week a friend brings Chelsea buns to eat, another friend arrives from overseas and is staying in Chelsea and your map falls open on the page where Chelsea is, each time you'll notice your intuition telling you what it feels about Chelsea as an area to live in.

Intuition diary

Use a simple diary to record when you used your intuition, how it felt and what you learnt from it. Did you follow your intuition or ignore it?

I used my intuition when...

....

How it felt

....

Did I follow my intuition or not?

....

What I learnt...

....

Listen to your intuition

Even when you haven't asked a question, you may suddenly think 'I'd love to be diving in that sea' or 'I'd love to draw that view' or 'I wish I could play the piano like that'. Those little fantasies mustn't be discarded because they are the key to something you love. They're your intuition telling you something. Start fulfilling some of those secret wishes and dreams and notice how much happier and more creative you'll feel because of them.

Things to do:
- **Start asking yourself questions and listening for the answers**
- **Notice where in your body, head or heart you feel your intuition**
- **Practise brainstorming – great exercise for your intuition, because you're not censoring your thoughts and feelings but allowing them to come.**

(See Body/Heart/Mind Types, Brainstorming, Choices, Decisions, Language, Listening, Questions, Synchronicity)

Language ●

'Do what you will, but not because you must.' Zen proverb

Often people I work with will choose a goal which goes something like 'I should tidy up my bedroom this weekend' or 'I ought to go to the gym tonight'. The moment they've said something like that, I know there's no passion there at all. Why 'should' you tidy up? Why go to the gym if it's an 'ought?' If there's no desire, then they probably won't complete their goal or they'll do it unhappily. Your language choice is a clue as to how you really feel about things and what will and won't work for you.

The **language** we use when we speak to or about ourselves is crucial. We can be very unpleasant and say horrible things to ourselves which we then believe, such as *'You're useless at parenting…', 'You can't dance…', 'No one likes you…'* Or we can use positive language to create affirmations, such as *'I'm beautiful'* or *'I'm confident'*. How we say what we say can either inspire us or put us off. Language can have a huge effect on our future.

'If I use the language "I'll have to floss regularly now", I don't want to floss. But if I say (and think) "I'm excited about flossing and my gums becoming stronger and healthier", I know I'll do it.'

Negative motivation
If you're asked not to talk about something you talk about it. If you tell yourself not to eat, you can't stop thinking about food. If you're told you can talk about something, you forget about it. If you tell yourself you can eat anything you like, you stop thinking about food so you don't get hungry. Because we focus on what we think about, it's important to focus on what you want rather than what you don't want.

Negative language
Similarly with language, 'should', 'have to', 'ought to' and 'must' are negative ways of motivating yourself. If you're saying 'I have to eat healthily' or 'I should keep this secret', you don't really want to do something, but are hoping that if you force yourself into thinking about it, it will become something you do. What happens is that sooner or later you'll rebel against this internal 'parent' telling you to do something.

Positive language
If your heart is in something you'll really want to do it. You'll use words and phrases like 'I really want to eat a delicious salad for lunch', 'I'd love to go to the gym today', 'I'd like to make my bedroom look all clean and cosy', 'I'm excited by being a size smaller'. There's nothing that will stop you.

Project: Start listening to the way you talk to yourself. How are you motivating yourself to do things? Using your intuition and language together, think about whether you really want to do the things you're setting yourself as goals.

(See Goals, Intuition, Motivation)

Laughter ● ● ● ● ● ● ● ●

When I was heavily pregnant with my second child, the midwife suggested that laughter might speed up the process. So I organised an evening of Cheers *and whatever other non-challenging American comedy series was on. I laughed so much that evening that I knew when I went to bed that something had happened. My wonderful daughter was born the next day.*

Whatever the science behind **laughter**, it can make you feel so much better in many ways. The benefits are enormous: less stress, less anger and more energy. The only question is: are you doing enough of it?

'It was so funny I laughed 'til I cried.'

Make time for laughter

If every moment of your day is booked up, there often isn't time for laughter. Laughter usually comes when you're relaxing, maybe even being spontaneous. Activities like the cinema, walks, music, sport, going to the pub or out for a meal with friends can bring laughter on. Make time for them in your life.

Laughing with others

Laughing in groups can enhance our laughter as we trigger off each other's shrieks and guffaws. We usually laugh when we're feeling comfortable with one another and then, in turn, we feel even more cohesive as a group. When we laugh with others there's a loop of bonding, laughing and more bonding. Before you get together with friends, know what your motives are for doing something – is it to laugh and have fun or (for example) to excel at tennis?

Dan had always loved tennis. He tried to organise a game of mixed doubles with friends (of very mixed abilities) as often as he could. He mainly enjoyed messing around, being silly and laughing with the others. One of Dan's happiest memories was when he and his friends had played in the rain and everyone kept skidding over and laughing as they hit the balls and the water from the balls exploded over them. Dan decided that he'd join a tennis club so he could play tennis more regularly. Suddenly, he was propelled into a world of hard-core tournaments and fiercely competitive matches. No one seemed to have any sense of humour about it. Once he even saw a man smashing his racket up in rage after a losing a game. This was the only time Dan actually found himself laughing at the tennis club – it was absurd, how could anyone take amateur tennis so seriously? Although his tennis was improving, Dan just wasn't enjoying it. He wanted to have fun playing, but everyone at the club was set on having a decent game – laughter wasn't part of their agenda. Dan soon left the club and went back to knocking-up with friends in the park. That was what he really enjoyed.

LAUGHTER

This is my daughter, son and me
messing about and having fun in a
beautiful garden one Spring.

Use laughter

Laughter is an incredibly creative tool because when you're laughing your judgement is suspended and your thoughts are free – you no longer critique every idea you have. The silliness that laughter can give you is a great skill. It's a shortcut to ideas. Have you ever listened to children playing make-believe? How silly are their ideas – and how creative? It doesn't matter what others think of you or if you're being 'childish'. Take 'childish' as a compliment. If you solve a problem that makes you money or helps you save a failing relationship, does it matter what anyone else thinks?

Laugh or cry?

Laughter is a release of tension, which is why it's so close to crying and at times the two can cross over; both are outlets of emotion that can come from a realisation, or a connection with other people, revealing the humorous and poignant side of life. Once you know what makes you laugh – go for it. But, if you don't feel like laughing, you can always cry. The advantage of crying is that it frequently has a soporific effect as well, helping you to sleep so you dream and your subconscious mind can sift through your problems.

Things to do:
- Work out what makes you laugh out loud
- Put some time for laughter and fun in your diary
- Think about the last time you really laughed out loud and what triggered it
- Write down which people, films, books, plays or TV programmes hit your humour buttons. How can you build more of them into your life?
- Think about laughing – when you laugh with others, do you feel more connected to them or are you happier laughing on your own?

(See Brainstorming, Connection, Creativity, Happiness, Intent, Relaxation)

Letting Go ● ● ● ● ● ● ●

It's one of those things – we go back to our family home and suddenly we're behaving like a five-year-old again. There's something about being back with our parents, in our old home, reliving the familiar smells and sights, that feels so comforting. Nothing seems to have moved on – including us. I become sleepy, quiet, demanding. I want to indulge myself in all the things I can no longer do as an adult. It would be wonderful to arrive there as me – awake, curious and helpful, but no one else has changed and to let go of them and wriggle free of the past in that environment I find difficult.

Letting go is about moving on from your parents, relationships, ambitions, projects, the bereaved – allowing yourself to be free of the past and its grip on you.
'I was so happy when I let go of the resentment I felt towards my mother for always putting my older brother first.'

What do you want?

Either because of the assumptions your parents made about you or the manner in which they treated you, many of us have unresolved relationships with our parents whether they are dead or alive. It may be because we still want more from them (either or both practically or emotionally) or it may be because we feel guilty that we can't give to them any more (either or both practically or emotionally), but whichever it is, in order to grow up and become our own person we have to let go of our past. We have to become people who don't want the approval of our parents or anyone else for the way we choose to live our lives. We also have to give up blame towards anyone else for whatever we feel isn't working with our lives because all these grudges and resentments do is hold us back and stop us from taking responsibility for our life and making it the life we want.

When you haven't let go

If you're still feeling dependent on your parents you're probably looking for love from them. You want to have their support and you blame them for whatever mess your life is in. But ultimately they're them and you're you and only you can change yourself and your life. You can never change them.

How to let go

If your parents are still alive, start becoming aware of the relationship you now have with them and the way they behave towards you. Think about not only their behaviour with you, but also with others. Look at them as objectively as you can, at how they conduct their lives now, not in the past. Get curious about them. Discover:

- **How your parents behave towards other people**
- **How your parents behave towards each other**
- **How your parents behave towards your siblings**
- **How your parents behave towards your children**
- **How your parents behave towards your partner**
- **How your parents behave towards you:**
  - **Do they still put you down?**
  - **Do they assume you'll do things for them?**
  - **Are they used to you being always available?**
  - **Do they say they love you?**
  - **Do they make time for you?**
  - **Do they listen to you?**
  - **Are they pleased to see you?**
  - **Are they critical towards you?**
  - **Do they always want to protect you?**
  - **Do they always include you in their plans?**
  - **Are they changing?**

Only you can change

As an adult you can now choose to be less affected by your parents' demands and less affected by them putting you down. You can never change them, but you can change the way they affect you. Once you've decided what you want from the relationship, how you'd like to be treated and the way you'd like to feel about them, you can set goals around your relationship with your parents and focus on what works for you in terms of how often you want to see them and when and where.

Letting go of the finished

When someone dies or a relationship is over, it can be very difficult to let go. There may be so much love and so many memories. You may want to seek professional help to get through it. In the case of a relationship, maybe it was preventing the growth of one or other of the parties and you have to feel strong about letting go of something that wasn't working. In the case of a bereavement, there may be guilt as well as unresolved issues. In these instances, time is a great healer, but you may want to rethink your identity in terms of who you are now as an individual.

Have you 'let go'? quiz

Think of a past relationship (lover, friend, family member) and answer the questions below:

- **Do you feel angry when you think about this person?**
- **Have you any regrets about this relationship?**
- **Do you feel guilty towards this person?**
- **Do you find yourself talking like a victim when thinking about your relationship? (eg it's their fault and not yours)**
- **Do you have conversations in your head (good or bad) with this person?**
- **Is this relationship affecting any of the areas in your Balance Chart?**
- **Do you find it hard to have other relationships as you are scared of repeating what happened with this one?**
- **Have your friends/colleagues/family told you to let go of this relationship?**
- **In terms of this relationship, do you live more in the past than the present and future?**

If you answered 'Yes' to more than five of the questions above, you have not completely let go of this relationship and it may be having an effect on other areas of your life and your relationships. Take one of the above questions that you answered 'Yes' to and think about how you can make changes in your life so that it will become a 'No'.

Letting go of the unfinished

Sometimes we have to admit that ambitions we had or things we started just aren't right for us and we may be hanging on to them to stop us having to do other things. It may be better to move on.

Having lived in Los Angeles and London, Noreen's ambition was to live in Sydney, but whilst back in London she met Greg and he asked her to marry him. Noreen was very unsure. If she married Greg she would have to stay in London and forgo her ambition of living in Sydney. After much umm-ing and ah-ing, she rejected him. But she hadn't counted on Greg's determination. Greg refused to take 'No' for an answer. He offered to take Noreen to Sydney and propose to her there. If she liked the look of the place, she could stay there and if she decided she'd rather marry him, then that's what they'd do. In Sydney Greg proposed again and Noreen decided that, although the place looked beautiful, it wasn't for her. When they returned to London it was as husband and wife.

Letting go of hurtful remarks

Often we hang on to things people have said to us or we have said ourselves – either to others or to ourselves. Forgiveness is key. People say things on the spur of the moment that they don't necessarily mean – just as you may have said some things yourself. Let go of hurtful things (said or received), rather than use them as a rod for your back.

Project: Write a letter to your parents thanking them for everything they've done for you and explaining to them who you are now and how you'd like the relationship to work. You need never send this letter, but it will help you clarify your behaviour from now on.

OR

Project Two: Write a letter to an ex-partner or friend or someone who has died thanking them for everything that you shared and forgiving them for leaving you. Let them know the impact they had on you and your life and how you appreciate the many things they did for you. Again, there is no need to send this letter, but it will help you clarify your feelings so you can let go. Then forgive yourself for not having been able to let go.

(See Acceptance, Assumptions, Blame, Boundaries, Change, Depression, Forgiveness, Guilt, Listening, Mirroring, Saying 'No')

Life Ambition ● ● ● ● ● ● ●

I had lunch today with a charming, thoughtful man who was telling me how he wants to start planning the future of his business rather than being swept along by market demands. I told him that it always inspired me if I visualised my ambition – so I could see it in my mind as pictures, or even create an actual collage. I suggested that he might want to do that, and that, at the same time as doing it, he might like to imagine what he wants people to get out of his company, so he could form a mental picture of their excited/grateful/happy faces too.

Your **Life Ambition** is what will inspire you daily and give your life a purpose. It's the goal you're aiming for – the pinnacle of your life. It could be that you want to move somewhere sunny and make jewellery or teach scuba diving or it could be a collection of smaller things, like walk Hadrian's Wall or create a family tree.
'My Life Ambition is to make the world a happier place.'

If you know your Life Ambition

Once you've discovered your Life Ambition, you can regularly use a Balance Chart (see page 77) to see how you are progressing towards your Life Ambition and how you want to move forwards. By imagining what the relevant areas of the Balance Chart will look like as a '10', you can use that inner inspiration to work towards that perfect number.

If you don't yet know your Life Ambition

If you don't yet know your Life Ambition, use a Balance Chart to take steps forward in your life until you have the confidence and the vision to discover your Life Ambition. By seeing how in control of the balance and progress of your life you are, you will slowly start setting bigger goals until your Life Ambition becomes apparent.

Project: Discover your Life Ambition using both these methods – and discover which one works best for you.

1 Go round your Balance Chart (Life Clubs version, page 77) imagining you were scoring '10' in each area. Once you can imagine what scoring '10' would be like, you can use those visions as the basis for your Life Ambition. Choose the two or three that are the most important to you to work with and focus on them.

2 Think about what you would like others to be saying about you when you are old. In particular, focus on what you'd like these four groups of people to be saying: your community, your family, your friends and your colleagues. Whatever they say will be your Life Ambition.

Project Two: Go through loads of magazines and find pictures that mean something to you, that make you feel happy or inspired or alive. Cut them out and make a collage of your Life Ambition – your future.

(See Big Picture, Goals, Intuition, Spider Diagrams, Talents, Values, Visualisation)

Lightbulb Moment ● ○ ● ●

A few months ago I was running a workshop in a large corporation and we were working on what we would say to motivate other people. At the close of this exercise a modest middle-aged gentleman who was almost hiding behind his beard, suddenly pronounced 'I used to think I had a negative, glass half-empty attitude to life, but doing this I've just realised that my attitude is actually glass half-full.' I can't tell you how happy his Lightbulb Moment made us both feel. Can you imagine how differently he'll live his life knowing that?

A **Lightbulb Moment** is when you have a sudden realisation about something – it's as if a light (anything from a 40 watt to a stadium) goes off in your head. You look to others as if you've just had a pleasant surprise. It's either something you've been thinking about beforehand suddenly reaching your heart or vice versa – something you've been feeling suddenly reaching your mind.

'My Lightbulb Moment was so exciting. I'd been wondering for ages why I wasn't as organised about my social life as about my work life and I now realise it's because they're in two different diaries – and I never look at the social life one.'

Bring 'em on

Lightbulb Moments are truly exciting and the more self-development work you do, the more easily you'll have them. Just keep a note of them when they occur otherwise you'll forget them. By helping you understand yourself, Lightbulb Moments are the key to changing both yourself and your life.

Things to do:
- **Buy a blank book in which to record all the Lightbulb Moments you've had whilst reading this book and will have from now on.**

(See Curiosity, Intuition)

Listening ● ● ● ● ● ● ● ●

I run a listening workshop in which, for a few minutes, you just sit and listen to someone else talking. You would think that was relatively simple and straightforward, but so many of us want to problem solve (and thereby control the conversation and the outcome of the problem) instead of listen. It's much more difficult just to listen and not butt in, but it's ultimately so much more rewarding – on both sides.

Listening can be anything from giving your attention to a sound to making an effort to hear something to really focusing on someone with your whole attention and carefully hearing what they want to tell you.

'When I really listened I realised they weren't going to tell me what I thought they were at all.'

Some reasons why we don't listen

Instead of listening to the person talking, many of us are listening to what's going on inside our head. You may recognise some of these ways of not listening.

- **What am I going to say next?: You're thinking about what you want to say**
- **Preoccupied: You're preoccupied by something completely different**
- **Looking for agreement: You want them to agree with what you've just said, but they're not, so you switch off**
- **I've got a great story: You can't wait to tell them your story – you're feeling competitive with your 'better' story – you want to win**
- **I can imagine that: You aren't really listening to what they're saying, you're listening to what you want to hear**

- **I've got some great advice:** Rather than listen to their problem, you solve what you think is their problem – you're the bright one with the solutions
- **I love a fight:** You listen out for flaws or weak points to attack and then jump in with your counter argument
- **I'm bored with this conversation:** If you're bored or uncomfortable you change the subject – or start joking
- **I want to be liked:** You're not really listening, just smiling and agreeing – then you appear supportive and nice
- **I don't want to appear stupid:** You don't understand, but, rather than appear stupid by asking for clarification, you switch off.

How to really listen to someone

1 Maintain eye contact at all times
2 Actively focus your attention on what's being said – it may help you listen if you imagine you're going to have to tell someone else later what you've just heard
3 Keep your emotions under control, whilst listening out for theirs
4 Understand what's being said, independent of your feelings about it
5 Listen all the way through to the end rather than interrupting or jumping to conclusions
6 When the person has finished talking, summarise what they said back to them – using your own words – to make sure you understood it and so they know you were listening
7 Listen out for the emotions and intent beyond the words that were spoken.

The benefits of listening

- Listening diffuses the situation – especially if there's a lot of anger or tension
- Others will feel warmer towards you and enjoy your company more if you listen to them – they will also trust you more
- Listening allows others to be acknowledged, making them more willing to consider an alternative or back down a little
- Listening helps others spot flaws in their logic when they hear their argument played back without criticism
- Listening identifies areas of agreement so areas of disagreement are put in perspective and diminished rather than magnified
- You'll enjoy the conversation more.

Listen to your mind

As well as listening to other people, you can listen to yourself. Over and over in our mind we can hear negative beliefs telling us not to do things because it won't work or because we're not good enough. But there are also positive beliefs in there. See if you can listen to them instead.

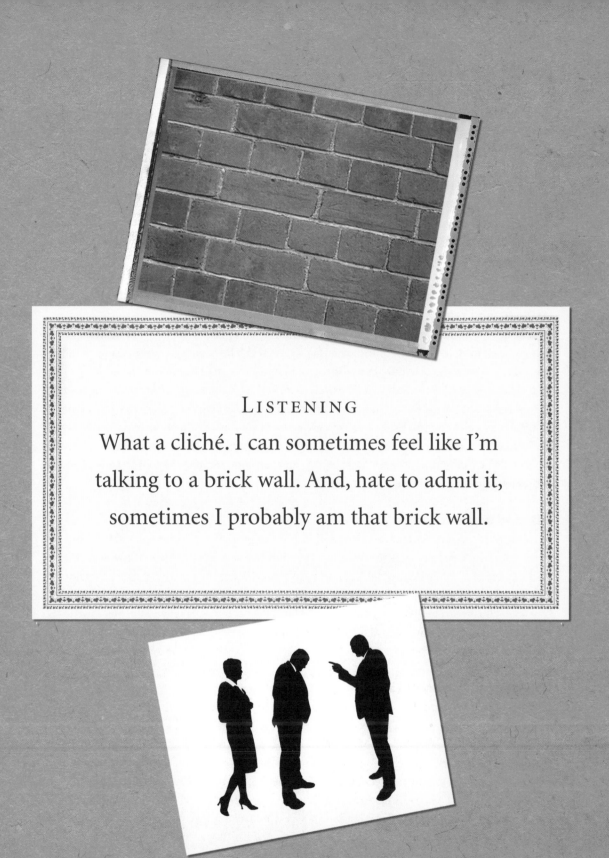

LISTENING

What a cliché. I can sometimes feel like I'm talking to a brick wall. And, hate to admit it, sometimes I probably am that brick wall.

Listen to your body

As well as listening to the ongoing monologue in your mind, you can listen to your feelings and you can listen to your body. Whether it's a growling stomach, not being able to sleep, a continual ache in your shoulder, a sore throat or anything else, these are all signs your body is trying to tell you something, yet most of us completely ignore them.

Nick and Patty had just got back from an exhausting day at work. Both of them were shattered. Nick listened to his body, excused himself and went to lie down on his bed for a quick power nap. Patty, although equally tired, decided not to listen to her body and instead battle on with what she wanted to do that evening. She had some chocolate and coffee to help her stay awake, which made her feel sick and headachy, rather than alert. In the end, Patty was so tired she fell asleep over the report she was reading anyway.

Listen to your family

We can take family for granted and assume we know everything about them. If you want to become adult in your relationship with your family, approach them as if you were strangers and really listen to what they say and observe them as they go about their lives. Listen to stories about their childhood and the next conversations you have, notice how present you are when members of your family are talking to you and what eye contact and body language you're using. Focusing on them may well bring you closer – are you giving them your whole attention? What would you like to communicate with them and what are they letting you know about them? Discovering each other could be a delightful process. See how you can open your family's eyes to who you've become and, at the same time, appreciate who they are.

Listen to your friends

Listening is the most important tool in a relationship, but relationships often seem to fall into patterns, in which one person is the listening ear and the other is free to offload the weight of their world. Occasionally it works symbiotically and you're there for them and, somehow, miraculously, they always seem to know when you need them, but those relationships are rare and should be treasured. Usually we find that we give to some, while other, completely different people, give to us. Being a good listener is a wonderful quality in a friend, but sometimes being the 'agony aunt' can become a pressure.

Listening isn't always easy

Listening when you disagree with someone can be very difficult, but, even when we want to listen to someone we like, it may be a pressure. Many of us have to listen to people all day at work and are exhausted by the end of the day. We feel that we just don't have the energy to really listen to our friends and loved ones. Maybe you have to let them know you're tired but will be there for them the following day – or at the weekend. It can also be difficult just sitting with an elderly friend or listening to someone who is going through a very bad time. You may feel you just want to get away and escape that overwhelming feeling of awkwardness and yet this listening is possibly the most precious you've done to date.

Being listened to

Ideally, once you start listening, the person you're listening to will realise how good it feels to be focused on and intuitively do the same intense listening back to you. You'll be role modelling listening. If it doesn't work naturally, just ask them to listen. Listening and being listened to both feel equally good. You get a deep connection which is fulfilling.

Listen to music

There are many benefits to listening to music and it goes without saying that some music is good for some things and other types of music for others. Music can relax you after an exhausting day or boost your confidence before an interview. It can also make you sleep better and, apparently, Mozart's piano sonatas can increase your IQ. And, if that's not enough, listening to music is one of the most pleasurable things you can do.

Project: Think about yourself as a good listener. Is listening something you enjoy, something that comes easily or something you find difficult? Practise. Take someone out and just listen to them really intently, with your ears, eyes and heart for 15 minutes, asking the odd question if necessary. Notice what you get out of the experience.

Project Two: Draw two overlapping circles, like the ones below and, in the relevant part of the circles, write down in which relationships you're listening, in which relationships they're listening to you and which relationships are 50/50. Think about what you could do to make all your relationships 50/50.

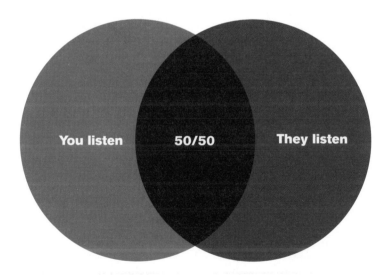

(See Absorption, Body Language, Boundaries, Compromise, Connection, Emotions, Focus, Intuition, Negotiation, Saying 'No')

Loneliness ● ● ● ● ● ● ●

I quite often dread being alone, especially before it happens when I feel as if I'm about to be abandoned. I remember when my son went off to university, I felt so lonely. I have three other children and a husband, so there was no need to feel lonely, but it was the idea of being deserted and having to cope alone – without him. My coach, the wonderful Gill Yourston (always great with perspectives), asked me to visualise the bleak landscape I felt I was in (a flat desert with almost no growth in it and thick, grey skies). In this landscape I found a decayed tree and she asked me to sit next to it (all in my imagination) and look at the dead sky. When it slowly turned blue I realised there'd be an end to my missing him.

Loneliness is being sad because you have, or feel you have, no friends or company. It's a feeling of emptiness and solitude.
'I feel so lonely even when I'm lying in bed next to her.'

We all feel lonely
Most of us have felt loneliness to a greater or lesser extent. You may believe you don't have enough friends, or don't know how to talk to the friends you have. You may feel that you get rejected whenever you try to make a new friend or that you don't know how to get intimate with friends you do have. You may feel that friends will leave you. Loneliness is often linked to change – whether moving house or job or changing yourself and your interests – when you don't yet know anyone who can support you.

Being rejected
Often we don't contact anyone because we fear that we'll be rebuffed. But what would be the worst that could happen if you phoned someone and they didn't want to talk to you:
- **They might put the phone down**
- **They might say they were busy**
- **They might tell you they were about to go out.**

And whatever they said might have been true and, even if it wasn't, it definitely is worth taking the risk, because they might say 'Great to hear from you.'

Overcoming loneliness
If you are extremely lonely you may find it difficult to have contact with other people and need to seek professional help. If you are going through a blip, here are a few ideas for ways to change your feelings of loneliness:

1 Talk to anyone you can – from your mum to someone in the local shop – and talk about them, rather than you. Listen as much as you can

2 Think of a club you might genuinely enjoy getting involved in (from a local badminton club to an Italian class). Go there with no expectations, but be prepared to enjoy it

3 Be curious about other people – take an interest in them and you will find that, given time, they may take an interest in you. Slowly break down the boundaries between you and them by being open and authentic

4 Imagine you were looking after your best friend (or the best friend you would like to have). What would you like to do with them today? Where would you take them, how would you treat them? Now, do all those things you'd do to a best friend – to you

5 Pretend this is your last day alone – ever. What would you do?

Divorced at 31, told by a match-making bureau at 38 'You're too old and you earn too much money – there's no demand for women like you', Rachael had been 'terribly lonely' for the 20 years since her divorce. She thought she'd gone past the point of no return and that she'd never meet a man – let alone one that was free. And she'd also begun to think she'd be no good at a long-term relationship. A Lightbulb Moment at a workshop made Rachael realise that the only obstacle to meeting anyone was her. But when you've got your life pretty well under control, things happen. Rachael met Neil at an all-girls lunch. He was the brother-in-law of one of her girlfriends and just happened to be there. They left the lunch together and haven't looked back.

Lonely in a relationship

If you're feeling lonely in a relationship, start talking – it doesn't matter if it's about the news or the neighbours, just start. And, start listening too, because relationships die when people stop listening. Do things together, build on what you loved doing together in the past. At the same time, discover yourself again as an individual and get involved in something you enjoy.

Project: Find someone lonelier than you to help. Notice how it makes you feel.

(See Authentic, Depression, Gratitude, Happiness, Life Ambition, Listening, Perspectives)

Luck ● ● ● ● ●

As well as luck being a state of mind, to me there do seem to be those who have good luck – regarding their family of birth and genes – and those who have bad luck. I definitely feel very lucky. I'm aware that some things have gone well for me all my life and I'm immensely grateful for those things – though, as we're in such a superstitious zone here, it can feel as if I'm tempting fate to allow myself to feel so lucky.

Luck is success or failure that has come about apparently through chance, rather than through any actions that you did yourself. It implies that the events that happened were beyond the person's control.

'I was so lucky in that match today – the wind was right behind me when I scored.'
'I'm always so unlucky, I won't bother buying a lottery ticket.'

Luckiness is a state of mind

Lucky people are lucky because they expect to be and vice versa. Luck is what you notice in your life, the perspective you choose to look at life through. If you assume you're going to be lucky, you look out for opportunities and you notice opportunities. Knowing you're going to be lucky, you act on the opportunities and create an even stronger feeling of being lucky. If you feel you aren't lucky you find failure in everything you try.

Become luckier

Lucky people...

- **notice and act upon opportunities**
- **frequently have large networks**
- **listen to their intuition**
- **are open to new experiences**
- **trust that the future will be good**
- **are relaxed about life**
- **are resilient**
- **don't dwell on 'bad' luck**
- **find the 'good' luck in 'bad' luck.**

LUCK as mnemonic

In terms of being able to create your luck, this mnemonic works well. 'L' stands for location, being in 'the right place at the right time'. 'U' stands for understanding, knowing what you want and what you can do to get it. 'C' stands for connection – in a networking way, who you are connected to and how they can help and 'K' stands for knowledge – the more you know about what you want to do, the better. Once those four (location, understanding, connection and knowledge) are in place, you've created a situation in which luck can thrive.

Luckiness as modesty

Sometimes it's easier to say that you were lucky than that you were brilliant and achieved great success. Or, conversely, to say that you or someone else was unlucky, rather than a failure.

Project: Think back over your life and make a list of everything lucky that's 'happened' to you. Did it just 'happen' or can you see your part in creating it. If you want to think about the 'bad' luck as well, see if you can work out what 'good' luck came out of the 'bad'.

(See Beliefs, Connection, Curiosity, Failure, Intuition, Language, Optimism, Perspectives, Planning, Relaxation, Success, Synchronicity, Trust)

Meditation ● ● ●

'Sitting quietly, doing nothing, spring comes and the grass grows by itself.' Zen proverb

I always find it difficult to brush my thoughts out of my head as I get carried away with the excitement of having them. I prefer replacing them with other thoughts. But then a meditation group I went to used music and visualisation and I found myself unbelievably calm. You can also feel calm and connected through looking at art and to me that's a kind of meditation too.

Meditation is a mental discipline in which you usually give your attention to one thing or the 'cosmic whole' and do not think about anything else in an attempt to get beyond the 'thinking' mind into a deeper state of relaxation or awareness. Meditation is used as a religious activity by most major religions. In Christianity, prayer (focusing on God) is seen as a form of meditation. *'After a good meditation session I feel like I can deal with anything without over-reacting.' 'When I meditated every day I felt so much calmer overall. It really helped me be in the present moment and not angry about the past.'*

Why meditate?
With continuous practice, meditation brings you peace of mind, clarity and a sense of fullness. You'll feel more accepting and less judgemental of yourself and others. After a while you'll notice yourself becoming less emotional and more logical and rational. It can also help with lowering blood pressure and general overall good health.

How to meditate
Find somewhere relatively quiet to sit where you will not be disturbed. You can sit cross-legged on the floor, but you can equally easily sit on a chair with your feet flat on the ground. Your eyes can be fully open or part open or fully closed and there should be a bright light in the room so you don't go to sleep. You can meditate for 15 minutes or longer at a time. The most basic form of meditation is just to surrender to the moment, relax, let go and do nothing. Just watch yourself silently. If thoughts come into your mind, observe them in a detached way and then let them go. Or listen to your breath and follow the in and out cycles. Feel the cool air coming in through your nostrils and the warm air going out. Or look at a flame and keep your attention on the way it changes and moves.

Does meditation have to be intense?
Modern meditation can be as simple as lying on the ground and listening to your favourite piece of classical music until your thoughts subside, your breathing slows down, your heart rate lowers and you feel the stress of your day drop away.

A few types of meditation

1 **Meditation on movement or posture** – go on a really slow walk and notice every time your feet touch or leave the ground or try t'ai chi or yoga

2 **Breath meditation** – focus on your breath and your 'Hara' (a Japanese term indicating a point just behind and below your belly button). Transferring your centre of awareness to the 'Hara' will quieten your thoughts and slow your breathing down. You can focus on your heart or your forehead instead

3 **Mantra meditation** – repeating the same words over and over again

4 **Meditation on an internal visual image** – visualise yourself on a beach or in a beautiful landscape, keeping your eyes closed

5 **Meditation on an external visual stimulus** – this can be a candle, a distant tree, a religious symbol, etc. It can also be a mirror. Staring intensely at a point just above your head, you see your body as a shadowy silhouette. Allow your eyes then to relax

6 **Meditation on a simple sound** – lying on the ground and listening to a tape of waves or a gong.

Project: If you don't already meditate and want to, find your nearest teacher and learn.

(See Absorption, Body/Heart/Mind Types, Breathing, Connection, Decisions, Emotions, Habits, Listening)

Metaphor ● ● ● ●

I'm a visual person – once I can see something I know how to proceed and I really enjoy using metaphors to problem solve. At school, in English, I dreaded having to think up a metaphor because I was using words and not pictures or feelings whereas now, just by visualising the situation I'm in, I find them easy and helpful to come up with. The best way to demonstrate how I use them is to show you how I calmed myself down when I felt a little under pressure from the deadline of a book I had to write. I felt empty and a little stretched and with no idea how I was going to manage.

My first metaphor for the way I felt was a wet and hairy purple jumper roughly hung out on the washing line, all twisted and rather too tightly pulled. Awful. This is the conversation I then had with myself:

Q. **How would I like to feel?**

A. **In an ideal world I'd like to feel on top of the situation, in control of the book and knowing I could write it in the allocated time-frame.**

Q. **What would a metaphor be for that?**

A. **This time the jumper might be dry and fluffy, neatly folded and ready to wear.**

Q. How am I going to get from the first metaphor to the second?

A. I had three ideas:

- **All jumpers do dry, so similarly, the book will get written**
- **The nicely folded jumper made me feel calm and peaceful, so I thought about where I could go to be peaceful when writing the book**
- **The mangled jumper had made me feel emotionally fraught, whereas the folded jumper made me feel more detached and cool. I thought about what could help me stay detached and not get too emotionally involved in the book.**

For fun I thought I'd have a go with another metaphor using the same problem. This time my visual metaphor was of an empty jar of honey. I even thought about having Winnie-the-Pooh staring rather despondently into me – not an ounce of creativity there. The metaphor I chose for knowing I could write the book was a full jar of lovely, pale brown honey with a smiling Pooh there looking fondly – and greedily – at me.

Q. How was I going to get from one metaphor to the other?

A. Again I had three ideas:

- **To get a full honey jar, maybe I needed some honey from somewhere else to replenish me. Could it be that I needed a weekend away or a trip to a spa, or a facial – something to fill me up with energy again?**
- **Maybe I needed help to fill the jar up – the creative input of others**
- **Or maybe it would just be easier to say 'No' to the book, so I could naturally fill up with honey again without the constraints of writing the book.**

I'm sure you can guess what happened, I decided to trust that the book would get written. I also made a sofa my calm writing home and decided to write the book starting from the end and working back to the beginning so I would keep my thoughts clear. I made a conscious decision that even though there was a time pressure I was not going to work all the time – to take days off here and there to replenish my energy – and, finally, I asked a few friends and wonderful writers, Laura Barnicoat (my gorgeous god-daughter), Andrea Blundell (a script writer and the first person I ever met through the Internet) and Annie Lionnet (one of my oldest friends and author in her own right) to help me write. The only thing I didn't do is say 'No' to the book, so here it is.

Metaphors are figures of speech in which you use a word or phrase and apply it to a different context to which it is not literally applicable. You picture one thing as being another.
'I'm "dying" to meet the new baby. From what I've heard, a "star" has been born.'
'The roofs were covered with a "blanket" of snow.'

METAPHOR

Anything can be anything. Those painted stones might have been a family, toys, soldiers, animals, a fairy story… or even just painted stones.

Play with metaphors

Metaphors are a simple way of understanding situations and looking at something in a new way. They are a creative way of solving problems and will open your mind to different thoughts. You'll discover how they will help you come up with unexpected solutions and inspire you to think outside of the box.

Peter, a successful photographer, wanted a change of career direction, but lacked the confidence, the motivation and the impetus to start selling himself all over again. He describes his feelings metaphorically: 'I'm surrounded by mountains and I'm going to have to climb one of them in order to get where I want to'. Peter started reminiscing about his childhood and the long walks he had when he was young. He remembered how he and his brother would push and pull each other up the hill or walk up the hill backwards. He could see his brother and him running up the hill in short bursts and then collapsing until they got more energy, whereas his parents would slowly and steadily tramp to the top. Peter started to understand that he was attempting a slow and steady climb up those mountains, sitting for several hours badgering clients he had previously worked for and leaving endless answering messages that he knew would never be returned. Metaphorically, it was leaving him out of breath and all too aware of the long path he still had to take before reaching the top. When Peter began thinking about himself and his brother and the fun they used to have, he started thinking differently. 'Maybe I could involve my partner in the process', he thought, 'and maybe I could make fun, casual phone calls, like walking backwards, rather than hustling.' Peter finally decided to 'run in short bursts' and that he would make two or three calls a day rather than spending hours at it.

Your Lightbulb Moment:
What metaphor best describes your situation? And, what metaphor would best describe your ideal situation? How will you get from one to the other?

(See Brainstorming, Creativity, Intuition, Listening, Planning, Play)

Mirroring ● ● ● ● ● ● ● ●

I want to introduce you to a fun exercise. You write a list of all the qualities you admire in other people – my mother's imagination, my daughter's logical mind, the Queen's discipline and so on – and then you think about how you display those same characteristics. For example:
- *I don't have the same imagination as my mother who can make up wonderful stories, but I know I can make up visual metaphors.*
- *I don't have a logical mind like my daughter, but (occasionally) I can organise things logically.*
- *The Queen's discipline I do find harder to recognise in myself. I know I'm very disciplined about the things I want to do, but not about the things I 'ought' to do – and rather wish I was.*

This game is wonderfully confidence-building, because after a while you start to realise that every time you admire something about someone, it's because you've noticed one of your values in them, so you're like that too. You can walk around giving people wonderful compliments and, at the same time, say 'Oh, that's how I am too' to yourself. It's a win/win.

Mirroring is when another person holds up a mirror to you and reflects back something of yourself that you either like or dislike.

'Being with you is like looking in a mirror – we're so similar in so many ways.'

Negative mirroring

It's sometimes easier to see how mirroring works if you think of someone you know really well – and really like, but who drives you mad in one aspect of their character. For example, let's say someone is really untidy and it upsets you. There could be one of four mirrors here – or all four:

- **Is it because you used to be really untidy and you've made a conscious effort to be tidy?**
- **Is it because tidiness is one of your values and they're upsetting it?**
- **Is it because, although you are very tidy in your home, your mind/desktop/diary is very untidy?**
- **Is it because tidiness for you stands for discipline (one of your key values) and they're clearly not disciplined?**

You drive me crazy

Because we are so closely connected in so many ways, it makes sense that our family members can mirror us. You can imagine getting really annoyed with your brother because he's so lazy when, guess what, although you're really hard working, you haven't been to the gym for months – so you're noticing his laziness as it reflects yours. Or your sister is making you cross because she's so self-centred and never asks about you or is interested in what you're up to. And maybe that makes you self-centred too, because otherwise you wouldn't mind if she didn't ask about you.

Will's brother arrived with a huge grin on his face. 'I've got three presents for you' he said. 'Can I have them now?' Will asked. 'No', said his brother, 'I'm going to drip feed them to you as the evening goes on.' 'You're such a control freak', said Will, realising as he said it that the fact that he'd noticed that his brother was controlling him was only because he wanted to be the one in control.

Positive mirroring

Because we mirror each other it can also be great fun being around your family. You notice their humour because it's your humour too. You enjoy their warmth, because it allows you to be warm. You love your father because he's so intelligent – and, of course, you are too. But let's say you admire someone because they're confident and you're finding it difficult to think about yourself as a confident person. Rather than thinking about confidence as being confident about everything and anything, break your life into areas and think about them separately. Maybe you feel confident about your knowledge of some obscure jazz musician or maybe you're totally confident about making soup. Be open to where the mirror is and what it's reflecting.

Search for the mirror

Sometimes the mirror is a bit more obscure, but it's always there to be discovered and, ultimately to open you up and to enable you to decide if you're living life according to your values or not. And, if you aren't, you can decide what you want to do about it.

Alison was sitting on a bus listening to a woman bitching about her neighbour. 'She's always meddling in my affairs', the lady was saying. 'I can't stand the way she pops her head over my wall every day…' and on and on. Alison got more and more annoyed listening to this. She couldn't bear the way the lady was being so unpleasant about someone instead of just confronting her and setting some boundaries. Why wasn't the lady being more honest? As Alison was getting crosser and crosser listening to this, she started questioning why she was getting so angry. She wondered what exactly the lady was triggering in her head. And then she saw the mirror. Alison too had been bitching a lot recently – about her step-mother. Her step-mother had been phoning Alison a fair amount and, instead of being honest and setting boundaries, Alison had listened to her step-mother moan on and on and then bitched about her to her friends. Alison suddenly saw that although one of her values was honesty, she was certainly not being honest with her step-mother. She felt a wave of compassion towards both the lady on the bus and her step-mother. From now on, Alison was going to live life according to her values rather than ignore them.

Project: Every day for a week, notice mirrors. Each time you appreciate or respect someone, think about where you too have that quality, and every time something or someone annoys you, think about what they're mirroring in you.

(See Change, Choices, Values)

Money ● ● ●

I grew up with divorced parents. My father, whom I spent the weekend with every couple of weeks, had a wonderfully lavish lifestyle and I would watch him on the phone for hours at a time to far-flung corners of the world. My mother led a very frugal lifestyle. Next to our phone at home was a sign saying '3 minutes on the phone = the cost of 1 Mars Bar, 10 minutes = the cost of 2 Mars Bars' (my mum loved Mars Bars). I think my character in many ways still reflects that split childhood. I am really parsimonious about certain things and don't spend money for months and months and then can go wild and buy an expensive pair of shoes or something equally extravagant.

Money is pieces of paper and coins that we give or are given to us in exchange for goods or services.
'Just give me money… that's what I want. Then I can give up work… have my dream life with a yacht… travel round the world…'

'When money
is not a servant,
it's a master.'

Indian proverb

What is money?

Even though the actual pieces of paper and coins have little or no intrinsic value, because money is so essential to our lives it has taken on a life of its own. We see money as:

- **Power**
- **Divisive**
- **Elusive**
- **Freeing**
- **Security.**

Yet, ironically the wealthiest often feel the least secure and the least free. They may have realised that money doesn't bring inner peace and that it can't fill the emptiness that many of us feel inside. The wealthy may see money as:

- **A responsibility**
- **A worry**
- **An obsession**
- **An addiction.**

How much money do you need?

Each of us needs (or wants) different amounts of money and each of us wants different amounts of money for different stages of our life. When you think about wanting money, think about what you really want it for. What would you do with the money? Is it what you really want? Would it really bring you enjoyment? Decide what you want it for and how much of it you want without being limited by beliefs and assumptions. Allow yourself to want the amount you really want.

Discover your financial beliefs

Earning money might be the main reason why you're working, but if, for example, you had parents who didn't value money and continually told you that 'Money is the root of all evil' or 'Money won't bring you happiness', you might find that even now that you have a great job that pays well, your finances are in a mess. Write a list of any negative statements that are going round in your head about money and find facts to prove how true or false these assumptions are. Show yourself that you value money – make a list of positive statements about money and read case studies about how money can change lives for the better. This is your life, not theirs.

Enjoying money

In order to enjoy money, there are five things you'll want to do:

1. **Learn to manage your finances wisely and educate yourself about investing – learn about our material world**
2. **Discover your Life Ambition so you know how much money you'll want**
3. **Understand your current assumptions about money**
4. **Know your current beliefs and emotions about money – they might come from your parents and upbringing and not even be your own**
5. **Trust that there will always be enough money.**

Project: Write a list of all the things that make you feel wealthy. How many of them are things that money bought and how many of them are things you have that money can't buy?

Project Two: Make a list of all the beliefs you have about money, for example 'rich people aren't nice'. You may have many of them – or just a few and they may be positive about money or negative. See if these views could be in any way causing you to block money from entering your life. It's difficult to become rich if you think money is what makes you a 'bad' person.

(See Assumptions, Beliefs, Excess, Life Ambition, Stress, Trust, Values)

Motivation ● ● ● ● ● ●

The other day I was running a workshop and I was pretending to be someone who didn't want to go to a party. I asked everyone there to write down what they felt would get me to go along. Most people in the hall wrote down things like 'You'll have such fun when you get there' (motivated by fun) or 'I'll come round and help you get ready' (motivated by being part of a team) or 'You only have to stay for 10 minutes' (motivated by taking things one step at a time). But there was one guy there who just wrote 'Think of all the free beer.' Wonderful. You can easily see what motivates him.

Motivation is what gets you to move towards the goal you want, the reason you behave in a certain way.
'I feel so motivated to climb Everest. I've seen a picture of the view from the top and I can't wait to see it for myself.'
'I'm motivated to see my sister because I feel guilty, whereas you're motivated to see your sister because you really enjoy seeing her.'

New Year's resolutions
Often what lets us down and stops us from doing things is losing heart. You know when you come up with a fabulous New Year's resolution and after a few weeks (or even days) have just totally given up on the idea. You've lost your resolve and consciously or unconsciously have chosen to stay as you are. Of course this happens at work too. You decide to step up, be particularly proactive, do something unexpected and suddenly you just give up. Maybe it's a response to negative reactions from those around you or maybe you've just lost your energy and conviction. Often when we choose goals that aren't really what we 'want' to do, but are instead what we 'ought' to do, we aren't fully motivated and lose interest – or heart.

We are all motivated
As babies we are highly motivated. Starting from when you were very small you taught yourself to walk and learn a complex language. Since then, you have continued to absorb an infinite number

of ideas, and you've built relationships and completed projects. You've stayed in relationships too – think how long you've known some of your friends for. So what kept you motivated each time? Think about all the things you've willed yourself to achieve in the past.

Emily liked working hard. Ever since she could remember she enjoyed succeeding at things. Emily knew that when she worked hard, things went well for her and when she stopped working everything seemed to slow down and fall apart. But at work, Emily had set herself some research to do and she was finding it impossibly difficult. Plus her boss wasn't giving her much time in working hours to do the research, so Emily had to snatch moments in the day and after work to cram in the extra research. One day Emily just felt herself giving up, which was unusual for her. She decided to think about all the things that usually motivated her. Emily remembered being a champion ice skater when she was small. She loved the praise she got from doing that. Emily remembered as well how lucky she felt when she won her championships. As Emily started thinking back, she could see how trust was important to her – she trusted that she would be lucky and that she was going to succeed. Emily also remembered how important it was to her to have a skating teacher there who checked up on her regularly, so she knew that accountability was key. She looked at her research and saw that three of her key motivators were missing. She had no praise from anyone, there was no one she was accountable to and she had forgotten to trust. Emily decided she had to explain to her boss how much this research could benefit the company – so that her boss would set her a deadline and she would then be accountable to someone. Emily then asked one of her closest colleagues if she would mind praising Emily whenever she had reached a new level of research and the colleague was happy to agree. Emily now felt she could trust again that everything would be all right. Emily had discovered her motivational tools and was once more up and running.

Your motivational tool kit

Each of us is motivated by different things. Here are a few things that you might be motivated by. Give yourself a score (10 = high) for each tool and find which ones work best for you – add your own too.

- **Advancement**
- **Fear**
- **Enjoyment**
- **Deadlines**
- **Responsibility**
- **Passion**
- **Rewards**
- **Competition**
- **Inspiration.**

Think about something you want to move forward in your life and see if you're using your motivators and, if not, how you can build them in.

Project: This week notice your achievements and what motivated you to accomplish them.

(See Accountability, Goals, Language, Life Ambition, Optimism, Success)

Motivation

Once you step onto the hopscotch,
you'll find yourself propelled forwards.

Negotiation ● ● ● ●

My children are world experts in negotiation:

'Mum, can you take me to the party? There aren't any trains going there.'
'I can't take you, sweetheart. Aren't there buses?'
'What about halfway. Can you take me halfway to the party?'
'What would be the advantage of me taking you halfway?'
'Or to Tom's and we can go together?'
'Darling, Tom lives miles away.'
'But Mum, it's late. You don't like me going out late on my own do you?'
'I'd rather you weren't out late on your own. What's wrong with staying at home?'
'Mum, it's a Saturday night and I want to go out. You went out on Saturdays when you were a teenager, didn't you? Can you at least take me to the Tube?'
'All right. I'll take you to the Tube.'
I'm never sure whether they just wanted me to take them to the Tube in the first place, and were softening me up, but whatever way it usually works – if not with me, with their father.

Negotiation is when two or more parties want to find common ground that all parties can adhere to.
'We're currently negotiating my salary increase.'

Satisfactory outcomes

Ideally when you negotiate you're looking for a compromise rather than a winner/loser situation. The competitive side of you may want to win, but negotiation is about both parties feeling satisfied and remaining on speaking terms. Key to negotiation is to:

- **Know what outcome you (and they) want out of the situation**
- **Find out as much as you can about the situation – both factually and emotionally**
- **Before negotiating, think, plan and brainstorm together so you're already part of the way there**
- **If possible, negotiate in a neutral venue**
- **Establish trust**
- **Keep positive**
- **Persuade with questions**
- **Only concede right at the end**
- **Be as creative as possible in your thinking – use stories, drawings, metaphors, perspectives, problem solving**
- **Before deciding anything – sleep on it.**

Listen

The Japanese are masters at silence. They use their silence to learn – observing and listening – and to push you into filling the silences. When you fear their silences is when you lose your strength and give away your hand. It's a wonderful technique to employ.

Knowledge is power

When negotiating, always find out as much as you can about your situation and the other side's situation. Once you know the strengths, weaknesses and needs they're negotiating from – as well as your own – it can help you enormously.

Project: The next time you're going into a negotiation – just listen. Notice how the other person will start conceding without you saying anything.

(See Creativity, Goals, Intent, Listening, Outcome, Perspectives, Planning, Questions)

Non-judgemental ● ● ● ● ● ● ● ● ●

A key rule when running workshops (as well as in life) is to be non-judgemental. I totally understand that that's a judgement in and of itself, but, if you want to change your life, it's vital to work with people who aren't going to judge you or your plans, but accept that they're what you want to do and encourage and support you. I first discovered the power of not being judged when I was younger and used to hitch-hike a lot. The joy of sitting next to someone and being able to tell them your ideas and plans and not have them put you down or remember some reason why you couldn't do that is liberating. Friends and parents often have you in a box of their making and aren't always as enthusiastic as they could be when they hear your plans.

Non-judgemental is accepting that other people have different views from yours and that their views may work well for them. It's accepting that there's no 'right' and no 'wrong'.
'My neighbour has told me that she's taken up smoking again. I'm trying to be non-judgemental, but it's such a waste of money and so smelly.'

To judge…

No matter how much we work at it, we will still judge others. We make assumptions about them and we may criticise them for being different from us or from how we would like them to be. A friend who has just left hospital after a knee operation wants to start jogging again. Do you want them to do whatever they want to do, do you sit there quietly wishing they'd let their knee settle first or do you let them know your views? Your feelings of responsibility may lead you to say something, rather than compromise your values, but if you let them know what you're thinking, you're casting your judgement. Have you taken their perspective into consideration?

'Do not judge your neighbour until you walk two moons in his moccasins.'

Cheyenne Indian proverb

or not to judge...

If there were no judgements, there would be no debate, no differences and no disagreements. As always, it's all about finding balance. If you want to, express your opinion tactfully and gently, but remember that others won't always agree. Allow them to think and behave differently from you.

Open up

Each of us creates and absorbs various social prejudices, which form our belief system. These beliefs are made up of what we already know or have experience of and they are a narrow way of thinking. Your frame of reference is in danger of becoming a fixed internal set of laws, governed by these narrow beliefs. The trouble is that beliefs of every kind, whether religious, political, artistic, or social, tend to crystallise into judgement.

Project: Notice all the judgements that go through your head all the time. Once you become aware of them it's much easier to decide if you want them or not.

(See Assumptions, Beliefs, Change, Listening, Perspectives, Values)

Optimism ● ● ● ● ● ●

'If I keep a green bough in my heart, the singing bird will come.'
Chinese proverb

I am so optimistic that sometimes I feel I should have a reality check. When I look back over the years at all the optimistic thoughts in my diary – not all of which have materialised – it can make me feel almost delusional. However, if I wasn't so optimistic I'd never be doing what I'm doing – and I love what I do, so I'm keeping optimistic.

Being **optimistic** is being hopeful and confident about the future. Most optimists believe that people and events are inherently good and so outcomes will be successful. Some optimists believe that whether or not people and the world are inherently good, you can make a positive decision about getting the best out of it. Optimism is one of the many components of happiness.
'I feel so optimistic about my meeting this week – I just know they're going to want to buy my product.'

Optimism motivates
When you're depressed, you are often so pessimistic that you don't do anything that could make your life better. In contrast, an optimistic person will usually take control of their lives, including, for example, looking after their body – possibly because they can see the benefit doing so will have in the future or because they're so looking forward to their future they want to stay alive and healthy to enjoy it. Optimistic people see the world as a benevolent place, make friends easily and enjoy social networking. Optimism has also been proven to lower the risk of death from cardiovascular disease.

Start thinking positively
An ideal balance in life is to be a mixture of both optimism and pessimism – using them both at appropriate times. Many of us are experts at pessimism and not so clear about bringing optimism into our lives. Which of the below could you adopt?:
- **An optimist would look forward to events and meeting people**
- **An optimist would see how they could connect with each person at a future date to the advantage of both**
- **An optimist would be thinking about all the exciting things that were happening today and tomorrow**
- **An optimist wouldn't worry about being disappointed or failing because they would want to see what good could come out of a situation that wasn't working**
- **An optimist would start noticing all the good things that are happening as well as the bad.**

Project: It is said that the only thing an optimist can't feel positive about is a pessimist. Think about what a pessimist could bring to the life of an optimist (eg caution, intensity, focus…).

Project Two: Think of something you would like to do, a goal. Circle the number below that represents how optimistic you feel about achieving this goal. '1' is pessimistic, '10' is completely optimistic. What could make you more optimistic?

1   2   3   4   5   6   7   8   9   10

(See Balance, Confidence, Gratitude, Happiness, Luck, Success, Trust)

Outcome ○ ● ● ● ●

Sometimes, even after a few weeks of attending, people coming to my workshops notice that their Balance Chart hasn't changed. So I ask them what they've been doing differently and the answer is always 'nothing'. As you know, if you don't do anything differently, your life won't be any different, and their lives are no exception. Each of us goes round and round living the same pattern, which I always imagine to look a bit like those wonderfully intricate Spirograph patterns. Patterns repeat and, if you want a different pattern, you have to do something differently – to carry on with the Spirograph metaphor – you have to move your pencil to another hole. You have to decide that you want a different outcome and, very deliberately, just change one element of your pattern so that when the pattern repeats it is a different pattern.

The **outcome** is the way something turns out. It's something that happens as a result or consequence.
'I want the outcome of this novel to be that they live happily ever after – and I want the same for my life too.'

Planning outcomes
Sometimes we forget that we can control our outcomes. We can create a list of things that we want to accomplish that day and we have control over them – providing we haven't set ourselves up for failure by writing down tasks that are too many, too complicated or too big.

Visualise endings
You can't change your character for a meeting, but if you imagine that meeting and, in your mind, plan it out as if it was a chess game – including achieving the result you want – you stand a much better chance of getting the outcome you want. What would you want them to be saying about you 15 minutes after meeting you? What is your purpose in talking to them? The same goes for the holiday you want. If you work through in your mind not only what you want for a holiday, but also all the potential problems, you stand more chance of having the holiday you want. Once you

know what you want you can plan it in your imagination. All it requires is for you to be as honest as you can.

Project: Imagine you're an actor who knows the end to every scene. You're never going to know the end to every scene, but you can decide what you'd like the outcome to be. Plan the outcome you want from everything – a phone call, a meeting, a dinner, the day – and focus on getting it.

(See Control, Failure, Goals, Intent, Patterns, Planning)

Patterns ● ● ● ● ● ● ●

Whenever someone talks about patterns, it always makes me think of Bridget Riley or Aboriginal art – maybe something spiral-like and peaceful for our sleep patterns and something circular and inward-looking for relationship patterns.

Patterns are when you repeat things over and over again in your life. They can be helpful patterns and they can be destructive.

'My pattern is that I'm never able to stick to anything – or anyone. I keep moving on. I'm constantly ruining relationships, career, security.'

Spot your patterns

- **Do you do the same thing over and over again and then regret it?**
- **Do you do the same thing over and over again and can build on it?**
- **Do you like your pattern or want to change it?**

Your good patterns are something you're always going to be able to go back and build on, whereas you might want to challenge your negative patterns.

When's a pattern a pattern?

The first time it may be an accident, the second time it may be a mistake, but the third time it is likely to be intentional. You have created a pattern. You can think back over your life and see where strengths recur.

When Jen was made head girl of her primary school she felt very proud and pleased, and, needless to say, was exceptionally conscientious. When Jen was made head girl of her senior school she couldn't quite believe it, the coincidence seemed too great. However, once again, she performed to the best of her ability. When Jen was given a special award for best all-round student at her college she realised that something she was doing was right. This was no longer just a coincidence. From that moment on, Jen had a different level of confidence; she could see that here was a pattern she could rely on for the rest of her life. At work she knew she would always be promoted and at home she felt she would be able to manage her family.

How good am I?

Fill in your own strengths in the chart, below. They can be anything from head girl, like Jen, to being good at drawing or swimming. Or even being brave or clever.

	As seen in childhood	As seen in teenage years	As seen in adult years
Strength	eg Jen head girl at primary school	eg Jen head girl at senior school	eg Jen promoted in first job

Relationship patterns

Many of us are attracted to and attract relationships and people who we feel are familiar – they remind us in some way of our parents. It's almost as if we're going out with the 'same' person over and over again. These people are all similar in some way – they may be unavailable, unstable, angry or unable to be intimate – and the relationship usually ends badly. Choosing these 'parent figures' to go out with can be an attempt to resolve an unsatisfactory relationship with your parent – only with someone who isn't your parent. And, as you can imagine, it isn't going to work. You cannot feel less abandoned or wounded or more loved by your parent through getting someone like them to love you. All it does is reinforce any feelings of inadequacy, inferiority and lack of trust that you might already have. Stopping this pattern involves accepting that you won't be able to get your parent's love from anyone else. Instead you may want to focus on forgiving your parent and letting go.

Looking back over the women he fancied, Anthony could see a pattern. Each time he fell in love with someone, they were never there for him, they were always unavailable in one way or another. Gabby had been coming out of a long relationship and wasn't receptive to starting a new one quite so quickly as she was still hurting and sad. Caroline was married and totally unavailable – even though she had flirted with him like crazy – and Martina just wasn't really interested in him because she fancied Mike. Thinking about his mother, Anthony could see she hadn't really been available either. Super bright, she flitted about from work to parties and never really seemed to notice him. Anthony even felt that she'd preferred his elder brother. Anthony realised he had to find a woman who was not his mother to fall in love with.

'No chicken will fall into the fire a second time.'

African proverb

Family patterns

Although we are individuals, we are all affected by the families who brought us up – whether we're adopted or not. We're affected genetically, of course, but we're also influenced by the beliefs, stories, rules and patterns of our families – whether spoken or implicit. We might be influenced by their illnesses, their problems and their addictions as well as their careers and successes. Sometimes we behave the same way as they do and repeat the pattern that has been going for generations and sometimes we consciously decide to do exactly the opposite and choose a new pattern of our own, even if it turns out to be not exactly that of our own making after all, but a pattern from another part of our family – the part that always broke the patterns.

Breaking family patterns

We often just carry on in the same way our family has always done – from the way we brush our teeth to the way we treat our friends – but we don't have to. The more family perspectives you explore, the broader your vision about who you can be can become. Many of us live our lives according to the stories we tell ourselves – stories about what we're good at and what we're not, about our interests and dislikes, about our ambitions and failures – and many of these stories may come from our family. And these stories don't just stop at our personality – they are also about the way we deal with life.

Family patterns in action

What did you learn from your family marriage patterns? Maybe your parents were divorced, so the story you got was that marriage didn't last. Let's say one of your sets of grandparents was also divorced, so that myth got amplified. And yet the other set of grandparents were happily married, so you can challenge the idea of failed marriage patterns and decide which part of the family you want to take your lead from. Similarly, what are your family success patterns? Maybe your parents didn't feel they were successful, maybe they told you that your part of the family wasn't going to achieve anything much – 'we never have and we never will'. Perhaps though, if you look at your cousins, they are all high achievers and doing well in their field, so what about borrowing them as part of your family pattern and forgetting what your own parents told you?

Bea was born in England to an English father and an Indian mother. A very tight-knit family, Bea somehow felt stifled. Every time they went to India to visit her large family, she was happy. Her mother relaxed and Bea could play with all her cousins and just have fun. The moment they returned to England, it was as if her mother put chains around her. Although she had almost as many English as Indian cousins, Bea hardly ever saw her English family – and, when she did, Bea's mum was very critical of them, so Bea felt trapped and isolated in England. When looking at her family tree, Bea could see that her mother was alone in England with no family and only Bea and her father as company. It felt as if her mother wanted to recreate this feeling of isolation for Bea, so that her daughter could mirror her life. Bea felt her mum was almost scared that Bea would love her English cousins and leave her. Bea, seeing this pattern her mother was creating, and also how large her English family was, could now help her mother open up to this other English world and thus free herself and her mother from her mother's self-inflicted 'prison'.

Behaviour patterns

You can learn a lot about yourself from the way people react to you. Are there patterns in the way people behave towards you?

- **Are they always expecting you'll help them with something?**
  - **If so, maybe you're stuck in a pattern of being the 'helpful' one.**
- **Are they always expecting you'll be up for a night out?**
  - **If so, maybe they think of you as the 'happy-go-lucky' one.**
- **Are they always expecting you to listen to their woes?**
  - **If so, maybe you're stuck in the pattern of being the 'Agony Aunt' one.**

Whenever people see you in a certain way, it's because you act in a certain way. Notice the pattern you're creating and the part you're playing in it and think of ways you can change those patterns. It may be just by setting a few boundaries.

Lifestyle patterns

Do you find you're over-eating, over-drinking, over-worrying, over-sleeping etc? Our lifestyle patterns are often to do with our excessive habits. The more conscious you get about how you indulge, the more your mind will kick in and wave a flag to say: 'look what's happening – there's a pattern'. Once you can consciously identify this pattern of excess – no matter what it is, you can begin separating yourself from the habit, because the habit isn't you. So, every time your mind now waves that warning flag, take three deep breaths and say to yourself 'I am about to overeat. I am aware that I'm doing this and that this isn't me, but a habit. I'm going to break this pattern.'

Project: Draw a simple family tree, just of the three most recent generations, putting everyone you have ever heard of on it – related by blood or marriage or partnership. Then, take any issue (eating, sleeping, drinking, money, confidence) that you have a pattern in and see if you can trace where that pattern you're following has come from and if, also within the same family tree, there's a pattern you would prefer to follow.

(See Boundaries, Excess, Failure, Forgiveness, Letting Go, Outcome, Stories, Synchronicity)

Perfectionism ● ● ○ ● ● ● ●

My perfectionism comes out most when I'm stressed. If we're having people round for a meal, for example, I want it to be 'perfect'. What does perfect mean to me in this context? It means that I don't have to cook when our friends are here; it means that all the food tastes good; it means that the table looks nice. That meal is all I can focus on for days – I can barely remember that we have to eat a few other meals leading up to that one. No wonder we hardly ever have people round – unless my husband cooks. Thankfully, he's not a perfectionist – at least not about food. But perfectionism can also be a wonderful thing. My son came back from the catacombs in Paris the other day marvelling over the precision, the order, the patterns. He loved the perfectionism.

'A beautiful thing is never perfect.'

Egyptian proverb

Perfectionism is when you want everything to be as good as it possibly can be – accurate, exact, faultless. Perfectionists like to be in control of everyone and everything.

'I'm such a perfectionist that when I meet people or go to places, all I can see is what is wrong – the dandruff on their shoulders, the crooked tiles on the wall. It's awful.'

'My perfectionism means that I'm always beating myself up about not being good enough.'

'When I'm relaxed I enjoy perfectionism. I notice it everywhere – beautifully written sentences, the elegant structure of a leaf, the composition of a photograph.'

What is 'right'?

Who says what's 'right'? Is it you or your mum or your dad or some other person in your childhood? We often grow up with such strict rules of 'right' and 'wrong'. We criticise others if they don't meet our high standards. We tell ourselves off when we set high goals and then don't reach them (because they were so high that no one could have). What if you could replace your 'wrong' with 'everything is perfect as it is'?

Hard to be perfect

If you're a perfectionist you'll find it difficult to take breaks and rest until everything has been done perfectly. You'll worry all the time that you (or they) are not getting it 'right'. When you're stressed you'll find you can't switch off, even when you get home after a full day's work, or at night when it's time for bed. Everything – even supposedly pleasurable activities, like holidays and social occasions – becomes a pressure, whether it's having to buy the 'right' presents or organise a 'special' family gathering. Somewhere along the line you'll have to compromise and then you'll beat yourself up about it.

Friends aren't perfect

Hopefully you can accept your friends, along with all their charming imperfections. It's all about not changing them (or even attempting to), but working out how you can change yourself.

Ed and Hannah had been friends since college, but Ed was beginning to find their friendship a strain. Hannah was always moaning – she never seemed to get any work, her other friends had deserted her, her boyfriend wasn't attracted to her anymore – everything made her miserable. It put Ed in an awkward position, because she depended on him so much for support. It was her passive nature that annoyed him most – she never made an effort to change things. Ed started thinking about himself – he always saw himself as an upbeat person; decisive and completely in control of his life. Just as Ed was starting to feel smug, it dawned on him why Hannah annoyed him so intensely – he couldn't control her. He couldn't make her happy or sort her and her life out. He couldn't make her perfect or her life all perfect for her. At that moment, Ed decided he was going to change and stop wanting to hold the reins on everyone and everything.

Drop perfectionism

Perfectionists usually 'know' that they're the only people who can do things. If that's you, let go. Make sure you're not the only one doing everything. See how you can take things a little easier. Have realistic expectations of yourself. Remember times when you were out of control and enjoying it and see how you can bring that laughter and fun back into your everyday life.

Oliver was doing well at work. He knew he was up for a promotion, so he was at work as much as he could be – doing everything the way he wanted it done. At the same time he had just got engaged to Phoebe and they were planning their wedding and buying their first home together. Oliver felt as if he was juggling three major things and was responsible for all of them. Phoebe would be upset if they didn't spend time together planning the wedding – plus he wanted it to be perfect and wasn't quite sure if Phoebe would manage that on her own. Similarly with house-hunting, Oliver wasn't sure if Phoebe would make the right decision on a home – he knew he had to see the houses too. At first Oliver noticed that he wasn't sleeping very well, he felt he was tired all the time and catching any sore throat or tummy bug that was going. Then Oliver started getting spots on his skin and realised the stress was causing him psoriasis. At this stage Oliver knew he had to stop something. Together with Phoebe he reviewed their plans and decided that there was no need to buy a house just yet as they were happy renting. They would get married and then move when all the kerfuffle around the wedding was over. Oliver had a word with his boss who helped him find someone to delegate to and design a working week for him, which would allow Oliver more time to be kind to himself – play some squash, go out with Phoebe to the cinema so he could laugh some more, or just go for a walk. Within months, Oliver's skin had cleared and he was sleeping through the night.

Things to do:
- Remember when you last 'let go' and relaxed and think about how you could do it again. Make time in your diary for you
- Think back to what's making you so tough on yourself and how could you be kinder
- When you're next beating someone else (or yourself) up, decide what 'right' is in this instance. Is it your 'right' or someone else's?
- Keep checking if you're taking on too much, if there are things you are doing that someone else could do, if there are standards you could drop a little.
- Discover who could help you out.

(See Change, Compromise, Control, Defensiveness, Failure, Goals, Mirroring, Planning, Procrastination, Relaxation, Sleep, Stress)

Personality Typing ● ● ● ● ● ● ●

I've mentioned the Enneagram before in Body/Heart/Mind Types. This time I'm going to tell you about another Enneagram facet, called 'sub-types.' When I can, I go to a group run by Rosemary and

Paul Cowan in London and it was with them, when we were working on 'sub-types', that I first heard this quiz[7]. I'm hoping it will whet your appetite for more Enneagram knowledge.

Personality typing is an incredibly useful way to help you to get to know yourself better and understand the others in your life. The Enneagram differs from most other personality typing tools in that its main objective is to enable you to grow both as a person and spiritually.

'My personality typing test helped me understand how different I am from the rest of my family. A silly example is how I like packing my suitcase in advance and don't take very much with me on holiday, whereas they all pack tons at the very last minute. I used to think they were just doing everything at the last minute to annoy me – now I know better.'

What would I do...? quiz

Imagine you're at the airport in France and have just been bumped off the last flight back home. The airline are saying that you'll have to stay the night in France and take the first plane the next morning. What would you do? How would you react? Take a moment to think. Be as honest as you can when answering these questions:

- **Would you find a cosy corner and make a home for the night? (see 1 below)**
- **Would you phone home immediately to let them know what's happened? (see 3 below)**
- **Would you link eyes with someone and make a plan together? (see 2 below)**
- **Would you go straight to the cafe? (see 1 below)**
- **Would you go to other airlines and ask if you could get a flight back now? (see 3 below)**
- **Would you have a meal and see if you could find someone to talk to? (see 2 below)**
- **Would you find out about other ways of getting back – train, boat etc? (see 3 below)**
- **Would you ask for a nearby hotel to be paid for and head there? (see 1 below)**
- **Would you sit in a nearby hotel lobby and see if you met someone there you could have a drink with? (see 2 below)**

How this quiz works

There are three different ways in which people get their energy. We all get our energy from each of the three ways, yet you will definitely put them in an order of preference. Imagine a three-legged stool with each leg a slightly different length: you will balance yourself on all three legs when you sit down, but one is slightly longer than the others so you sit leaning towards that one more and towards the shorter one the least. Once you know where you get your energy from you can use this knowledge to understand yourself and your relationships with others better.

[7] More information on Enneagram groups can be found at www.enneagramworldwide.com/london-enneagram-centre/

The three energy types

1 Self-preservationist

If you wanted to look after yourself and take care of all your creature comforts, you're a Self-preservationist. These hunter-gatherers have an in-built need to survive. You'll probably stick near the food at parties, collect something or other – be it books or toy trains or make-up, be in control of your finances and take your own pillow with you when you go on holiday.

2 Sexual

Those of you who wanted to lock eyes with someone else, get your energy from one-to-one conversations and from intimacy, and are perpetually searching for someone to bond with. The Sexual type craves intense relationships – even eye contact energises you. Think of the depth of the ballroom dancer's gaze or remember those people who glue you to the wall at parties. That's the Sexual type.

3 Social

You were probably desperate to get back to your clan at any cost. As a Social you get your energy from groups or thinking about how you relate to them. Family, friends and any other groups are very important to you. And, as your focus is on the greater world, manners are very important too – you see them as oiling the wheels.

How it works

There are actually 27 different Enneagram sub-types, but these are the three main ones – and even this amount of knowledge can show you how each of us are so very different. For example, in a friendship you may only want one good friend, while others need gangs of them, or hundreds of acquaintances. You may feel drained by an intense one-to-one conversation, whereas others find it stimulating. Similarly, you might thrive in a group situation, or simply feel overwhelmed. Keep noticing who you (and others) are and what you (and others) like.

Suzy was a high-powered marketing professional who disliked both shopping and cooking. Her family's fridge was often bare – not great with three children. Her husband Oliver, also highly successful, loved supermarkets, delicatessens, street markets and cooking. But Suzy's upbringing led her to believe that as wife and mother she should shop and cook. Furthermore, as Suzy hated the process so much, she couldn't quite believe that Oliver really enjoyed it – she thought he was simply being kind to her by offering to do it. After an Enneagram meeting both were immensely relieved. Suzy (a Social) realised she could take Oliver on face value – he clearly did love shopping – and so she would never have to think about food again and Oliver (a Self-preservationist) could do what he loved.

Project: Start becoming aware of which type you are and think about how this knowledge could affect you both in your career and out of it.

(See Body/Heart/Mind Types, Compromise, Listening)

Perspectives ● ○ ● ● ● ● ● ● ●

If you see me wearing green it could be because I wanted some help from my Scarlett O'Hara perspective. I found Scarlett one day – thanks to some great coaching – and she has been invaluable ever since, though I find she's done such a good job on me that I don't need her services as much any more. Of course, it isn't really her I wanted in the first place, but Rhett and his 'I don't give a damn' attitude, but I love Scarlett's feistiness and her stubbornness and the way she truly doesn't care about very much apart from herself and Tara. That Scarlett perspective is what I think about when I'm about to do something I'm dreading – whether it's giving a talk to masses of people or going to a party where I'm not sure whether or not I'm going to know anyone. I imagine I'm her and suddenly it seems easy.

Perspectives are a way of looking at something – a point of view.
'My mother's perspective is always more positive than mine, so I borrow it occasionally.'

Perspectives are useful

Usually we can only understand another's perspective by listening carefully and checking that we've got it right, but if you're having a discussion and you can see the situation from both sides – their perspective and yours – it's a wonderful skill to have; a great way of avoiding arguments. And, even better, if you can make sure they've understood your perspective too.

Time perspectives

A useful perspective can be time-travelling. Sadly we haven't got a Tardis, but we can do it in our head.

- **Future perspective: Imagine going forward 20 years (or as far forward as you can go – some of us can't go more than six months) and, from that perspective, looking back at your current life and seeing what's working for you and what isn't. You could even give yourself some advice from that future perspective – maybe you can imagine what you'll be like in 20 years and what you've learnt.**
- **Past perspective: Go back 20 years (or as far as you can go or find it easy to go) and think about how much you've learnt and how far you've come. Remind yourself of all your achievements and again look at your current life and see what's working better than it did before and what's worse. Once you know what the situation is, you can decide what your next step will be.**

Using these perspectives can help you plan your life.

Amplifying perspectives

If you're not feeling like doing something, there are some amplifying perspectives which might help you. Which inspires you more?

- **Worsening perspective: Imagine the situation you're in has got much worse – as bad as it could get. (For example, you're having a row with your landlord, imagine this situation getting worse and worse. Your landlord is now so cross, he's kicked you out – you have nowhere to go, nowhere to live and he's taking you to court for arguing with him.) What could this situation inspire you to do next?**
- **Improving perspective: Imagine the situation has got much, much better. (For example, you're struggling with learning Italian. Imagine that suddenly you've understood just how Italian works and you're fluent – you're good enough to be an interpreter, the Italian just flows from your lips.) What could this situation inspire you to do next?**

Fun perspectives

Ask a small child what they want to be when they grow up and they might easily say: 'a giant' or 'a tortoise' – they have no problem imagining perspectives and they don't censor their ideas. By applying unusual perspectives to your life you can find answers, guidance and help from places you least expect it.

Vanessa had friends coming round for supper and had no idea what to make. She really didn't know these people very well and felt a little nervous. Vanessa decided to use some perspectives to help her. She started by imagining she was the Queen. What would the Queen serve people? Vanessa laughed, quite obviously the Queen wouldn't cook – she'd have a chef. Vanessa thought 'I could do the same thing. I'll buy a ready-prepared meal from the delicatessen around the corner. I'll get some salads, hams, olives, and a few things I've never tried before.' Vanessa knew that would work. She'd feel relaxed as she hadn't cooked, plus the variety of food would break the ice. To take a different perspective Vanessa imagined she was Oliver Twist – how would he cater for Nancy and a few friends coming round. Vanessa imagined he'd not have much of a kitchen to cook things in – probably just one pot, so he'd make something simple and filling – soup, bread and cheese. That would be easy too and nice and warming. For her final perspective Vanessa thought of Popeye. Of course – anything with spinach… quiche, pasta, soup… Vanessa liked the idea of the soup, bread and cheese best – and she'd make a spinach soup. Simply by using her mind differently she had solved her problem.

All perspectives are you

Every idea you have, every perspective you choose is yours anyway. There are so many more ideas in our heads than we ever use or know are there. By finding different perspectives – from your father to Madonna, you can solve problems and simply think differently.

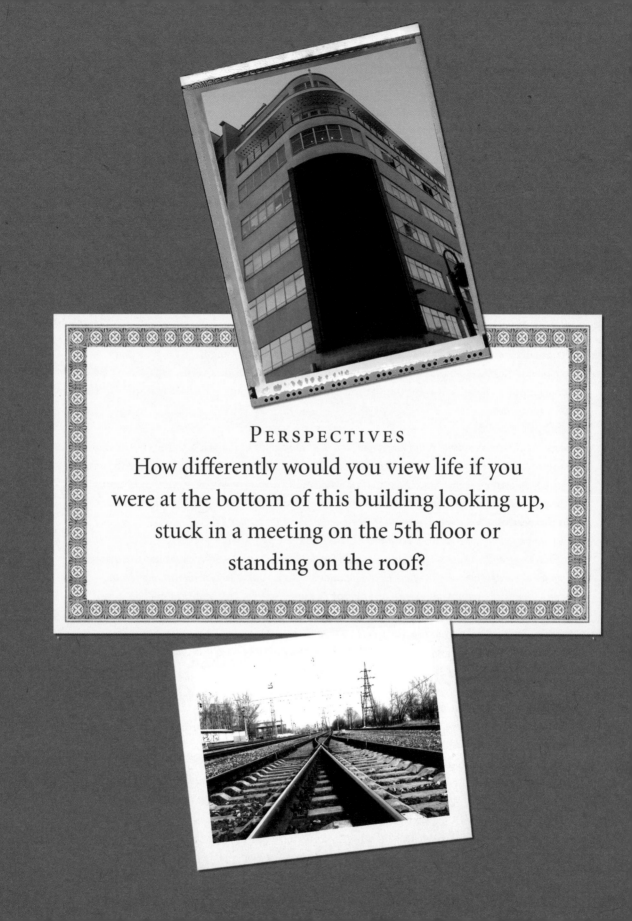

PERSPECTIVES
How differently would you view life if you were at the bottom of this building looking up, stuck in a meeting on the 5th floor or standing on the roof?

Getting into perspective

In order really to think yourself into a perspective, ask yourself as much as you can about the person you're thinking about, the person whose perspective you'd like to have:

- **What am I like?**
- **Where do I live?**
- **What do I do?**
- **What's important to me?**
- **What catchphrases do I use?**
- **What are my priorities?**

Really see if you can imagine that person and then ask them what they'd do if they were in your situation.

Focus outwardly

If you are feeling metaphorically tied up in knots, focus on other people, because concentrating on someone else's problems or dilemmas can help you gain perspective. As soon as you are put into the position of helping other people, suddenly everything you've been through becomes useful, constructive experience and will build empathy and compassion. Listening to others will ultimately help you change your train of thoughts.

Escape for a while

Another way to escape your own storyline is by watching a film or reading a book. Soap operas also involve us in different narratives, revealing a host of unfortunate characters all fated to suffer various disasters along the way, and watching that can make us feel part of another community with similar issues to our own. We can not only see their perspectives on life, but also put our own into perspective.

Project: Take a situation you're worrying about or a decision you've got to make and are stuck on and find as many different perspectives on that situation or decision as you can. Some will be the same as the one you've got now and others will be different. See how your views develop and change.

(See Brainstorming, Change, Failure, Listening, Metaphor, Planning, Play, Stories)

Planning ● ○ ● ● ● ● ● ● ●

Sunday evenings is my planning time for the week. I sit quietly with my ever-shifting three-month plan and decide what I'd like me, and anyone else who's working with me that week, to have accomplished by Friday. It gives us a structure for the week and a wonderful list to tick off as we achieve things.

When you **plan**, you define your aims and objectives, develop strategies and set goals for the years ahead. You then put a timescale in place for achieving those goals.
'I believe in planning ahead. I've already planned for our retirement and we're only just in our thirties.'

'He who fails
to plan, plans
to fail.'

Proverb

Fail to plan

It's so easy to sit in your comfort zone and hope that someone else will organise your life for you. Maybe they'll decide what we're doing at the weekend and for our holidays and even when we're going to bed. Sometimes this backfires and we sit at home at the weekends waiting for our family to return from whatever they've planned, wondering why we didn't organise our weekends so we too had something to do. Or we end up on the trip they planned wishing we'd said we didn't know if mountain climbing was really our thing.

Why plan?

Once you decide to plan your days and break down your time into conscious slots, not only will you be far more efficient, but you'll feel better too – satisfied that you're really using your time to the full. No matter what your plan is, whether it's to relax and exercise more or to work harder, doing what you intend to do feels good. Wasting time doesn't. The feeling that you have no plan and aren't managing your time effectively can feel draining and like a wasted life.

Plan at work and at home

Perhaps at work you thrive on structures, schedules and deadlines and at home find yourself lost without a plan. This could even be what is keeping you at work late, because you feel safe there. But what's stopping you creating plans like that for home? Decide what it is that makes your work-life successful and use these work skills at home too.

Samantha had just moved out of home into a house share with three friends, all of whom had hectic work and social lives. They didn't have time to cook in the evenings but would usually just grab something or make some toast before heading out for the night, inevitably ending up at the local kebab van on the way home. Samantha was not happy with this arrangement and found herself cooking enormous quantities of food alone, which she then ate too much of, too quickly. She decided to talk to her friends and persuade them to plan the weekly meal schedule so that they could at least have dinner together once a week. They found that this brought them all closer together and made them feel healthier – gradually, they all fell into better eating habits, cooking together, and even inviting other friends over.

Plan to succeed

If you've got a Life Ambition, you can plan to achieve your goal by breaking it down into smaller, manageable parts and setting up deadlines for each of those parts of it until the whole is achieved. Your plans can be broken down into five year, one year, six month, three month, one week and one day. Using a Spider Diagram can be very helpful. What's important is that you're planning for something you want to achieve. If you haven't yet got a Life Ambition, just plan for as far ahead as feels comfortable.

Plan your day

If you look at a television schedule and see how the day can be broken down, hour by hour, into so many different programmes, it's quite revealing to see just how much we can pack into one day, if we're organised. Do the same thing. See how it helps you to plan your day like a television schedule or do it backwards and write down where you are spending each half-hour of your time so you can see how you work. To get the most out of your days, you'll want to look at how you could structure and plan your time. If you're a late-night person, start making plans for the next day in the evening or in bed that night. If you're an early morning person, you'll want to go through your diary first thing in the morning.

Create a time sheet

Either fill in the time sheet at the beginning of the day, as if you were at school and had a timetable, or fill it in as you notice what you're doing during the day. Choose which one works for you.

Keep a balance

Watch that your plans don't become too tight though – as always, it's all about balance – football on Monday, cinema on Tuesday, Spanish classes on Wednesday, pottery on Thursday and book club on Friday, with a visit to the parents and catching up on sleep at the weekend is no way to live. Make a conscious effort to plan time in for you, but not necessarily 'doing' time. 'Being' time is just as important.

Keep plans fluid

No matter how rigid and in control you like feeling, stuff happens. Things might happen that affect our society in which case you might want to revisit both your business and home plans, or things might happen to you and your family. There's suddenly a massive change and everything is up in the air. Keep fluid, alert and optimistic. Open up to what the changes could bring.

Plan time for spontaneity

The trick is not to make your diary too full so that there's no time left for spontaneity. There's nothing better than just taking off without a plan and seeing what happens. It's ironical to think that you have to plan time for allowing things to evolve, but you do. Plan time for spontaneity with your friends and partner too.

Make time for plans

Sometimes we feel stale and that our days are full up with things that we no longer want to do, such as routines that are no longer necessary and leave no time for pursuing our plans. What routine might you like to change? Lying-in in the mornings? Watching television every night? Reading the papers every day? Checking your emails every 10 minutes? See what you can cut out. Once you've created your plan you'll find that there are things you can let go of to make time for what you really want to achieve.

Create a time sheet

	M	T	W	T	F	S	S	
6.00								
7.00								
8.00								
9.00								
10.00								
11.00								
12.00								
13.00								
14.00								
15.00								
16.00								
17.00								
18.00								
19.00								
20.00								
21.00								

Lydia had a full-time job, but her real ambition was to write a novel. She'd already successfully organised her life and found herself a job with less demanding hours. At work, Lydia only looked at her emails three times a day so she could focus on the things she needed to do. It meant that Lydia accomplished everything she wanted to do in the available time so that she could get home in the evenings as early as possible. Every evening Lydia got home about 90 minutes before her partner and would 'kill' time in front of the TV and cooking a meal for the two or them. Once Lydia knew what she wanted to do, it dawned on her that this could be fantastic novel writing time. When her partner came back they could start cooking together and Lydia would already have a few hundred words under her belt and feel good about the rest of the evening.

Using metaphor in planning

This planning technique is a visual aid, which will help you plan your time simply and effectively. Imagine first a glass jar. Then imagine filling it with three of the largest stones you can. The glass jar looks pretty full, doesn't it? But, of course it's not. Take a whole load of pebbles and watch as they slip down the sides of the stones through the cracks and fill up the jar more fully. Now it looks full, doesn't it? Needless to say more can go in. Next take some sand and tip that in so it goes in between all the stones and the pebbles and reaches the top of the jar. Full at last...? Or not. Finally take some water and pour that in. Now it really is full.

In your imagination, try this experiment the other way round. Put the water in the glass jar first, then the sand, then the pebbles and then the stones. What happens? There's no room for the stones.

Metaphor explained
- glass jar = your day
- stones = your priorities or goals
- pebbles = necessities of life
- sand = little tasks
- water = technical stuff

The glass jar and stones...

The glass jar stands for your day. The stones are your three priorities of the day – the three things that will make your day feel worthwhile if you achieve them: 'Today I want to plan my week, go for a long walk and write part one of my proposal'.

The pebbles...

The pebbles are all the essential things you have to do – eating, sleeping, shopping, commuting, meetings, clubs and committees. They are your fixed commitments, the things you'll do anyway, no matter what else happens.

The sand...

The sand is the fiddly, little stuff that you'll have to do – paperwork, paying your bills, tidying your home, vacuuming, dusting, waiting around for others. Little things that feel like they won't take long, but can do.

The water...

The water is anything technical – emails, texting, phoning, surfing the net, watching television and so on. They may only take a few minutes each, but there are lots of them.

Days of water

On days when we don't make a plan, it can feel as if our day is full of nothing but sand and water as the day fills up with annoying, inconsequential things to do or crises that suddenly appear or visitors or never-ending phone calls that stop you getting on. These things all have to be done, it's just that it's important to fit in the things we want to do as well in order to feel truly fulfilled.

The glass jar model

The stones are the foundations of your future. They are your goals, the priorities of your present and future life. By taking time to decide on them, you are deciding what's important to you. Because if you plan your day by first scheduling in the stones, all the lesser priorities will fit in around them and happen anyway. Choose a maximum of two goals for work, study or other people, and then make sure you've chosen one for you – something you really want to do.

Taking stones further

You can use the stones metaphor to plan for your life, your year, your week and your next hour as well as your day. There's something simple about having three goals and achieving them gives you a great feeling of satisfaction.

Finally... plan sleep

If you go to bed thinking about how much more work you have to do tomorrow – and it's not yet clear exactly what that work will entail or when you can do it – your mind will naturally whirr, prematurely kicking you into action in preparation for the dreaded tomorrow. If you're feeling like this, plan the next day as best as you can by simply writing a list of everything you can think of. Then draw a line under your plan for tomorrow and get some sleep.

Project: Take your Life Ambition and plan how you're going to make it happen. If you don't have a Life Ambition, go round the Balance Chart (see page 77) and choose an area you'd like to succeed in and then work out a plan for doing that.

Project Two: Use the stones metaphor to plan each day next week.

 Your Lightbulb Moment:
Where does your life structure need to be tightened up?

(See Choices, Control, Decisions, Focus, Goals, Intent, Life Ambition, Outcome, Prioritise, Spider Diagrams, Time Management, Visualisation)

Play ● ● ● ○ ● ● ● ● ● ●

I love the way 'planning' and 'play' are next to each other in this book, because I'm not so good at one and great at the other and yet if I don't plan, I don't get any time to play. To me play is everywhere – in my work, being with friends and family, when I write. I love all sorts of play – going on swings, playing cards, visiting funfairs, meeting people, icing cakes, tennis, dancing, talking, laughing, skipping, getting lost – anything that is fun. Play and fun are my key motivators. Whatever I do I like to build something fun into it or it ceases being something I want to do and becomes duty – and then I'm lost and have to turn to that other 'p' entry, 'procrastination'.

Play is when you amuse yourself by engaging in an activity that will give you pleasure and enjoyment.
'My 10-year-old would say that out of all his toys, he loved playing with his Lego best.'

Follow a child
When you play with children you can really understand what play is about. It's being totally absorbed, mesmerised by whatever is in front of you – whether it's watching a caterpillar crawling slowly across the path or throwing stones into the sea. There's no space in your brain to use to look back at your life and start regretting or to look forward and plan. You're just there – in the present moment of time.

When play stops
Many of us lock ourselves away. We're no longer to be found tinkering in the garden shed; these days we're behind our computers, televisions and mobiles, hardly interfacing with life at all. The distractions of new technology are seductive – suddenly we find ourselves pulled away down a black hole of Internet links, rather than getting inspired from more direct experience of the world around us, yet this bodily static play is no substitute for being fully involved in life.

Jackee had a degree in set design under her belt, but, unable to get work as a set designer, had ended up designing titles for an Internet news channel and stuck behind a computer screen all day. She had thought that it would be an exciting job, but soon knew that sitting behind a computer wasn't doing it for her. One week Jackee had a Lightbulb Moment and understood what wasn't working for her. It was that she was missing the three-dimensional reality of life. 'Computers are so two-dimensional', Jackee said. 'I want to be able to use my whole body, not just my hands. There's nothing physical in my job.'

Play starts
Play starts by being in the present moment. It begins with casual smiles with people on the bus or banter with shopkeepers. Playing is about interacting, meeting new people and opening yourself up to new experiences, making space for surprises and adventures. In order to play, let go of your inhibitions, your certainties and preconceptions – just be. Then anything can happen. Many of us think that it's not our place or role to act in a different, spontaneous, or creative way, somehow

imagining that if we stepped beyond these imaginary boundaries, we might cause concern or embarrass ourselves. But we won't.

Stretch yourself

Start getting curious about life – snoop into what others are reading, listen to what they're talking about, go to places and exhibitions and plays you'd never usually go to and open your mind. Follow your intuition; if a poster for a film intrigues you, go and see it. Play is opening your mind up to the fact that there may be more than one way to do things and it's a willingness to have fun. Play is also a chance to experiment and learn from others and everything around us.

Say 'Yes'

Saying 'Yes', whether to marriage or simply a cup of coffee, is always a leap into the unknown. We have no idea what marriage will be like and we're not sure if we're going to like the coffee the person makes. We hold our breath and go for it. Whether it's a trip to the races when you were going to do the ironing, or a visit to a salsa class when you were going to write that report, somehow 'Yes' feels exciting and decadent. Only you can know if you want to say it, but give it a go and see what happens.

Make space to play

Going out at least two nights a week is something to make space for in your diary. Doing different things and seeing new people will give you energy and make you feel more accepting the next day, when you're back in your work routine. Do you remember the last time you stayed up all night at a party? That satisfying feeling of walking home with friends, exhausted, listening to the dawn chorus and going to sleep in the morning as the sun's coming up. Pushing yourself into social situations that might scare you will make you feel alive again.

Add in surprise and celebrate

When was the last time a friend surprised you? When did you last surprise a friend? How much fun could you add to your social life? How can you celebrate? Think back over all the celebrations you've experienced, both your own and other people's. What stands out? What was it about that karaoke bar that had you laughing for hours? Was it making a fool of yourselves together, or the singing and the music? Perhaps your favourite memory is of a hen night where you sat and talked for hours. Or was it that post-football all-night party on the pitch? What stands out for you? Once you know that you can recreate it.

For Mike, a picnic was the ultimate kind of play. You never knew where you were going to end up eating and just how delicious the food would taste when eaten outside. Mike and his family loved going on picnics and their memories of each of these special events were very detailed because the facts of each picnic were inscribed on the canvas on the back of the picnic rug. Mike and his family would record the landscape in which they were sitting and the food they were eating as well as the date. That rug for them was a celebratory possession, filled with all the good times their family had had together. To Mike, a picnic epitomised fun: eating outdoors, simple food, good company, sun, fresh air and memories of picnics past.

Let your body play too

See exercise as a much-needed playtime – fun for your body. The reason many of us don't exercise is that we haven't found a sport that suits us. We associate sports with teamwork, tight-fitting Lycra clothes, claustrophobic gyms or aggressive competition. But it doesn't have to be like this – there is a sport for everyone. It may be badminton, t'ai chi, Nordic walking, jiving, mountain climbing – be creative with your definition of sport and find a form of exercise you'll love and get health benefits from. Think of exercise as a real thrill. Surprise yourself and your body with occasional challenges.

More physical play

Some cultures do far more hugging than we do, particularly when meeting strangers, but most people will respond positively to a hug. What are you waiting for? Physical contact is very playful.

Project: Think back over all the fun you've had, both on your own and with other people. What stands out? That trip to the playground? That bicycle ride? That boat race? Watching that singalong film? What did you enjoy about it the most? Do it again.

(See Absorption, Choices, Creativity, Curiosity, Decisions, Relaxation, Saying 'No')

Prioritise ● ● ● ○ ● ● ● ● ●

Sometimes I'm asked what the most important things in my life are and I find that an impossible question. Clearly health has to come at the top because without your health you are nothing and yet health seems so obvious as a top of the list item that I'm more interested in what follows. Only I'm not really, because of course people have to come next – family, friends, colleagues and then work or hobbies. Needless to say there are days when I would happily put work at the top of the list and other days when work isn't even on the list. The question I'd rather answer is 'what's the most important thing for you right now?' Now, that's more interesting.

Prioritise is when you decide the order in which to deal with a series of items or tasks according to their relative importance.
'Although I've been invited to a party I'd love to go to, my priority for today is to finish writing my book.'

Time is finite

We only have 168 hours a week for everything – including sleep – and yet there are so many things we have to fit into our day, which is why we often feel so stressed and pressured. Our to-do lists seem to go on forever. It's very important to know what you're going to focus on or your energy will be wasted. Once you're able to prioritise, you'll know what you want from each hour, day, week, year and even life. Sometimes it pays to multi-task, especially when we have to do things (for example, exercise) that we don't really want to do.

Wasting time

Brenda knew she had to start taking some exercise; she was eating far too much at odd times of day because she had to work long night shifts. She had friends who took dance classes and who loved going to the gym, but she couldn't get inspired to join in. She didn't want to spend her precious free time on sport. Then one day, Brenda saw a girl sweeping past on her bike – it brought back memories of how she used to enjoy cycling around at university. She realised that cycling might be a way around her problem. Brenda invested in a bike and started commuting to work on it. This meant she was exercising, while also getting to where she wanted to be, so it didn't feel like a waste of time. When Brenda had to work night shifts, she felt a wonderful sense of liberation, cycling home through the quiet city, before everyone else was up.

First things first

There are many ways of deciding what's important for you to be doing with your day. It could be by:

- **Tossing a coin, throwing a dice etc**
- **Deciding what you'd enjoy doing**
- **Knowing if there's an imminent deadline**
- **Going back to your Life Ambition plan and seeing what comes next.**

Interruptions

Often when we're in the middle of something we get interrupted and we lose our concentration. It's then when it's good to ask yourself 'What's the most important thing I could be doing with my time right now?' That question will help you find your priority.

Project: At the beginning of each day for a week, ask yourself 'What's the most important thing I could achieve today?' and do it.

(See Choices, Decisions, Focus, Goals, Intuition, Life Ambition, Planning, Spider Diagrams)

Problem Solving ● ● ● ● ●

About 20 years ago a friend of mine and her husband were pouring over endless brochures wondering what dishwasher to buy. As they were decision-making, my friend's sister, an ex-heroin addict, popped by and asked them what they were up to. When they told her they couldn't decide on a dishwasher, she looked at them and said 'Rich man's problems'. Since then, that has become one of our family mottos. If it's a 'Rich man's problem' we just make the decision and move on quickly.

Problem solving is the mental process used to find solutions to situations that have to be dealt with.
'How do you solve a problem like Maria?'

Do you know what the problem is?

You know when you're in the middle of a difficult situation and you can't find the root of the problem? Each problem seems linked with each of the other bits of the problem so you really don't know where to start. It's as though you're in a jungle of thick intertwined roots and high canopies; every step forward trips you up and you can't see the horizon. You need clarity in a situation like that. Describing your problem as clearly as you can allows your mind to process the information in order to begin solving it.

Suzy was looking for a new job. Most weeks she set as her goal that she was going to send out her CV to loads of new companies. But at a problem solving workshop, Suzy suddenly sat bolt upright with her face lit up. 'I've just realised', she said, 'I've been trying to solve the wrong problem. I don't need a new job, I need a new home. I hate my flat. Once I'm happy at home, I'll feel like going home more and I won't spend so much time at work, so everything will be fine.'

Get curious

There are many different ways to solve your problems, but all of them involve getting curious about who you are and what you want. Both perspectives and metaphor can help you problem solve too, as can brainstorming. When your mind feels free and open you can put two unrelated things together and invent something new, as Johannes Gutenberg did when he took the wine press and the die-punch and came up with the printing press. If you can dare to look at your problem with a child's perspective – using an open mind, looking where everyone else is looking and seeing what no one else can – as if you knew nothing, that's always the way to start.

Trust

A huge part of problem solving is learning to trust. You've put your problem in the coffee maker and filled it up with water – your ideas. Now let it heat up and bubble whilst you have a shower, go for a walk or allow a few days or weeks of not thinking about it and trust that the answer will come. The inventor, Art Fry, was an engineer who had discovered a barely sticky adhesive at his work that no one else knew what to do with. Fry wanted to use it for something but also had no ideas. It was only when he was at church singing in the choir, wishing his bookmark wouldn't fall out of his hymnal, that inspiration hit and he invented the Post-It.

Jack had a problem. He was bored with his wife, Fiona. He felt their relationship had gone stale and he didn't really enjoy being with Fiona any more, plus he didn't feel he could talk about it with her. Jack had a journal he kept for things he wanted to think about and in it he wrote down 'Bring fun back into our relationship' and a few obvious ideas – go on holiday, Friday night dates, listen more, go somewhere we can laugh together. Jack then left the problem to incubate without attempting to solve it. He just trusted that the answer would come to him. A few days later Jack was relaxing in the swimming pool. He'd just swum his routine lengths and was pretending to be a dolphin, flipping around for fun. In that moment he knew what he would propose – he and Fiona needed to have a fun project they could do together. They both loved films, so he decided that every Sunday they would find a new film to watch, from different countries around the world. Together, they began to explore all these different cultures and learnt new things about each other, as they bonded over the films they liked and disliked. It sparked their imagination and they began to plan possible trips to the places they had travelled to through film. Suddenly they felt like a pair again.

Five ideas for problem solving

1 Break down the problem into as small components as possible and solve these individually
2 Get help from friends
3 Attempt to prove that the problem can't be solved – when your proof collapses you may find you're on the way to a solution
4 Look at what's already going right
5 Brainstorm ideas and put these ideas into different themes – this might show you a way forward.

LIFE model

The LIFE model can be used to solve problems or set goals. When you're using it, make sure that you want to solve a problem that you can affect the outcome of, bearing in mind that you can't change anyone else. For example 'How can I make my son revise harder?' is a problem that only your son can solve. 'How can I stop worrying about my son not working?' is a problem you can solve.

Mnemonic

LIFE is a mnemonic. Each of the four sections, Living, Ideal, Fuel and Energy, contain lots of questions that you can ask yourself in order to solve your problem. Ask them in the LIFE order, rather than skipping around or it won't make sense.

L = Living (your current situation)
I = Ideal (your 'ideal' situation)
F = Fuel (what 'fuel' do you need to help you?)
E = Energy (taking the first step)

Living

Living is your current situation and helps you define the problem you really want to solve. These questions will give you an overview of the situation and help you see it clearly before deciding what you want. Often just by getting that overview, what you have to do then becomes obvious and straightforward.

- What's annoying me?
- What is really going on?
- What am I reacting to?
- What are the facts?
- Could things be different?

Ideal

Ideal is the problem solved, it's the situation you want – your 'Ideal' outcome. Be totally realistic when you answer these questions, otherwise your 'Ideal' isn't going to work. For example, if you want to win the lottery, you have at least to enter it. Once you know what outcome you want, you'll find your problem has far less of a grip on you.

- **What do I really want to achieve?**
- **What would my ideal outcome be?**
- **How can this situation work for me?**
- **How can it work for all those involved?**
- **Is my Ideal goal realistic, and within my capabilities and budget?**

Fuel

Fuel is about finding ways to achieve your 'Ideal'. The fuel you'll want is unique to you depending on your problem, so these questions are a chance to get creative and think of as many different solutions as possible.

- **What will help me tackle my problem and achieve my Ideal goal?**
- **Is there any more information I could get before I start?**
- **Who might be able to help me?**
- **What could I do to help myself?**
- **What resources are available to me and might I want (money, training, experience, advice, information, etc) in order to achieve my goal?**
- **What could be my first step?**

Energy

Finally, these Energy questions are about moving forward. You have almost solved your problem intellectually, and it's time to be proactive.

- **What are my next steps going to be? (You can even list them in order so that you can start doing them straightaway)**
- **Where and when will I take my next steps?**
- **How will I know when I have reached my Ideal solution? How will I be feeling, looking, thinking as I near my goal? What changes in me and my life will there be?**
- **How committed am I to this Ideal goal? How confident am I? If my commitment and confidence is not 9 or 10 (high) on a scale of 1 to 10, what is blocking the way before final take off? Who or what could help me get my commitment and confidence higher?**
- **How will I feel when I reach my Ideal outcome?**

At every office meeting Tim felt slighted and angry, but he didn't feel right about saying anything. After the meeting he would always spend the next couple of hours raking unproductively over all the conversations, feeling negative, upset with himself for not taking action and wondering if he'd ever change. Using the LIFE model, on 'Living' Tim asked himself why he didn't speak up with the team at work when he had the chance. He knew intuitively it was better to deal with things when they arose rather than letting them snowball. On 'Ideal' Tim decided that he didn't ever want to stew over lost opportunities again and was going to speak his mind. When working through the 'Fuel' questions, Tim worked out that next time he was going to listen carefully in the meeting and deal with the issues there and then. Plus, if there was any back-biting, he decided he was going to remind them of team-meeting policies about putting statements into a definite context and that they can only move on through the agenda when overall clarity has been achieved. Tim was confident and committed and knew that the only thing that he wanted left on the agenda was action points and that he had the 'Energy' to see that through.

Project: Take one of your problems and work through the LIFE model with it.

(See Brainstorming, Choices, Decisions, Metaphor, Perspectives, Spider Diagrams, Values)

Procrastination ● ● ○ ● ● ● ●

I don't think I've ever procrastinated so much as when I was writing our workshop on procrastination. They say you get what you focus on and, in this case, it was definitely true.

Procrastination is putting off doing tasks and actions until a later time.
'I procrastinated so long over buying the plane tickets that when I finally got round to it, they were all sold out.'

Problems with procrastination

Procrastination is often seen as a joke, but is a serious problem which can lead to overwhelming stress, missed opportunities, uncontrolled work hours, resentment and guilt. While most people have the potential to procrastinate, about 20 per cent of us are what we might call chronic procrastinators. If you procrastinate, you've probably already noticed how there's fallout in every area of your life. You may not pay your bills on time, you'll miss social engagements because you forgot to reply to an invitation or buy tickets in advance, you'll file your taxes late and give gifts you bought on the way to the party at the only shop (or petrol station) that was open. You can imagine how being a procrastinator destroys your relationships – everyone has to pick up the pieces after you.

'If not now – when?'

Jewish proverb

Why procrastinate?

Although fear and indecision are often said to be the main reasons for procrastination, they aren't at the root of what makes us procrastinate. There are three main reasons why we procrastinate and fear and indecision fit into each of them:

1 we want to do things perfectly

2 we feel overwhelmed by the task

3 we rebel against what we have to do.

Your procrastination quiz

Once you've done this quiz you'll know what's stopping you and you can decide if you want to move forward or not. Make a note of what you answered ('a', 'b' or 'c') to each question.

1 What's stopping you?

    a I'm frightened of getting it wrong

    b There's not enough time

    c I've got better things to do.

2 Can you start straight away?

    a No, I need to plan more

    b I don't know where to start

    c Yes, but I don't want to.

3 What are you frightened of?

    a Not getting it right

    b It taking up too much time

    c I'm not frightened.

4 Are you feeling indecisive?

    a Yes, I'm worried about going down the wrong path

    b Yes, there are too many decisions

    c Yes, I don't know if I really want to do it.

If you answered mainly 'a's, read about **Perfectionism** overleaf, but also read **Overwhelm** (if you answered any 'b's) and **Rebellion** (if you answered any 'c's).

If you answered mainly 'b's, read about **Overwhelm** overleaf, but also read **Perfectionism** (if you answered any 'a's) and **Rebellion** (if you answered any 'c's).

If you answered mainly 'c's, read about **Rebellion** overleaf, but also read **Perfectionism** (if you answered any 'a's) and **Overwhelm** (if you answered any 'b's).

PROCRASTINATION

Sometimes we have a green light and act
like it's still on red.

Perfectionism

Many procrastinators are perfectionists. Are you so scared of not doing something perfectly that you indefinitely put it off? Can you imagine how difficult it is to book a holiday if it has to be a perfect holiday? Or how difficult it is to tidy your desk if you haven't got a perfect filing system? The pressure of having to get everything right can leave you paralysed.

Do it

Remember that a less than perfect step taken today is better than a perfect step that never happens. And often you'll find that when, with your 'imperfect' steps, you've completed that task, the finished result is at a level you didn't even know existed when you first set out, that is far beyond your original idea of 'perfect'. And, if it isn't, see it as 'good enough', and enjoy it. Winston Churchill used to 'spoil' his blank canvasses by just daubing a spot of paint anywhere to get him started. Do the same thing. It stops you thinking 'I have to be perfect.' If you're a perfectionist, just start.

Overwhelm

If you find you're easily overwhelmed it may be that you feel deprived of time. You've convinced yourself that if you start writing your book or learning your new language, you won't have time for anything else you like. When we feel like this it's because we're seeing the big picture and not the small steps in front of us. We see that huge blockbuster novel we want to write instead of seeing each tiny step: character list, plot synopsis, chapter breakdown and so on.

Delegate

Rather than asking yourself 'How can I finish this huge task?' just say 'What small step can I do right now towards my task?' as it will stop the task feeling so overwhelming and get you started. Use a Spider Diagram to break your goal down into small tasks. Or find someone to delegate to. They can help you get started or may be able to take the entire task on. Have a go at using a time sheet as well, then you can see how much time you really have left for your task every day.

Rebellion

Procrastination often has its roots in childhood. As children we like to think for ourselves and take initiative – it's a normal part of growing up. But if you were a child with overly authoritarian parents (or teachers) endlessly telling you what to do, at some stage you probably felt either unable to make decisions for yourself – because they were all made for you – or you became a rebel – someone who didn't do what you were told or someone who left doing things until the last minute. Now, as a grown-up, you can't make decisions for yourself or you look for distractions whenever you think you have to do something. You check your emails, read blogs, make cups of tea – anything that means you don't have to get on with the task in hand.

Just thinking that you 'have to do' something, starts off your rebellious streak and this rebellion may lead to procrastination, although, ironically, the thing you are rebelling against is now something you want to do. You're the adult – you can decide.

Every time Olivia sat in her living room she felt guilty and insecure. There were bookshelves propped up against the walls that had been waiting for months to be assembled, along with piles of books she had never read, lying around collecting dust. Somewhere in her heart, Olivia didn't really want to hang up her shelves, nor did she want to be surrounded by books. She was convinced that all sophisticated grown-up people should have books in their house, but reading wasn't really an important part of her life – she just thought it 'ought' to be and that she 'should' have bookshelves. Once Olivia realised that she was rebelling against herself by not putting them up, she knew what she had to do, decide whether she was a grown-up who had books, or a grown-up who didn't. Olivia decided to sell her bookshelves and give the books to charity. Her house felt clear and empty, ready for her to design it according to what she loved. She designed a whole area for her music system, and had her old vinyl record covers framed and hung them on the walls and suddenly it began to feel like home – her home.

Dump it

When you notice yourself procrastinating, start by asking yourself if you're rebelling. If you're avoiding learning French, for example, is it because you don't want to? Well, you don't have to – you're in control of your life, nobody else is. Most of the things you put off or decide to do in life, are things you chose to do or not do. You chose to present the brief you know will put you in line for promotion. You chose to take on the work of an extra member of staff while they were away on holiday. You chose to leave your job and become self-employed. If you've forgotten exactly why you chose to do them, make a list entitled 'Why I chose to do…' and see if you can't see each entry as a treat or a goal, rather than a job or a task. And, if you constantly find yourself faced with things you can't bear to do, ask yourself what made you say 'Yes' instead of saying 'No' in the first place.

 Your Lightbulb Moment:
If you were no longer procrastinating, how would your life be different?

(See Accountability, Boundaries, Choices, Control, Decisions, Fear, Goals, Guilt, Intent, Language, Perfectionism, Planning, Saying 'No', Spider Diagrams, Stress)

Questions ● ● ● ●

It always makes me smile remembering when my eldest son asked me 'Why did God create stinging nettles?' It was one of those questions for which I truly had no answer.

Questions are sentences worded to elicit information.
'You ask so many questions and they're all good ones. I'm having to think really hard.'

What questions?

We use questions all the time in everyday life. There are many types of questions, all of which are designed to elicit certain responses and, because your brain will always try and find an answer to any question, it's important to know what each question is doing. Here are a few examples of different types of questions:

- **'Will you pass the butter?'**
  - **This question demands an action, not an answer.**
- **'Do you know James?'**
  - **This question requires a 'Yes' or 'No' answer.**
- **'What can be known with certainty?'**
  - **This question starts a philosophical debate.**
- **'Don't you know the way?'**
  - **This question expects you to feel ashamed.**
- **'What kind of friend am I?'**
  - **This question wants you to think about yourself.**

Forward-moving questions

Outcome questions are asked in order that you can understand what you're thinking and feeling so that you can then focus on solutions. These questions are distinctly different from everyday questions, which often start with a 'why?' and can leave you feeling negative about yourself. For example:

- **'Why are you going on a diet?'**
  - **This everyday question asks you about the present situation – it makes you reflect on the negatives and maybe even the past.**
- **'What do you hope to gain by losing weight?'**
  - **This forward-moving question makes you think about the future and fills you with anticipation and confidence that the weight loss can happen.**
- **'Why haven't I been promoted yet?'**
  - **This everyday question makes you feel guilty and at fault. It supplies you with an answer that makes you feel bad about yourself.**
- **'What can I do to get promoted?'**
  - **This forward-moving question will have you thinking about future solutions and allows for the possibility that you will get promoted.**

Ask yourself questions

Rather than waiting to be asked forward-moving questions, you can always ask them of yourself. Have a go at these:

- 'What did I feel about....?'
- 'What did I think about...?'
- 'What do I want from this situation?'
- 'How much do I want to do that...?'

Project: Practise using forward-moving questions on a friend. Ask them beforehand if they'd mind you doing that and, afterwards, what they felt about the questions.

(See Connection, Curiosity, Focus, Listening, Perspectives, Prioritise, Problem Solving)

Regret ● ● ● ● ● ● ●

The one regret I have career-wise is that I never worked for a magazine. In my teens I helped out at an indie magazine called Roots *in Edinburgh and had some of the best moments of my life there. I loved the buzz, the pressure, the teamwork of creating that monthly magazine and the fact that there was a completed product at the end of it. But I've got that same buzz, pressure and teamwork now in a different way and it's important to recognise that. Plus I've created a little newsletter and who knows what might happen to that one day…*

Regret is feeling sad, guilty or disappointed about past acts or behaviour that you now wish you hadn't done or about something that has happened to you – for example, a loss or missed opportunity.
'I bitterly regret staying in that job for so long – I was going nowhere and learning nothing.'

Move on

Most of us have regrets – over our behaviour, over a job we didn't get, over a partner we let go, over our childhood, over our family relationships and on and on; but, rather than regret, think what you've learnt from everything you've done. Think especially of the good things that came out of what went 'wrong' and then focus on your future.

Learning from regret

Sometimes regretting your behaviour may mean that you won't repeat it. Regret can be a motivator to stop behaving badly and has been proven to work amongst those who regretted binge drinking. What you regret may well also indicate future choices. Study your regrets and see what you can discover about yourself from them. The very fact that you've regretted something may point to your future. Check also if there are any patterns of regret; do you also have the same regrets, for example, about partners you've let go of? Are there changes you want to make in order for you to be able to move forward, leaving your patterns behind?

Letting go

Sometimes regrets about our families are the biggest and most difficult to let go of. Many of us have regrets over unresolved relationships with our parents, whether they are dead or alive.

Busy, busy, busy

You may also regret not having been there for your friends or having been unpleasant to them for no (or not much) reason. Sometimes, when you fall in love or throw yourself into a period of work, you can stop communicating with your friends. Hopefully they'll still be there for you when you want to re-balance your life.

When George met Chloe he became utterly infatuated with her and began to neglect all his old friends. He suddenly hadn't enough time for anyone else, and began ignoring calls from his best friend, Sam. George devoted all his energy to Chloe, taking her to the pub, to the cinema, away for weekends, as if no one else existed. It had been a few months now since George and Chloe had started going out and then, one weekend, Chloe lied to George about something and he suddenly realised that perhaps she wasn't the right woman for him at all – he'd made a huge mistake. That Saturday George sat at home feeling sorry for himself. He'd ignored his friends and cut them out of his life for the last few months and now he felt lost. In his state of despair he didn't know who to turn to. He felt ashamed to go 'crawling' back to his friends. Just as he was feeling completely overwhelmed with sadness and regret, the phone rang – it was Sam. He'd phoned to find out how George was. It was as if he'd heard George's cries and responded. George had learnt a lesson – never again was he going to let his old friends out of his life for someone else.

Regret you're not like others

If you regret you're not like someone else or don't behave like them, see if you can't adopt them as a role model for you. There's so much you can learn from others that you can incorporate into your life.

Project: What can you learn from your regrets? Make a list of them and see if they're to do with guilt, envy, both or neither. If they're related to guilt, forgive yourself and others. If they're to do with envy, find out where and how that can motivate you.

Regret	Guilt	Envy	What did I learn?
Eg I didn't spend more time with my dad whilst he was alive	He would have liked me to	Other friends with fathers still alive. I now wish I'd known him better	● Always seize the moment ● Work out my priorities in life ● Remember what we had ● Forgive myself ● Found out if I can enjoy their dads too.

(See Beliefs, Choices, Depression, Envy, Forgiveness, Guilt, Letting Go, Patterns, Procrastination, Saying 'No', Stories)

Relaxation ● ● ● ● ● ● ● ●

I'm not sure I'm terribly good at relaxing, though I sometimes think I don't allow myself to relax because I have a fear that once I start relaxing I won't want to do anything else. To be fair, I do sometimes relax. I love beaches and pools – anything where there's water. I remember the most wonderful place I think I've ever been to – in terms of relaxing – was with my great friend, Annie Lionnet. We were in our twenties in Mexico and came across a hotel right next to the emerald green sea. The hotel had not only the most stunning pool, but in the middle of this stunning pool was a cocktail bar with seats so you could sit under a straw roof and sip your margarita. In those days we could only afford one cocktail at most, but I think when we first saw that scene, after the cheap hotels we'd been staying in, we both thought we'd arrived in heaven.

Relaxation is when you're free from worries and stress and feel calm.
'The doctor told me that if I relaxed more my blood pressure would be lower so I'm going to leave work earlier and have a massage once a fortnight.'

Stop

Life can be so serious. Work and responsibilities seem to take over and we don't want to stop in case we miss out. Slowly, little niggling problems and worries build up and gather momentum, and the longer we ignore them, the worse they get and so we carry on and on working. None of us can sustain life without relaxing – we all need time to unwind and fulfil our creative potential. Relaxing brings new energy and ideas into your life.

Ruby was in a job she loved. She wanted to be there all the time so she could see everything that was going on and keep learning and learning – she really didn't want to miss anything, plus she could see that her all-encompassing knowledge made her invaluable. For two years Ruby soldiered on with only a two-week break at Christmas when she stayed with her family. But it began to tell on her. Ruby started feeling weepy, got cold after cold, became slightly tetchy and changed from a wonderfully creative person into someone who could only see the task in front of her. Her input became uninspired and reactive. With the encouragement of her boss, Ruby decided to go to a spa for a week and do nothing except plan future holidays. It was just the break Ruby needed. She came back smiling and full of energy and with two holidays booked – one to visit family in the Far East and one to visit a friend in New York. Plus as soon as she got into work Ruby instantly had a new idea for organising something. Once again she felt inspired. Relaxing gave her brain a chance to try new angles whereas pushing had kept it stuck.

'How beautiful it is to do nothing, and then to rest afterward.'

Spanish proverb

Plan time for you

Whatever your job, build time in for regular breaks where you can relax and not think about work at all. If you're at work:

- **Stretch**
- **Walk round the block**
- **Shut your eyes for five minutes**
- **Read the paper**
- **Visualise your dream holiday**
- **Listen to your favourite music.**

If you're not at work, even simple treats can help you relax:

- **A lovely long bath**
- **A game of tennis**
- **A trip to a museum**
- **Being scared in a horror movie**
- **Reading a good book.**

If you're working really hard, punctuate your week with short, but regular time out slots. Try something new – something you'd never normally dream of doing.

Suit yourself

Many of us aren't aware of how we relax, but if you know, pursue your own interests without worrying about getting friends and family to enjoy them too. Be independent. Spend time on what relaxes you, whether that's getting on with making something creative, or managing your local hockey team, and respect and support those around you in getting on with whatever it is that they love doing. If you feel like it, you might want to dip into their world and, at the same time, introduce them into what you love.

What's your body saying?

Sometimes you may notice you're feeling tense – you've got tension in your shoulders or your head is hurting or you're grinding your teeth. If you deal with your body's physical stresses as soon as you become aware of them, you'll notice you find it easier to relax.

Jane noticed that whenever she was feeling tense, she dug her heels into the ground. She became stubborn and entrenched in her views. Both physically and metaphorically she dug herself in. Once Jane noticed what was going on, she could make a conscious effort to flatten her feet and move her toes to the top of her shoes. Jane could see that she instantly became more relaxed and, in the longer term, her relationships improved and that she became more flexible when dealing with people.

Instant relaxation

Just take a couple of minutes to be in the present moment. You'll find your energy will rise and you may even notice things around you that you hadn't noticed before. Enjoy these two techniques:

1 If you're cutting carrots (for example), simply repeat in your head 'I'm cutting carrots' as you cut the carrots and notice how your mind instantly relaxes. You can do the same thing with anything you're doing – brushing teeth, walking, drinking tea etc.

2 Breathe slowly and deeply. Take a deep breath, hold it for a count of three and then slowly breathe out. Just continue breathing like this until you feel more relaxed.

Relaxing long term

Having clear weekends where you can do what you want – whether it's rushing around trying to fit everything in or doing nothing, is also vital, as is taking holidays. Keep noticing what makes you relax. Is it:

- **a glass of wine**
- **a hot bath**
- **reading a good novel**
- **making a plan so you know what you're doing**
- **chatting to friends**
- **lying down doing nothing**
- **keeping the weekend free so you can be spontaneous**
- **a dangerous sport**
- **hugging the person you love?**

Which of these really turns off your mind? Make a list of all the things that work for you and do them as often as you can.

Project: Think about relaxation. Start with the big picture: your dream holiday. What would you like it to be? Then work your way down. What would you like to do monthly? Or weekly? What would a relaxing weekend be like? What relaxes you instantly? Looking over everything, is there one thing you could do that would help you relax more and worry less?

(See Body/Heart/Mind Types, Breathing, Listening, Planning, Play, Routines, Sleep, Stress)

Roles ● ○ ● ● ● ● ●

At Christmas when we were young, my brother Paul's role was to hand out the presents and make us laugh. Paul has the best sense of humour of anyone I've ever met and my mother and I would be in hysterics as every present was accompanied by a five-minute comic monologue about what could be ascertained about the giver and the recipient from the packaging. Of course, as there were only the three of us, we all played lots of roles within the family, but Paul was slightly forced (probably because he was so good at it) into that of family entertainer.

A **role** is the function assumed, or part played, by a person or thing in a particular situation. The position of a person in a group.

'My role in this family is cook, washer-up, food shopper, clothes shopper, nappy-changer, party planner, duster, vacuum cleaner, table layer, clothes washer... I don't know what isn't my role. And it's exhausting.'

Roles and assumptions

From the moment you were born, assumptions were made about the role you were going to play in your family. Boys love football and aren't meant to cry, girls are meant to be helpful and pretty. These roles carry on until adulthood – Mums are meant to be good cooks and keep everyone happy, Dads are meant to earn enough money to keep everyone. Grandparents are meant to be loving and seen but not heard, and on and on it goes. These may seem old-fashioned assumptions, but they (or their equivalent) are very much present in things we read and think.

Personal roles

There's a high probability that no one ever asked you what roles you wanted within your family; it was just assumed that as you showed a natural inclination to something or even once expressed an interest or just got on and did it, that that role would be your role. These roles are often the boxes we're struggling to get out of. Were you 'the artistic one... the responsible one... the caring one...' in the family you were born into?

Personality vs function

As children our roles are usually to do with our personality (scientific, funny, cuddly etc). As adults our roles are more to do with our tasks (the cook, the bread winner, the clothes washer etc). Even at work we have our assigned roles within our team. You may be the energiser or the encourager or the opinion giver or the information giver. When these roles work, they work brilliantly. There's no questioning over who books the holidays or takes out the bins. But when they work badly and one person feels stuck in a role, it can be a cause for resentment. Ideally roles should be challenged and kept fluid so they can change as you change and grow. Keep talking about them so you can communicate how you're all feeling about your roles.

Query roles

Overleaf is a chart that you can do on your own or with your partner or other family member or colleague ('X'). You may find that many roles are interwoven so it will throw up lots of other possibilities. Keep open to change.

My current role

··

What do I gain by having it?

··

What does 'X' gain by me having it?

··

What would I gain by losing it?

··

What would 'X' gain by me losing it?

··

Is the role still necessary?

··

Could the role be shared?

··

Meeting new people

It can be liberating meeting new people at a party or on a course or in a new job. Even though you may very quickly move into a role, it could be that you invent a new one for this particular group of people. At home you could be the 'serious' one, but within this new group you could decide to be the 'joke teller'. Conversely, you may want to avoid your familiar pattern of falling into 'clown' role and telling jokes all the time. What could keep you sombre and sober?

Project: Create a list of all the things it's been assumed you are and assumed you'll do – both personality and task roles – and question if you want them any more or not.

(See Assumptions, Beliefs, Change, Choices, Inner Child, Intent, Personality Typing)

Role Models ● ● ● ● ● ● ●

I had never consciously thought about role models, until I met Matt, a friend of my eldest son, who worked with me in his gap year as I was starting Life Clubs, my business. Matt was inspirational in the way he studied Steve Jobs, the founder of Apple. There was nothing Matt didn't know about Steve or the development and history of Apple and all our learning came from Steve. Matt would suggest I didn't talk about things until they had happened and then launch them as events in grand Apple style and that, at this early stage, I keep focused on one product rather than diversify. We were the blind leading the blind – an 18-year-old boy and a woman who had written books most of her life – but Steve was our entrepreneurial role model.

A **role model** is a person who is looked up to as an example and their behaviour imitated by others.

'My mum has always been my role model in the way she was so independent and encouraged me to be so too.'

Learn by watching

As parents, we can forget that what children want from us is not for us to tell them what to do, but for us to be perfect role models and then they can learn all they need just by watching us. Children simply need to be shown the ropes and they will copy. If parents scream, they scream. If parents are angry, they're angry. If parents are calm and loving, then that's how they'll be too.

Grown-ups can learn too

Our role models aren't heroes in every part of our life, but they have something about them that we admire and want to copy. Your best friend might always be incredibly diplomatic and that's something you'd want to copy – even if they aren't always punctual (something you wouldn't want to copy). There are no perfect role models – we aren't perfect as people – we're flawed and scarred and wonderful. But each of us has a little bit of perfection and you can look up to us for that one thing even if you don't look up to us for anything else.

How does it work?

Inside you is a confident as well as an under-confident person. In fact, there are many personas waiting to come out. Sometimes you need a little help to reach those confident parts of yourself that you don't usually access and one way to do it is by imagining how someone else would act, and copying them. That way you can appear confident until your real confidence kicks in.

Who do I want to be?

You can experiment with all sorts of role models in order to access and explore the different facets of your own character and see which one fits. To see how it works, think of a forthcoming event that you're slightly dreading. It might be going to a costume party – the idea fills you with fear, but you secretly wish that for once you could get into the spirit of it and approach the event creatively instead.

Step by step role modelling

1 Think about the fancy dress party and who's attending
   - Who would the guests like to meet?

2 What attributes would you like to have?
   - Friendly and likeable? Good at flirting? Charming?

3 Decide on a role model
   - Would it be your brother? – he's always funny and charismatic. Imagine that you have his confidence. Or could you imagine yourself as James Bond – smooth, charming, casual, insouciant? Or what about Madonna? She would automatically be the centre of attention, despite the fact she'd probably be completely indifferent to everyone else around her.

4 Get into your role model's frame of mind – how will they approach the situation?

- What would they be thinking?
- How would they be feeling – about themselves, about the other guests?
- What's their attitude towards this party?
- What would they wear?
- How would they make an entrance?
- What would their intro line be?

Make-believe

Not unlike acting, role modelling encourages you to access a part of yourself that's normally dormant in the situation. For once, allow yourself to behave out of character and go a bit further than you would normally. You'll find that you can behave differently if you're being someone else. Experiment. Try out all sorts of different people in order to access and explore the different facets of your own character. Give yourself the confidence to tackle a situation that would normally fill you with fear. Push yourself – enjoy getting into the role and imagining how someone else would be feeling.

Grant was inviting some potential new friends home for a dinner party. It was the first time he'd actually thrown a dinner party – usually friends just dropped by – and he was nervous. He decided to put on an apron and be the chef for the evening and put on a bit of a show. He served all his guests with a flourish, imagining he was a renowned chef casually cooking at home for once. By adopting another persona, Grant enjoyed himself far more than he thought he would and felt both confident and creative about his success.

Learn from ourselves

We don't always need to look to outside role models. We can sometimes help ourselves by acting as if we are the person we want to be, rather than the person we are. By thinking yourself into being the person you want to become, you will build up confidence and begin to succeed where previously you had felt you were failing. By acting confidently you will become your own role model and able to do everything as yourself.

Brendan had problems with staff who were undermining him, both to his face and behind his back. Brendan was becoming increasingly under-confident and feeling he didn't know how to handle being 'a boss'. He hadn't wanted to adopt a confrontational stance and yet he knew it was what was needed in this situation. Brendan knew that he had an 'aggressive/assertive' side to his personality and that, although he hadn't wanted to use it, now was the time. Brendan worked out how he could use it and yet retain his integrity. When he finally plucked up the courage very calmly but deliberately to give Jim, the ring-leader, an ultimatum, Brendan couldn't believe Jim's response – Jim started to cry and vowed to change. His bluff had been called. Months later Jim was still in awe of Brendan. And Brendan, by becoming his own role model, had worked out how to be more assertive and yet remain himself. His ideal life – peaceful, happy colleagues and a smooth-running office – was beginning.

Project: Think where in your life you would like a little more confidence and who you imagine has the kind of confidence you want. Then work out how it would feel being that person and how you'd approach the situation you're in if you were them. Use their energy to get you to the next step.

(See Beliefs, Change, Confidence, Creativity, Perspectives)

Routines ● ● ● ● ● ● ●

I find going on holiday a really helpful time to challenge and change my routines. One of my naughtier routines is eating a bit of chocolate after every meal (except breakfast). That routine gets forgotten on holiday and, when I come back, I find I don't even think about chocolate for quite a while. Conversely, I love to go swimming every day on holiday and so, when I return, for quite a time I go swimming every day – until somehow the routine gets broken and then…. of course, I've stopped.

Routines are structured patterns of activity that are regularly followed.
'I couldn't survive without my routines – it means I know what I'm doing when and gives me a feeling of comfort and security.'

Why routine?
Many of us live routine-based lives, broken up into clear, bite-size proportions. We walk the dog at 6.30am, have breakfast at 7.30am, start work at 9.00am and on it goes throughout the day. It may be a hangover from our childhoods when we were forced to go to school and operate with routines or it could be dictated by work, but most of us feel more comfortable with routines even if – as on the weekend or during holidays – the routine is different. Routines stop us from feeling disorientated, unfocused and fearful.

The right routines?
Your days may be full up with things that you no longer want to do. Maybe they're full of routines that no longer challenge you. Think about your night-time. What routines do you do every night? Do you feel you have to watch television so you can calm down? Or read a book in bed and have a long, cleansing shower before you can sleep properly? Or have a few drinks to stop you thinking about the day? Are these routines really necessary? If you look at your day you may find that your routines could be simplified allowing you time for spontaneity or to do something you want to do.

Gabby's morning routine started with having a shower and then getting dressed. Gabby somehow felt dirty if she got dressed without getting washed first, but sometimes Gabby wanted to go for an early morning swim, and having a shower and then getting dressed first were just taking too much time. Gabby didn't know what to do. A friend of hers suggested that instead of showering and dressing before swimming, Gabby find some sort of sports kit to wear to go to the pool in. That way Gabby wouldn't have to put her clothes on or have that 'dirty' feeling. Once the idea was suggested, Gabby was up for starting a new routine.

Build in 'chores'

There are many things that we don't like doing. It could be dusting or filing or cooking or even exercising or writing. Instead of battling with them, add them to your routine. The more you build things in as a routine, the easier you'll find it to keep them up, and the more rewarding it will be.

Fran was not keen on exercising, but knew that keeping fit was something she 'should' be doing. Fran decided that her walk to work was half-an-hour and that was all the exercise she would do. Fran surprised herself every winter by being the only person who didn't get sick. Being regularly outdoors and using her body kept her healthy, fit and happy. Fran now revels in her walk, doing it whatever the weather and seeing it as her time to think and feel much more in touch with nature.

Routines help balance

Building in a routine will help you keep your ideal balance too. If you don't put things in your diary you often don't do them. Write in what you honestly want from life. Book in 'sacred' time for yourself, for your family and partner, for spontaneity or for whatever you want. Then arrange a specific time every week to pay your bills and do your paperwork. Even book in a time slot for household chores, so you don't spend the entire weekend doing them. Book in your time – otherwise life slips away.

Keep on track

Attending a weekly course also keeps you on track. Whether it's a course at the gym or a life drawing class, enormous discipline is required to work on our bodies or be creative. Even when we have writer's block, with no thoughts in our head, or physical lethargy, when we have no will to move, we have to push through and routine is a great help. Both structure and routine are very important parts of the creative and physical process.

Project: Go through each of your routines – your mornings, lunches, days, evenings, weekends, holidays and think about what works for you or not. If routines are no longer necessary, throw them out. Make time for new things to happen.

(See Balance, Control, De-cluttering, Excess, Habits, Planning, Prioritise, Relaxation, Sleep)

Saying 'No' ● ● ○ ● ● ● ● ● ● ●

Sometimes I feel I say 'No' too often. I get into my comfort zone and when my husband arrives home on a Friday evening and says, full of excitement and anticipation, 'Let's go out', my immediate instinct is to say 'No'. It's with much inner struggle that I say 'Yes' (sometimes) and, of course, we have a wonderful time and I regret even having thought a 'No'.

Saying 'No' is when you reject a proposition, giving a negative response.
'No. Going to see your old school is the last thing I want to do with my time this weekend.'

Not about being selfish
Sometimes life can seem totally out of balance in that all you seem to do is help friends or acquaintances. It's as if you're in debt to your friends and every spare minute you have belongs to them. What is it that makes you say 'Yes' when someone asks you to take them to the airport, or if you could help them clear their attic? Of course you'd rather say 'No', but then you would feel guilty. So, you say 'Yes' to them and 'No' to yourself. You help them, rather than help yourself. And you end up doing something you don't want to do, then feeling stressed, and resenting the person you're trying to help. Saying 'No' takes practice, but is essential if you want to have some time for yourself to do what you want to do. See it as energising, rather than selfish.

A full diary
Other times people don't ask for your help, they ask for your company. Even so, there are some things you want to be able to say 'No' to. It may not be practical to accept every invitation and request, as you could end up taking on too much and then burning yourself out. Is your diary full because:
- **you have problems with saying 'No'**
- **you like to feel in demand**
- **you genuinely have to attend lots of meetings?**

Each week leave some time for yourself and if you feel your week beginning to crowd in on you, take a step back and explain that you've got too much on.

Get used to saying 'No'
Saying 'No' isn't a question of never helping anyone else, it's finding the balance that suits you that's vital.

Tash loved her yoga classes. It was her time for herself, her time of feeling fluid and connected. In her enthusiasm, she told her friends repeatedly about how happy yoga made her feel until one day when one of her close friends, Jessica, asked if she could come too. Instinctively Tash knew she didn't want Jessica to join her – exercise for her was a private experience and she enjoyed just 'zoning out' and releasing tension on her own. But Tash couldn't bring herself to say 'No' and told Jessica she would be delighted to have the company and support. For the rest of the week Tash dreaded the class and began to resent Jessica. Predictably, Tash stopped enjoying the yoga. She felt confined and inhibited by Jessica's presence, but, instead of saying anything to Jessica, Tash switched classes and started going on a different day, making some sort of feeble excuse to Jessica. But the new class wasn't nearly as convenient and so Tash's resentment grew and she stopped attending the yoga as frequently. Jessica was also offended because, had she been asked, she might have joined Tash in the new class. Gradually their friendship drifted apart, all because Tash hadn't been honest enough – or able enough – to say 'No'.

Listen to your intuition

A lot of misunderstandings are caused by our inability to be honest with each other – and with ourselves. If only Tash had listened to her instinctive intuition and said 'No', she would have been able to keep that 'me' time for herself and Jessica would have found another class to go to. Listen to those inner nudges of intuition, which are begging you to say 'No' and do it.

Say 'No' to your thoughts too

It's also essential to say 'No' to those negative, self-doubting thoughts that inhibit you from achieving your potential. Make a list of them ('I want to say "No" to my under-confidence', 'I want to say "No" to thinking I'm rubbish at relationships'…) and notice every time you have one of those thoughts and just say 'No. I'm not thinking like that any more.' Keep practising – you'll get better and better at it.

At work and at home

And if you're good at saying 'No' at home, next time say it at work instead. What can you say 'No' to at work that really isn't a priority? Unless it's a total emergency, next time say 'No' to staying late at work when you've promised a friend you'll see them that evening. It'll be difficult – especially if you've never said it before – but it has to be said. And if you're good at saying 'No' at work, practise saying it at home.

One night Judy's boyfriend asked her to make sure he woke up at 5am the next morning. In the past Judy had done this for him but it had meant that she'd had a very bad night's sleep worrying all the time that she wouldn't wake up. This time Judy said 'No'. She calmly said to her boyfriend that he had to take responsibility for his early morning himself, put in her earplugs and had the best night's sleep.

Worrying they'll say 'No'

Linked with saying 'No' is a worry that others will say 'No' to you. It stops us asking lots of questions, especially 'Would you like to go out?' But, rather than assuming that they won't want to come, just ask them and find out. At worst they'll say 'No, I'm busy' and even that shouldn't stop you asking them again. They might be genuinely busy and the next time they'll be free. Rather than assuming that people won't want to be friends with you, assume they will.

Saying 'No'
By saying 'No' to traffic, that road can be
comparatively empty.

Say 'Yes' instead

Saying 'Yes' can be a very creative thing to say, because enjoyable and unexpected things happen from saying 'Yes'. Our first instinct is to put up shields against new challenges, quickly finding some excuse that holds us back – 'I promised Ivan I'd go shopping with him' or 'I have to finish something at work' and on and on it goes. But if you just throw caution to the wind and live your life in a more open, spontaneous way, you might find it's more fun. The whole point of saying 'Yes' is just to say it, to be completely unlike the usually cautious person you are and embrace the day as it comes. It may mean changing your routines and getting more organised so that you have time for the 'Yes' bit, but it's worth it if it makes your life more exciting and enjoyable.

'Yes' to me

And sometimes it's important to say 'Yes' to being alone with yourself. It may be that you want to escape reality for a bit, or throw yourself into something and become totally absorbed. In an instant, you'll feel utterly free to be yourself. Make time in your diary for you. Give yourself space. Learn to prioritise your creative moments.

Saying 'No' = Saying 'Yes'

In the first column write what you want to say 'No' to and in the second column write down what you will therefore be saying 'Yes' to.

I'm saying 'No' to...	Which means I'm saying 'Yes' to...
eg 'being a taxi service to my children'	eg 'spending more time with my partner'

Your Lightbulb Moment:
What in your life would you like to say 'No' to? What stops you from saying 'No'? What would make it easier to say 'No'?

(See Beliefs, Boundaries, Choices, Confidence, Decisions, Intuition, Planning, Routines)

Sleep ● ●

We live very near Big Ben in London and it can be disconcerting to be reminded by those chimes just how late it is – and I'm still awake – and, on those nights when I can't sleep, just how long I've been awake for. I'm a bit of a night owl and tend to go to sleep around midnight every night. I wait for Big Ben to strike 12 chimes and then turn out my light. One night a week though I like to have my light out by 8.30. It gives me a big boost to have one good night's sleep.

Sleep is a natural state of rest and unconsciousness from which you can be woken. It affects both your physical and mental health and is essential if your body is to function properly.
'No one really understands sleep yet and how it works. All we know is that it's good for you.'

Listen to your body
Sleep is vital. Sleep keeps us young and gets rid of those bags under our eyes. Sleep softens our bad tempers. Sleep makes us human. If you're rubbing your eyes or your eyes are bloodshot red or dull and listless or even twitching, your body wants more sleep. If you're overdoing the caffeine – think chocolate too – or eating more food than usual, your body wants more sleep. Listen to your body.

Difficult to go to bed
Nothing goes right when you're tired, but when you are tired it's difficult to make the decision to go to bed or to take that power nap. The night can seem like an opportunity for escapism – suddenly here you are, at home, with your own space, with hours stretching ahead; finally, you can do what you want. And yet without sleep, you won't be able to use your spare time as effectively as you could. It's so essential for your wellbeing to be rested.

Your sleep kit
We spend about one third of our life sleeping, so make sure your sleeping environment is right. Only you will know your 'princess and the pea' situation and whether where you sleep is comfortable enough – check if you've thought about these:
- **a good mattress**
- **curtains that block out the light**
- **earplugs**
- **nightcap (to put on your head) and flannelette sheets if you're cold.**

Remove distractions
Having a television in your bedroom is a temptation to stay up watching programmes you could easily do without. Or you might fall asleep with it on and then all night it will form a low-lying irritant, a sort of white noise intruding on your sleep. Television can appear soporific, but is often a stimulant, as are reading magazines and newspapers before you go to sleep. Books are ideal as they can help you escape inside your imagination, which might encourage you to doze off if you're tired. Of course, it depends on the book – it's a great feeling staying up until the early hours glued to a novel, but if you need to go to sleep, read it on the way to work or in your lunch break instead.

'In sleep we are all equal.'

African proverb

Sharing room

Sharing beds or rooms with others can be difficult – they might snore, groan, thrash around, hog the covers or come in when you're asleep and wake you up. No matter how much you love someone else, if they're interrupting your sleep, it's probably going to create a rift in your relationship unless you do something about it. If you've already tried sleeping with two duvets, wearing earplugs and putting a bolster of pillows between you, you may want to check if specialist books and practitioners can help you.

Siestas

Sometimes sleeping during the day can help you relax and makes sleeping at night easier. It also gives you extra energy for the afternoon. Different countries structure their day differently. Maybe a short siesta will work for you – sleeping for a few minutes can be more beneficial than sleeping for an hour. Experiment until you know how much sleep you want.

Grace loved her sleep. As a child, bed had always been presented to Grace as a treat rather than a punishment and so she enjoyed going to her bedroom. Grace saw her bed as a safe place, with its crisp white sheets and warmth. Every evening Grace had the same ritual. She had a hot bath and then went straight to bed. In bed, Grace would write a list of what she wanted to do the next day (everything from packing her son's trainers for school to finishing the report) – prioritising three goals. She would then draw a line under her list, read for five or so minutes, and go to sleep. Usually Grace was in bed quite late, having worked right up to her bath-time, but once a week she went to bed at 7.30pm to catch up on a week of not sleeping quite enough and allowing her to read for an hour or so. Every Wednesday evening, when Grace worked late, she'd have a catnap during the day. Grace would lie down (or sit if there wasn't anywhere to lie), close her eyes and clutch her keys tightly in her hand. It took her 10 or 15 minutes to fall asleep, and then the moment Grace dropped off, her keys would fall out of her hand and wake her up. This split-second of deep sleep was enough to leave her refreshed and ready for the rest of the day and yet still able to sleep soundly at night.

Get worn out

The top tip for sleeping well is to increase your energy during the day, by exercising and eating well, so that you tire yourself out and then naturally drop into a genuinely deep sleep at night.

Insomnia

Rather than treat the symptoms of insomnia, treat the underlying cause. Many of us have brief periods of insomnia, especially at certain times of our life, but if your insomnia has been going on for several weeks, you might want to seek appropriate help. Start by following these tips:

- **When you feel tired, go to bed**
- **Avoid large meals or lots of drinks before bedtime**
- **Nicotine, caffeine and alcohol all impair sleep**
- **Avoid taking long naps in the daytime**
- **Use bed for sleep and sex. Eat, worry, watch TV and work out of bed**
- **Avoid doing stressful jobs just before bedtime**

- Get up at the same time every day – even weekends
- Make sure the light, noise and temperature of your bedroom work for you.

Your Lightbulb Moment:
Notice what you do when you're feeling sleepy. Is it go to bed?

(See Breathing, Laughter, Listening, Planning, Relaxation, Stress, Worrying)

Spider Diagrams ● ● ● ●

You know when you write a list, and think of something you want to add in the middle of it, you sometimes don't want to cross things out or squeeze them in because it will make it look messy? Of course, one of the great things about computers is that you can alter lists, but even freer than that is a Spider Diagram where you can add things in no matter how far into your list you've got. I find it a fantastic tool – fun, creative and inspiring to use. I often start working on a workshop with a Spider Diagram and Genevieve and I used one the other day to get clear about all the many activities we do.

A **Spider Diagram** is a way to organise your thoughts using a diagram on which you can put words or images.
'I use Spider Diagrams when I'm in a lecture to take notes or when I'm going to write something. I use it to make sure that I've covered everything in the topic.'

What do I do?
Start with your problem or task or topic in the middle of the page and, as you think of them, draw legs (with 'to do' steps or ideas) out from the centre to the sides. Each leg is a different part of the task or problem or concept. You could even use different colours for each section and decorate it, which will help to clear your mind and focus on the task in hand. It's a creative way of gathering your thoughts.

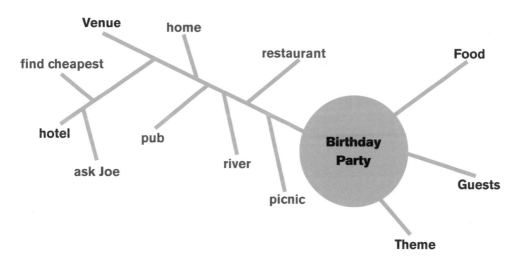

1 Put your target in the middle and then break down your goal into many legs.

2 For example if your goal is to have a birthday party, you would write 'birthday party' in the middle of the spider's body

    a One 'leg' might be the venue

    b Another 'leg' the type of food

    c Another 'leg' might be the guests

    d Another 'leg' might be a theme for the party.

3 Add 'hairs' to each as you start to really think creatively.

4 For example if you take the venue 'leg', coming off it might be 'hairs'

    a One 'hair' might be hotel

    b One 'hair' might be restaurant

    c One 'hair' might be home

    d One 'hair' might be pub

    e One 'hair' might be river

    f One 'hair' might be picnic.

5 Then you add 'finer hairs' to the original 'hairs'. For example, if you take the hotel 'hair', coming off it might be 'finer hairs'

    a One 'finer hair' might be a task, find cheapest

    b One 'finer hair' might be another task, ask Joe

    c One 'finer hair' might be another task, check local hotel and so on...

Life ambition

Spider Diagrams can be used to inspire you into thinking about what your life purpose is. See yourself as the 'sun' or 'spider's body' in the middle and then draw out of it legs which are things you love, for example 'sky diving', 'shopping', 'animals' etc and just keep adding things. Your hairs for 'animals' for example, might be 'grooming', 'caring for', 'breeding', 'walking' and so on. Once you have the diagram in front of you with everything you love on it, you can see how things link up or are repeated to give you ideas for your future. Or you can create a Spider Diagram using the Balance Chart as a foundation. You add the hairs to note what you'd like to be doing in each area of your life.

Project: Use a Spider Diagram to solve a problem in your life – from how to decorate your room to finding your Life Ambition. See how it could help you.

(See Goals, Life Ambition, Outcome, Planning)

Stories ● ● ● ●

Oh gosh. I tell myself lots of stories, from the deeply dramatic – how difficult it is to be first generation English – to the simple – I'm no good at cooking, or even, I'm no good at telling stories. What are the advantages to those stories?

Stories can be factual or fictitious, or a mixture of the two, and are created to amuse, excuse, interest, instruct or forgive the teller – in this case yourself.
'When I discovered I was adopted, I realised all the stories I'd been telling myself about myself had to be re-thought. Who was I?'

The stories we tell about ourselves
Each of us has many stories that we tell about ourselves. We're no good at tidying up, we're no good at sticking to a job, we're no good at making new friends and so on. Our stories are our beliefs and we do a good job of using them to protect us. We do also have stories that show how good we are: we're good at running, we're a good listener, we're good at skiing and so on. Those are the stories it's helpful to keep and the kind of stories you want to discover more of.

Using stories to solve problems

When you're feeling stuck, it often helps to turn your issue into a story by imagining it happening to someone else. It can give you a new perspective on your 'story' and possibly also solve your problem. You could even tell your story as if it was a fairy story.

Michelle was overwhelmed by all the stuff she'd accumulated in her years of marriage and family life. She didn't know where to start throwing things away. It was such a massive problem and felt to her such a waste of money just to chuck these precious, almost new baby clothes and toys away. Michelle wanted them to go to a good home. As she was sitting with her husband, Michelle decided to tell him a story about 'Julia' who couldn't throw out her old baby clothes. As Michelle got more and more involved in 'Julia's' story, she realised that there were lots of people around – neighbours, friends, family and friends of friends who were having children and that she could give the toys and clothes to them. Plus she could see if there was a local charity who specialised in looking after single-parent families who couldn't afford many new things and pass her lovely toys over to them. By looking at her life through a story perspective, Michelle had solved her problem.

Jack was in a job he hated. His boss was mean to him and gave him the worst jobs to do. When Jack told his friend, Ella, about the situation, he cast himself as a Prince, trapped in a tower with an evil wizard who kept casting malicious spells on him. The Prince felt his strength and energy being sapped and yet he didn't know how to escape. Ella suggested that the Prince, being ultimately good and therefore stronger, could escape from the tower using stealth or possibly could find an ally to help him, maybe the person who brought him his food every day? Jack could see that there were indeed a few means of escape open to him. He could use every available minute to try and look for another job or he could find someone in the organisation to help him move sideways. Or he could escape with the sandwich man into a totally different life – maybe that of an entrepreneur.

Project: Each time you tell yourself a story there's a reason you're telling yourself that story and there's an advantage to you to keeping that story. Once you've found the reasons and the advantages, you can decide if the story is really helping you or not. Think about some of the stories you tell yourself and fill in the chart below.

> **Story I tell myself** eg **That I find it difficult to make friends**
>
> ....
>
> **Why do I tell myself that story?** eg **To let myself off the hook if I don't make friends**
>
> ....
>
> **What are the advantages to keeping that story?** eg **To give me an excuse for staying at home and not trying to make friends. So I can feel unloved and sorry for myself**
>
> ....
>
> **What action am I going to take?** eg **I'm going to change my story to 'I find it easy to make friends' and see what happens**
>
> ....

(See Advantages, Assumptions, Comfort Zone, Metaphor, Patterns, Perspectives, Victim)

Stress ● ○ ● ● ● ● ●

I can feel when I'm about to get really stressed. I start noticing that my teeth are almost permanently grinding – my jaw is so tense – and I feel thirsty all the time and my head wants to explode. Once I'm aware that it's happening, I do what I can to calm down, hold back on working quite so hard for a few days, sleep more, stop doing whatever it is that's stressing me and, thankfully, I'm better quite quickly.

Stress is a state of mental or emotional strain or tension (symptoms include headaches, irritability, nausea, withdrawing, higher heart rate etc) which can occur as a result of unfavourable or very demanding conditions. Stress has become an umbrella term for all our emotional problems which can be comforting, as it's familiar and universal, but be wary of dismissing everything as 'stress' and failing to work out what the root of the problem is.

'I feel so stressed out all the time by the amount I have to do and the time I have to do it in. It's as if a huge weight was sitting on my head.'

What happened?
Stress can start in any part of your life and it can be hard to work out how it all began. Your worries build up all at once into a blur of impossible challenges, designed to catch you out.

How does stress start?
Most of our life can create stress in one way or another. Relationships, for example, are an entire area that can bring on stress – from trouble with your in-laws to a boss who is forever putting you

'Tension is who you think you should be. Relaxation is who you are.'

Chinese proverb

down and not valuing you. Or you feel as though no one is listening to you and that can create a well of frustration. Some of us feel ignored even in our most intimate relationships. Our lovers may not be as romantic, intense, involved, open, or honest as we would like them to be, or they may not be pulling their weight.

Making decisions, too, can be very stressful. Some of us get stressed by the pressure of feeling we have to know everything about something before we can take action. Others of us worry if we still have the ability to make the necessary decisions. We may feel undermined by our peers, by our families and by ourselves and our limiting beliefs.

How does stress work?

Stress is designed to help you in life, acting as a quick, temporary reflex to push you in the right direction when you're under pressure. When your body gets stressed it produces chemicals to prepare your body for an emergency. If these chemicals are produced at a moderate level, the stress will help you perform better – think of a cave man running from a wild animal that's hunting him down. They will make you more alert and can help you with that job interview, or get over stage fright or win the 100-metre sprint. But ultimately these chemicals are designed to make it easier for you to fight or run away, they are not designed to help you in a busy office or an overcrowded train or stuck in a traffic jam where you can neither fight nor flee. When the chemicals are produced in such static situations, instead of helping you, they can have the opposite effect and start wearing you down.

Am I becoming stressed?

The first thing is to become aware that you're feeling stressed. It's not always easy to spot, but you'll start noticing your own particular stress patterns. It could be that you start biting your nails, grinding your teeth, feeling unreasonably grumpy about little things, or perhaps you've got an irritating song stuck on your mind. Stress often makes you feel tired and tearful, and to make matters worse you'll be more susceptible to catching every cold and 'flu symptom going – you'll notice you're feeling run down.

How does stress start?

The symptoms of stress can be triggered by minor hassles such as being late, losing your keys, a deadline at work, or larger, perhaps more complicated problems involving relationships, or poor health. If we have to face these challenges singly we can usually tackle them; it's only when they start accumulating that things can get worse.

What are stress symptoms?

Stress produces physical symptoms, such as:

- headaches
- skin problems
- nausea
- indigestion
- fatigue.

Stress can produce emotional symptoms too. You may experience:

- **anxiety (eg worrying, sleeping problems)**
- **fear (eg indecision)**
- **anger (eg road rage, physical or verbal aggression)**
- **frustration (eg hurling objects)**
- **depression (eg withdrawn, tearful, loss of sex drive).**

These feelings can start to escalate, as they feed on each other. Your behaviour might change and become more extreme and then you dislike the way you're acting, which makes things even worse – it's a difficult cycle to escape.

When is it time to take action?

Think about how stressful your life is. Are you aware when you have a particularly stressful period coming and what you can do to prepare yourself for it? If you're prone to stress, there are always things you can do to help yourself.

Just stop

If you notice yourself becoming angry or upset, just take time out – even if it's only for five minutes. Time out for you might be:

- **getting a drink of water**
- **walking round the block**
- **reading**
- **breathing deeply**
- **stretching**
- **phoning a friend**
- **listening to some music**
- **having a quick nap.**

Experiment until you know what will calm you down. Then you can carry on with what you were doing. In the long term, review your diary and see what you can de-clutter and start saying 'No' to. Make your life more how you want it to be and keep relaxing.

Eat well

Stress is reduced by eating a healthy, balanced diet, including lots of complex carbohydrates, such as wholemeal bread and jacket potatoes, to help with your mood swings. A diet including plenty of fresh fruit and vegetables with a minimum salt and sugar intake will help support your immune system fight off any colds. Alcohol, junk food and smoking might appear a solution, but they will only exacerbate the problem further. Stimulants, such as sugar and caffeine, weaken your natural defences. The effects of caffeine on the body can be similar to the effects of stress and anxiety, so replace coffee and tea with herbal tea, fresh fruit juice and water. Drinking water will help you rehydrate your body, as will being a bit more physical (and that includes a simple stroll to the shops) and relaxing a little more. Don't feel guilty about relaxing, it's vital you recharge your batteries. Get enough sleep and have fun. Spend time on you.

Laugh

One of the best antidotes for stress is laughing and having fun. Even simple treats like laughing out loud over a funny sitcom or reading a funny book can help you deal with stress. Make a point of hanging out with your friends who make you laugh most and see if you can make them laugh too.

Project: Create a stress diary to help you discover the things that regularly make you feel stressed and how you cope with them. Each time you feel stressed fill it in and see if you start noticing patterns and common themes. If you regularly feel stressed, seek professional help.

Date

....

What's made me stressed?

....

How do I feel – physically and emotionally?

....

What do I think is at the root of the problem?

....

What are my early stress symptoms?

....

How did I act in response to what's made me stressed?

....

How did I make myself feel better?

....

(See Anger, Breathing, Change, Choices, Control, Depression, Fear, Patterns, Perfectionism, Perspectives, Procrastination, Relaxing, Trust, Worrying)

Style ● ● ○ ● ● ● ○

When I was buying a carpet for the sitting room of the first flat I ever owned I had no idea whatsoever what colour to choose. I love colour and I could have had any colour and have been happy. I remember asking a friend what she thought and her reply was 'Anything that you'll look good on when you're lying on it.' That was great advice. My carpet ended up a grey-ish pink and (though I say it myself) I felt I looked good lying on it.

Style is your own distinctive way of doing something.

'Your style is great – I always love the way you appear to have just thrown something on and yet still look stunning.'

Finding your style

Ask yourself how you would like people to describe you when they think of you and how you would like to feel. For example, would it be:

> Boyish...Sensual... Relaxed... Soft... Exotic... Cluttered... Bold... Gracious... Minimal... Masculine... Elegant... Eclectic... Feminine... Provocative... Modest... Structured... Original... Learned... Dramatic... Creative... Assured... Stylish... Tailored... Colourful... Sexy... Bright... Traditional...

Find the adjectives that you think best fit what you'd like to be and you have found your style.

Using metaphor

Use metaphor as another way of discovering your style. Think of a box of writing implements – pens, pencils, coloured and black, ball point pens, magic markers, crayons and so on – and think which one most represents you. Are you a relaxed, casual blue biro or a formal, suave fountain pen? Or a blotchy, untidy blue biro or a smooth flowing, sophisticated fountain pen? Or one of those coloured pencils with four colour leads in them that you can swivel around – unexpected and fun? Or something completely different?

Deliver your style

Once you've decided on your style, use it. Each time you want to buy something, whether it's a t-shirt or a pillow case, ask yourself 'Is this exotic and relaxed?' or 'Fun and casual?' or whatever adjectives you have decided are you.

Your style at work

Even if you're working at home, look as if you're about to head the boardroom table as it will give you the confidence to deal with important phone calls. Wearing your pyjamas may be fine on a writing or thinking day, but won't push you out of your comfort zone.

Using your style

If you visualise your Life Ambition, you're probably either wearing a 'power' outfit – or are totally relaxed in jeans and a t-shirt. What makes you feel you have to wait until you've achieved what you want to achieve to start wearing what you'll want to wear? Dress like you want to in the future and you'll start becoming your own role model now.

Your style in the home

Your environment is so important. You want it to reflect the way you're feeling. Is there a space that's yours that you can do up to echo your values and style? Many of us live with style 'dictators' and have to sneak in things we like so we don't 'ruin' the look they have created. See if you can't compromise and find a way of bringing your visual fantasy into your home.

Martina lived with Neil, a very fashionable designer. The home Neil had created for them was white and minimalist. There was a space for everything so there were no ornaments or anything on display. It was difficult for Martina to look after, but it also wasn't really her. Martina loved chaos and warmth and there was nowhere in their home that reflected those values of hers. One day, Martina went shopping and bought herself a white vase with a pink heart on it. She felt it was her first step towards making a part of their home her own.

Project: Keep a file of magazine cuttings. Every time you see something – an item of clothing, an interior, a book cover, a photograph, a piece of furniture, a picture of a hairstyle, a postcard – you like, put it in your file. Before long you'll have an inspiring place to turn to whenever you want to brainstorm anything to do with your style.

(See Body/Heart/Mind Types, Creativity, Intuition, Personality Typing, Role Models, Values)

Success ● ● ● ● ● ●

If you asked most of us the meaning of 'success', we may well think of Richard Branson or Nelson Mandela, but not of ourselves. Success is big stuff. But actually success is little stuff too. I wanted to work today until the battery in my laptop ran out (about three and a half hours) and I'm almost there and feeling successful. Needless to say I've been distracted a little by the Internet and done a few quizzes (all in the name of research), but by and large I've done what I wanted to do. Success is completing anything you set out to achieve. You can boil an egg successfully or sharpen a pencil successfully or do one of the projects in this book successfully. Of course you can aim for the big successes, but keep celebrating the little successes on the way – they're what you're doing now.

Success is completing what you set out to do.
'What a success story you are. You've stopped smoking – from 20 a day to nothing, just like that. That's incredible!'

Change perspective

There are always two ways to look at any situation. The 'I've failed' way and the 'I've succeeded' way. When we make a meal, for example, that isn't up to our usual standard, the perfectionist in us can start beating ourselves up about it. If, however, we were to turn it around and say 'Wow. I made a meal in under 20 minutes which was edible', you can suddenly see the success in it. Decide which perspective you'd like.

'Everyone who is successful must have dreamed of something.'

Maricopa Indian proverb

Why we fail to feel success

There are many reasons why we don't appreciate the success we've achieved.

- It may be too easy (for example, going for a walk)
- It may be that our goal is too open-ended that we can never complete it, so there is never a success (for example, 'I want to be a very good person')
- Our goal is too big (for example, 'I want to start a global empire'), so it will take a long time to complete
- Our goal doesn't align with our values, so we don't really want to achieve it (for example, 'I want to win the marathon, but my value is equality').

How to become more successful

Shift your perspective so you start noticing where and when you are being successful. Once you allow yourself to feel successful, the more you'll notice your successes and the more you'll feel successful and the greater challenges you'll then feel inspired to attempt which will then lead to bigger successes. Be aware of what you're doing successfully. Success is an attitude or habit you can develop.

Notice your achievements & feel successful

Set even greater challenges

Feeling successful so take on greater challenges

Succeed at greater challenges so feel even more successful

How will I know when I'm successful

If you've done something you wanted to do, you'll know you've been successful. But if you have a Life Ambition that seems a little distant, if you answer the questions below you'll know when you've hit success.

When you're successful...

- What will you look like?
- What will you feel like?
- How will someone else notice the difference between your new and your old self?

And break your Life Ambition down, so you can succeed at a little bit of it every day.

Fear of success

As with fear of failure, when we fear success it's because we see it as instantaneous. It becomes a fear of change. 'What if I'm so successful my friends don't like me any more… I get recognised in the street…' and so on. Only in very rare cases does success on a grand scale happen instantly. Usually it's a slow process and happens step by step. Just focus on the next step and be successful with that. Don't let fear of success petrify you.

What qualities do successful people have?

You'll rarely find what you might call 'successful' people sitting around procrastinating. Successful people are determined, committed, focused, feisty and enthusiastic. If you don't feel successful, act as if you are. Find what qualities successful people have in your eyes and copy them.

Mirror, mirror

Choose five people who you think are really successful and decide what it is about each of them that makes you feel they are really successful. Write down your thoughts on each of them. Now think about those qualities with regard to yourself. Where do you mirror them? And what does it show you about what success means to you?

Use role models

Imagine yourself as the successful person you want to be and start acting and making choices as if you were that person. How do you think you'd be different from now if you were successful? Would you be more confident? More decisive? More relaxed? Start by making one choice a day as that successful 'you' and see what happens.

Be successful now

Look around you and see if there are any unfinished tasks that you could finish today. Just do them – or at least one of them. Know what you want to achieve and take action. Feel successful as you're doing it. Focus on the job in hand, so you're aware of doing it and aware of finishing it – multi-tasking can take away from that feeling of achievement.

Your Lightbulb Moment:
What success do you allow yourself to dream of? How can you make that dream bigger?

Project: Every evening this week spend a moment reflecting on the successes of your day – from arriving at work to eating a healthy lunch.

(See Achievement, Confidence, Failure, Goals, Intent, Life Ambition, Perspectives, Role Models, Spider Diagrams, Values, Visualisation)

Synchronicity ● ● ● ● ●

Synchronicity or coincidence happens all the time, but we don't notice it unless we want to. Like the autistic boy in The Curious Incident of the Dog in the Night-time[8]*, Mark Haddon's great novel, when we start focusing on things, we notice 'three red cars parked in a row' all the time. I remember whenever I was pregnant, all I saw everywhere were pregnant women and now I hardly see any. I firmly believe that when you want something really badly and you're really ready to get it that you will. I'm lucky. People and things pop up for me in an unbelievable way. Even my husband who is the balance in my life and the voice of rationality says to me that he finds it incredible how frequently the coincidences in my life happen. I simply think it's about noticing. The more you focus and notice, the more you'll see them happening. Then you'll trust they'll happen and then you'll notice them happening even more. It's also important to know exactly what you're looking for. If there's any doubt in my mind that what I think I'm looking for is what I really want, the coincidences won't happen. I have to be totally clear about what it is I want.*

Synchronicity is when two or more events which have no reasonable grounds to be together happen at the same time in a meaningful way. In other words, they were unlikely to happen together, but they did.

'I was just talking about Helen and how I hadn't seen her for a long time when she phoned – what incredible synchronicity.'

Global synchronicity

You may have noticed how you've had a thought and seen something similar – if not the same – in the paper or on the Internet the same day or thereabouts. There are definitely trends and thinking patterns that are around at any one time. A clear example of this is Dennis the Menace, a cartoon of a very young boy who first appeared in 16 newspapers around America one day and coincidentally three days later in the *Beano* in the United Kingdom. Although one was blond and young and one was brunette and older, they both wore stripy jumpers and had the same name. The two different creators claimed there was no causal connection – the concept was somehow in the air. It may have just been that two guys deeply in tune with the atmosphere of 1951 both wanted to show that children had become the centre of adult focus in a post-war world. And maybe Dennis was the popular name of the year (apart from the fact it rhymes with 'Menace').

Use synchronicity

When you're feeling despondent about something you're doing or aren't sure you're on the right track, just start noticing any coincidences that are happening to you. For example, you are worried about whether the business you've just started is the right one for you. Become aware of synchronicity – out of the blue, do you get an email praising you for what you've just done? Or do you get an email saying that something you made has broken? Are there queues outside your shop in the morning or do you have no customers all day? Keep noticing signs. What's important is which signs you notice.

---

[8] Haddon, M. (2004) *The Curious Incident of the Dog in the Night-time*, London: Vintage Books.

Love sick

Sometimes when we're in love, we notice signs all the time – often too many. We may read into coincidences things that aren't really there, but we want them to be there. See if you can use your intuition at the same time as these coincidences arise to check if they're real coincidences or wishful thinking.

More in tune

Synchronicity often happens at powerful times – births, deaths, personal crises. It could be because we're more aware of life at those moments or because we're more focused in our thinking.

Ten days after his father died, Ed was with his wife in hospital at the birth of their first child. A somewhat blinkered man, Ed had never thought about synchronicity or intuition, but at the time of the birth he somehow felt his father was present. Ed left his wife for a few minutes and went to buy that day's paper, and excitedly found an enormous photo of his father in the obituary section. As he was showing it to his wife in the delivery room, the anaesthetist walked in and said 'Are you his son? My husband worked with him for years – great man.' Suddenly it felt to Ed as if his father really was present. What were the chances of the huge obituary of his father being in the paper on the exact day Ed's son was born and the anaesthetist's husband being a colleague of his father?

Project: Calmly and gently, start watching out for synchronicity. Decide you're going to notice something and write down each time you do notice it. It could be once a week or once a month or several times a day. When you get skilled at observing it, start just focusing on things you'd like to occur – 'I'm going to phone my mother' or 'I want to see Alice' – and see what happens.

(See Connection, Creativity, Focus, Intuition, Trust)

Talents ● ○ ○ ○ ● ● ● ●

I had parents for whom age was not an issue, which was just as well as I've always been a late starter. I had just turned 50 when I realised how I could combine all my talents and create a career that is perfect for me. Luckily my father was a huge fan of the American artist, Grandma Moses, who only started her life's work as a primitive painter when she was in her mid-seventies. Grandma Moses was the family role model and, thankfully, in her terms, I'm still a baby.

Your **talents** are your natural aptitudes and skills. If something makes you feel happy when you just do it, if it's something you're drawn towards – that's a talent of yours – something that makes you special and something you'll probably want to carry on doing.
'You are so talented. The way you spin that ball when you bowl is amazing.'

Naturally talented

As children we are naturally creative and use our talents without thinking. Designers, writers, chefs and soldiers simply took the way they used to play dressing-up games, making up stories, cooking magic potions out of ingredients from the garden and creating fields of battles with their soldiers and carried them through to the next stage; essentially making a career out of playing. You probably used your imagination in many ways too, perhaps to create wild and crazy brick monsters or to build sandcastles or to find the best hiding places. Or maybe your childhood was spent careering down hills on your scooter or on the back of a pony.

Talents get overlooked

Our talents often get squashed by teachers or parents who don't want us to have skills that are different from theirs – talents they don't understand. Or maybe – if our talents are very different or alien from theirs – they didn't even notice or recognise that we had them.

Hidden talents

Without the help of an inspiring parent or teacher, something happens. At some stage we leave the world in which we enjoy the things we're naturally good at – whether it's designing zoos, chatting to friends, bicycling or decorating our bedrooms – and start compromising; losing sight of who we really are. We become self-conscious about using colouring pencils and sliding down slides and don't want to get our hands dirty any more. It's often at this time that our confidence nosedives as we compare ourselves unfavourably to others and decide that we're just not good enough at the things we love.

Your talents are your future

When you really love doing something, it's usually because you have a talent for it. It's these talents, or gifts, that make you unique and that want to be used. Usually, only doing something using these talents will make you feel as if you have the Life Ambition that you want and will make you feel satisfied.

Finding your talents

If you could go back in time and remember everything you enjoyed throughout your life, you could follow that talent through and see how and where it reoccurred in your life, like a theme. And you could bring it back in again now. These themes can be quite vague.

- **Enjoyed eavesdropping on my parents when they were chatting to friends**
  - **What can that tell you about yourself?** Do you love intrigue or was it being involved in everything that was going on or simply discovering what grown-up life was all about or just being interested in people? Could that translate into working with people, in HR or as a doctor or therapist? Or might you enjoy being a private detective or part of the police force?
- **Really liked roller skating**
  - **What can that tell you about yourself?** Did you enjoy being outdoors, or were you good at balance and precision? Or was it the performing aspect that appealed to you or doing things physically? Or was it the freedom or the individuality? Might you like to be on stage or doing something outdoors or any career so long as it's being self-employed?
- **Kept pet mice successfully**
  - **What can that tell you about yourself?** Was it about caring? Or about being different? Or being in charge? Or about giving and receiving love? Could being a nurse or a vet be relevant to you or anything managerial or supportive?
- **Used to spend lots of time building forts or tree houses**
  - **What can that tell you about yourself?** Might you have enjoyed using your imagination? Or was it the actual making that was important? Or the logic that you used or the patterns you could create? Might that translate into architecture or design or the army or building?
- **Liked playing in the sandpit**
  - **What can that tell you about yourself?** That you liked getting your hands dirty? Creating something out of nothing? Designing a landscape? Imagining an interior? Perhaps it was that directness of seeing what you'd created physically in front of you, and suddenly being aware of living in the present moment. Could that translate into pottery, gardening or sculpture? Could making sandcastles translate into building something – be it a family, a new business or a home? Or could it simply mean that meditation is something you'd want to build into your adult life?

Remember what you really enjoyed (and may still enjoy) doing without worrying about whether you can earn a living from these talents or not. They may be the key to your future career, but they may just be interests that you want to bring back into your life in the evenings or at weekends.

Talents

We all have the potential to bloom.

Nicola loved colours. When she was very small she occasionally went shopping with her father to choose paints for redecorating their house. One of her favourite things to do was watch the different colours of paint being mixed together by the shop assistant to create the colour they had chosen from the chart. Watching the colours swirl thickly together into the right mix was mesmerising. Nicola also loved colouring-in and drawing. As she grew up she got slightly more inhibited about her drawing skills, but still loved colour. For a teenage birthday she asked for a huge set of colouring pencils, which she always kept in the order they arrived in. Nicola loved the rainbow pattern of the colours, something that fed into her developing style and flair for design. In her late teens, Nicola had combined her love of colour and decoration and would pour over interior design books day and night. By her twenties Nicola had studied interior design and was working in the field.

Forgotten what you loved?

If you can't remember any more what you enjoyed doing as a child, you could start by looking through old photos of your childhood and talking to people who've known you for a long time. Once you start thinking back and doing a bit of research you'll find things come up that you'd forgotten and, as always, brainstorming with friends about the things they loved as children will add to your collection of memories.

Think now as well as then

As well as thinking back to the past, you can think about talents you know you have now as an adult – whether it's being practical or sympathetic or good at maths or French or a natural leader.

Think future too

You can look forward too. Without censoring your thoughts explore what you would love to do if time and money were of no consequence. What would your fantasies be? How would your talents emerge?

Max had just left university. He had studied politics, but wasn't sure he was interested enough in politics to want a job in the field. He really didn't know what he wanted. Max thought back. As a child he had enjoyed drawing plans of towns and playing with toy cars. When he looked forward, his fantasies were to become a DJ and to drive round the world. When Max thought about the talents he had, he knew he was good at getting along with people and could throw a fun party. From his friends and family he learnt that others saw him as having excellent people skills and a great sense of humour. Max decided to use his people and party skills to earn money in the catering world. He built up a reasonable reserve of cash and at the same time planned his trip around the world, going on car maintenance courses and reading voraciously around the politics of each country he was going to visit. Max arranged for different friends to come out and travel with him through various countries. When he finally left, Max owned a reliable car and had saved enough money to last him six months. He took with him his laptop and a contract from a radio station to broadcast his adventures weekly. He was on his way.

Project: Discover what you can learn about yourself from your talents. Make four lists – one list of the things you enjoyed in the past, one list of the things you enjoy now, one of your fantasies for the future and one of what others would say you were good at. What can you can learn about yourself from all this information? Make a Spider Diagram of you and all your skills and talents. Brainstorm.

(See Assumptions, Beliefs, Brainstorming, Creativity, Life Ambition, Mirroring, Patterns)

Time Management ● ● ● ● ● ● ● ●

I first became interested in time management as a child when I read Cheaper by the Dozen[9], *by Frank Gilbreth Jr and Ernestine Gilbreth Carey. It's a true story about a time and motion expert and his 12 children and by the end of the book you start noticing exactly where your time is going. I now time tasks I find boring (eg ironing shirts – under four minutes) and, every now and again, I see if I can beat my record. It adds another dimension to something tedious and makes me smile at my competitiveness.*

Time management is about how to manage (make the best use of) your time. It may involve electronic devices, diaries, clocks, time and motion studies or any other system that you can use to plan and prioritise.
'You are so good at time management, you know what you're going to be doing every minute of your day.'

Empty your mind
A good place to start managing your time is to free up your mind from remembering everything you want to do. If you write tasks down, you create space in your mind to focus on what you're doing, rather than what you want/have to do.

What do I want to spend time on?
Time is finite. Even if you get out of bed an hour earlier or go to bed an hour later, there are only 24 hours in each day. In order to know where you want to put your energy, think about the balance you want to have in your life. Think about your life divided into the headings below and fill in roughly what percentage of your day (ignoring sleep) you are spending on each area (use the '%' in the left column). These percentages don't all have to add up to one hundred, instead think about each one as a percentage out of one hundred. Then, under each of the 10 areas, fill in roughly how much satisfaction you get from each of these areas (use the '%' in the right column). Again, think about the percentage of each area out of 100 per cent, rather than them all adding up to 100 per cent.

[9] Gilbreth Jr., F. B. and Gilbreth Carey, E. (2002) *Cheaper by the Dozen*, London: Harper Perennial.

Time Satisfaction

	Time spent	Satisfaction gained
Home	%	%
Creativity	%	%
Health & Fitness	%	%
Rest & Relaxation	%	%
Friends & Social Life	%	%
Work	%	%
Family	%	%
Money	%	%
Spirituality	%	%
Love & Romance	%	%

If you look at the percentages you've put for each area and compare them, can you now see what you'd like to be doing with your time?

Helena had just had her first child. She had decided, even before she had the baby, that she would go back to work as soon as possible. Helena loved her job and didn't want to leave it for more time than she had to. But, when Helena thought about each area of her life, she could see she was spending about 70 per cent of her time with her baby, about 20 per cent of her time looking after the home and about 10 per cent of her time with her husband. There was really not much time left for anyone or anything else. Helena then thought about how much satisfaction she got from each area of her life. She wrote down that she got 100 per cent satisfaction from being with her baby, but only 5 per cent from looking after her home and, when she thought about her work, she scored it 75 per cent. High, but not high enough to give up the joy she got from her family. Helena did decide to tweak her life a little though. Having scored that she got 100 per cent satisfaction from being with her husband, she found someone who could help her look after her home and someone else who could do a little baby-sitting, so she could occasionally spend some more time alone with her husband.

How can I get more efficient?

There are many time management tools and techniques. You can set goals to focus you, fill in time sheets to check that you're not wasting your time, plan your days and work out your priorities. There will always be some things that waste your time and it's good to know how to deal with them.

What can waste my time?

There are five main things that can stop you getting on with your time:

- ● **Waiting**
  - ● **If you find you're constantly waiting for people, work out how you can change that situation. If you can't change it, always have with you easy, unimportant tasks or something that you want to read or think about.**
- ● **Interruptions**
  - ● **Acknowledge that you're being interrupted and, when the interruption is over, focus again on your task. Be aware that what you want to do after the interruption may not be what you were doing before the interruption.**
- ● **Too much to do**
  - ● **Sometimes you find you've planned your diary so you have too much to do and are rushing around like mad. Keep your diary de-cluttered – make sure your days are planned and manageable and have time for you in them.**
- ● **Being unable to say 'No'**
  - ● **Having to do things for others when you want to do something for yourself can seem like an enormous waste of time. Schedule time for helping others into your diary rather than give your precious time away.**
- ● **Procrastination**
  - ● **Not getting on with whatever you want to do is an enormous time waster.**

Time management tool: 80/20 rule

Many use the 80/20 rule to help them prioritise. This rule states that 80 per cent of tasks can be completed in 20 per cent of the time you have available and the remaining 20 per cent of tasks will take up 80 per cent of the time. Using this principle to sort tasks into two parts, you then do the 80 per cent of tasks very quickly in the 20 per cent of time so you have more time left to do the tasks that will take more time and commitment. This 80/20 split works with everything. Twenty per cent of the people you know will be the ones supporting you through thick and thin. Twenty per cent of the work you do will bring in 80 per cent of the income. Twenty per cent of the Internet surfing you do will be useful. Remember this rule whatever you're doing. Are you doing the 80 or the 20 per cent?

Time management tool: do, delegate or defer

Anything that takes less than two minutes to do should be done there and then, because it would take the same length of time (two minutes) to defer the action. So, if, for example, you're reading an email or letter that requires some action, either:

- ● **Do it (if it takes less than two minutes), or**
- ● **Delegate it, or**
- ● **Defer it.**

There is no point in opening an email and then closing it again, only having to open it and reply to it some time later. If, on the other hand, the email or letter does not require action:

- **File it for reference, or**
- **Throw it away, or**
- **Incubate it for possible action later.**

Time management tool: the urgent/not urgent grid

Each task you have to do gets put into one area of the grid. Anything in 'Urgent' and 'Important' is prioritised and done personally. Anything in 'Urgent' but 'Unimportant' is delegated, anything in 'Not Urgent', but 'Important' gets an end date and is done personally, and anything that is 'Not Urgent' and 'Unimportant' is dropped.

Urgent/Important	Not Urgent/Important
Done now by me	Create an end date and then do myself
Delegated	Drop
Urgent/Unimportant	Not Urgent/Unimportant

Project: For a week use each of these time management concepts in turn and see which you find most helpful.

(See Boundaries, Focus, Goals, Outcome, Planning, Prioritise, Procrastination, Saying 'No')

Trust ● ● ○ ● ● ● ● ● ● ●

I think many of us have had childhoods in which we potentially could have learnt not to trust, but it's so important to get through that story and move on, because trust is the foundation of every successful relationship. I feel beautifully safe with my husband because I trust him so implicitly. I feel like a ship coming back to a harbour. It was, of course, partly to do with the two of us laying careful foundations, but also to do with just trusting that everything was going to be all right.

Trust is when you rely, depend on or place confidence in someone or something. Or when you have a confident expectation or hope of something happening.
'I trusted you with my friendship and you ran off with my partner.'

Trust yourself

We so rarely trust ourselves. We don't trust our memories…and check up what we thought we knew. We don't trust our bodies…and falter as we climb. We don't trust that we'll be creative or have original ideas. Just relax. Think 'can do', and learn to trust yourself.

'Love is giving someone the ability to hurt you but trusting them not to.'

Proverb

Maddy decided to splash out on a personal trainer. As the weeks went by, she noticed she got a bit fitter and definitely felt more energetic, but the most exciting thing for her was learning to trust her own body. Maddy lives most of the time in her head and thoughts, but even she had noticed how she was often not even really aware that she had a body. When one day at the gym, Dirk, the trainer, asked Maddy to put the back of her head onto a large plastic ball and then walk her feet forwards until she was in a sort of crab-like position, Maddy was in total fear. All she could think of was 'what if the ball slips away from under my head?' or 'what if my head crashes to the ground?' Dirk, noticing Maddy's fear, looked at her, said 'Trust your body' and, there and then, Maddy walked confidently forward until she turned into a crab. Once Maddy allowed herself to trust her body she found that it knew just what to do. That was a turning point for Maddy – she now pays much more attention to her body and trusts it to climb over rocks and jump from great heights.

Trust in relationships

When you're with someone who understands you and with whom you don't need to say anything but just feel totally relaxed and comfortable, life feels blissful. In those circumstances, it may seem unbelievable to think that relationships are something you need to work at consciously, but you do – and you have. It takes time to build a true friendship. We can have many acquaintances, but deep understanding and trust is rare and to be treasured, because once it's gone, the relationship is over.

Building trust

Open and constant communication is the most important thing in building trust, as well as making sure you're not confusing this relationship with a previous one. You may have been out with someone who kept letting you down, but that doesn't mean this person is going to. Here are a few hints to building trust:

- **Listen to each other** – Listen to what is not being said as well as what is being said and listen to the tone in which things are being said. For example, if someone says to you 'You'll regret having met me', whether it's in fun or not, keep your wits about you. Many a truer word is said in jest. Also, listen to what their needs are, so they can feel safe with you.
- **Communicate your feelings** – Let them know what you're feeling and what you need in order to feel secure.
- **Be honest** – Trust requires total honesty.
- **Keep your word** – Let people know what you're going to do – and then do it.
- **Understand how they may be feeling** – If they're feeling nervous or upset, see if you can understand their perspective.
- **Focus on what's happening now** – Don't bring past pain of jealousy, abandonment or guilt into this relationship and don't make up future disasters that haven't happened. Remember this is a different person – or, if it isn't a different person, at least it's a fresh start. Talk honestly about any old pain you have. Once the pain is acknowledged by the other person you can let those thoughts go and they can understand why you're feeling the way you are. Look at where you are in the present.

- **Spend time together** – When you're together it can be easier to feel your attachment to each other. When you're apart, you can drift into worrying about previous relationships or where the relationship is going.
- **Watch out for signals** – In war, trust often has to happen instantly. In peace time it may take a little longer. Keep checking that you can trust them – are they willing to share? Willing to be open? Are they reliable? What language do they use? Do children and animals like them? Do your friends like them? Trust is something that can take a while to develop, so be patient. Remember that you're building a bridge and not a tower.

Picking carefully

Some of us always pick the 'wrong' people to trust. We go out with people who have let countless others down and think we can 'change' them and it will all be okay. Maybe we don't really want to be in a relationship, maybe we don't feel worthy of a healthy relationship, maybe we don't trust ourselves or maybe we enjoy being a victim.

Building bridges

Think of all the things and people you trust – it could be certain people, or books, or pets, or houses – anything or any place that you feel is safe. Write them below in the first circle. In the second circle write down anything you don't trust, but would like to. Think about what would help you get those things or people across the bridge so that you can trust them.

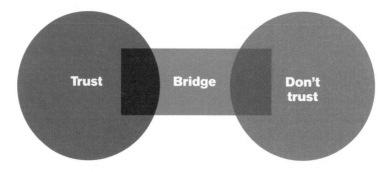

 Your Lightbulb Moment:
Which part of yourself have you yet to learn to trust? What could you do to move you closer to trusting it?

(See Boundaries, Change, Choices, Letting Go, Listening, Patterns, Perspectives, Stories, Victim)

Values ●●·●●●●●●●

One of the courses that I've been on helped you find one of your ultimate values visually. I thoroughly enjoyed that and I still have this image of running along the beach (freedom) firmly in my head. I love beaches at all times of the year, but this particular image is of a beach in winter so it's pretty deserted.

Values are your judgement of what is important to you in life – your principles and standards of behaviour.

'Our values are totally opposed to each other. I can feel the temperature of the conversation rising.'

What are values?

Below are a list of a few values, some of which may be yours. If you read through the list slowly, you'll notice which values belong to you as you'll suddenly feel a 'thump' in your heart or the pit of your stomach or you may get a little flustered. When you've made a list of all the ones that resonate with you, and possibly added a few more, put them into an order of importance for you.

accuracy	balance	belonging	calmness
cleanliness	commitment	control	creativity
daring	directness	excellence	freedom
generosity	helpfulness	humour	imagination
independence	inspiration	joy	knowledge
love	mastery	moderation	neatness
openness	order	philanthropy	presence
reliability	resolve	responsibility	security
self-discipline	sensuality	tact	tenacity
thrift	tolerance	trust	wealth

Why are values important?

When your values are conscious and clear, it's easier to make decisions and to tell whether something is right for you or not. For example, if your value is reliability you may not want to go out with someone who is always late or forgetting things, no matter how much they appeal to your independence value. Your values will help you decide what you want from every aspect of your life because everything that means a lot to you springs from your own personal value system. Your values are what give you your sense of identity. They govern the things you do and if you are happy or unhappy it's because you're working with or against your values.

Are values always 'good'?

Each value has a positive and a negative. You may find it easy to understand that 'integrity' is a 'good' value to have and yet those who have integrity as a value may not be prepared to compromise what they say or do, may speak out when it would be more polite, and perhaps more sensitive, not to and may well end up hurting people they care about as they believe in telling the truth. Similarly, generosity could be seen as another 'good' value, as you could not only be materially generous, but you may also be someone who extends themselves to others. But the flipside of your generosity may be that your giving can be controlling – manipulative even, whereas allowing someone the opportunity to give can be very selfless, very generous. Whenever you are aware of a value you hold, just check out what its flipside is and be aware of that in your character too.

How do I find more of my values?

Your values are revealed in everything you say or think. Just start by describing a perfect day or something that annoys you. After every statement ask yourself 'What's important about that?' until you get to your value. You'll soon start noticing your values all the time.

Eg 'I don't like people being late'
'What's important about that?'
'It makes me think they don't respect me'
'What's important about that?'
 'I think people should take care of each other'
'What's the value there?'
'I suppose thoughtfulness – and respect could be another value'

Can I change my values?

Our values can be shaped by the experiences we go through. Compassion and charity, for example, can grow directly from our own failure or suffering. Or you may have a friend, relative, teacher or famous figure whose values you admire and would like to emulate. You can look back and work out where each of your values comes from and see how they're evolving and can keep on doing so. Simply ask yourself – 'Is this what I believe or what I used to believe or what I was taught to believe?' Some of your values may be obsolete or stand in the way of your happiness so you can throw one out and adopt a new one to help you in your plan for the future.

Finding values from others

Often the key to our childhood values is not to be found within our own family, but in the other families we knew. Our family might have been kind and loving, but our best friend's family might have been so much more fun or relaxed and it's in those memories of other people that often the key to who we are and what we want from life can be found.

Josh's parents were divorced and he lived with his mother and sister in a flat. Although Josh was happy and felt very secure, his life was not exactly exciting and pretty much female (and rule) dominated. Josh's favourite place to go was to his best friend's house for the weekend. Chris lived on a farm and there were four children – three boys and a girl. There, Josh could drive a car over the fields, play Murder in the Dark, eat tea whilst watching television and practise throwing pitchforks around. In Chris's home, Josh felt free and unrestrained. He could be himself and at the same time watch and learn from, Josh felt, a family that had totally 'got it right'. Josh knew that was how he wanted to live when he was older; that what was important to him was not rules, but freedom, excitement, spontaneity, being relaxed and unrestrained.

Things to do:

- Discover some of your values. Think about your favourite day or what it would be like to rule the world and keep asking yourself 'What's important to me about this?' until you find some of your key values.
- Think where in your life you're not living life according to your values. Go through your Balance Chart (see page 77) to check.

(See Compromise, Control, Happiness, Intuition)

Victim ● ● ● ● ●

We all take it in turns to play victim. My husband will come home from work and say 'I'm so tired, I've been working such long hours this week.' And I'll say 'I've made some simple supper but I didn't really want to cook after rushing round having meetings all day.' We're both playing at being victims and neither of us is taking the time to say to the other 'Poor you – what a tough day.'

A **victim** is classically someone subjected to hardship, mistreatment – or worse. In this context it's someone who blames everyone else for what happens in their world.
'He's such a victim. All he does is blame everything on his parents getting divorced 20 years ago.'

We're all victims
There is a victim inside all of us. We become victims to get love, support and guidance when needed. Sometimes we use our victim status too much and start blaming others and the world for all the things we don't like about our life. Even when we receive love, support and guidance it makes no difference, we have become a victim. And, because of the huge power victims can command, being a 'victim' can become addictive. If we want to get out of the seductive qualities of being a victim, it's up to us to realise the advantages we're getting from the role and change.

Do I think I'm a 'victim'?
Some of us take being a victim to extremes so that we don't have to be accountable for our life and actions. Victims don't feel in control of their lives. They feel sorry for themselves and use language that conveys self-pity and direct blame onto others and the world. To understand if you have fallen into your 'victim', listen to yourself:

- Are you blaming other people for the sadness in your life and for everything that's going 'wrong'?
- Do you see life as unfair and feel that everyone else apart from you gets the breaks?
- Do you see yourself as really unlucky – 'everything bad always happens to me'?
- Do you turn to your friends and family for support but do not take on board what they say?
- Do you tell the same sad story over and over again?
- Do you enjoy the attention that you get from others when you tell them your stories?

- **Do you control your relationships by making others feel sorry for you?**
- **Do you notice that people don't want to be long-term friends with you?**

It's not all bad

Being a 'victim' has its advantages. By moaning about our lives, we can distance ourselves from our problem. It can be a highly manipulative role – we get both power as well as sympathy from others and it gives us the safety of not being accountable. However, being a victim holds us back from moving forward, accepting and enjoying our lives and feeling in control. If you are regularly using your 'victim' mode, then you are holding yourself back. You are also risking your relationships, because although at first many of us like to help victims, after a while it can be frustrating to keep trying to help someone who does not want to be helped.

Stop being a victim

Instead of being a victim, become your own hero by being aware of yourself. Listen to your language and when you hear that self-pity emerge, transform it by accepting, asking and acting.

1. Accept

The first step to getting out of 'victim' is to accept. Accept what has happened. It is in the past and there is nothing that can be done to change it. It may be something that has been done to you by someone or it may be that you feel you're very unlucky. Rather than waste your energy by blaming, understand your position and do what you can to change it.

2. Ask

Once you have accepted what has been given or done to you, ask yourself *'What can I do to move forward?'* The answer may be to do nothing – to accept what's happened and forgive – or it may be a practical solution, such as 'move house', 'seek medical help' or 'tell them not to control you anymore'.

3. Act

You now have a solution, so act on it. Carry it through and instead of being a victim, become your own role model.

Victim in a relationship

Sometimes even the strongest of us will find ourselves falling into the role of being a victim. This can happen when we want to get attention or feel the other person is uncomfortable with our strengths. If you notice yourself changing to make others happier, think about how you're controlling now.

Your Lightbulb Moment:

What is your inner victim stopping you from doing?

(see Anger, Authentic, Beliefs, Excess, Language, Optimism, Patterns, Stories)

Visualisation ● ○ ● ● ●

For me, visualising is just seeing pictures in my head. I know for others it's hearing sounds or words and for some it may be smelling – or it could be a mixture of all of them. If you think you can't visualise, right now, close your eyes and imagine a pizza in front of you – your favourite kind of pizza or, if you don't like pizza, your favourite food. How you imagine that pizza is how you visualise (remember how you've done it) and I'm sure you've probably started salivating too, because our mind and body are so inter-connected.

Visualisation is to imagine something – to form a picture of it in your mind.
'I find that visualising a beautiful landscape really helps me to relax.'
'I keep on visualising tomorrow's interview with me getting better and better at answering the questions.'

Negative visualisation
Most of you will be masters of visualisation already – of the negative kind. How often have you left home and imagined the house burning down because you left the oven on or climbing in through the window because you forgot your keys, when you have neither left the oven on nor forgotten your keys. You may well also imagine relationship scenarios that make you jealous which also have no foundation and just worry you. All these visualisation skills can be put to more constructive use.

Positive visualisation
It has been proven that if you lie on the sofa and visualise exercising, let's say swimming, the muscles that you would use to swim begin to move. It's only a small amount, but this willingness of your body to act on what your mind dictates, proves the power your mind has over your body. Mind and body are inter-connected. Positive visualisation is a very powerful tool and used by many in their lives – and by doctors to help with infertility and other health care treatments.

We all visualise differently
Some of us use words, others pictures, others noises and smells or feelings. There is no one way to visualise – do whatever suits you. One way of discovering how easy it is to visualise is to close your eyes and imagine the place you live in. Go in through the front door and just see how you're imagining your home. Is it with words, pictures, through smells, noises or feelings? Whichever it is – or maybe it's a combination of all of them – use that for other visualisations.

Process visualisation
There are two main ways of visualising. One is what we call 'Process' visualisation where you start at the beginning and go through the process. Visualise boiling an egg. In process visualisation you'd start by getting the egg and putting it in the water. You'd visualise the water boiling and then taking the egg out and finally eating it.

Result visualisation
In 'Result' visualisation, you're visualising a result as if it had already happened. So, for example,

you'd first imagine eating the delicious boiled egg with your dippers in your kitchen with the sun streaming in, and then you'd think about what you'd have to do to get to that stage. You'd then go into 'Process' visualisation and visualise making the egg.

The power of the mind

If you can visualise your Life Ambition in as much detail as you can as a finished result, it's an extremely helpful and motivational tool. Visualise your future as clearly as you can by thinking about:

- **where you'll be**
- **what will be happening around you**
- **who you'll be with**
- **what you'll be looking like**
- **what smells there'll be**
- **what you'll be hearing around you**
- **what you'll be seeing**
- **how you'll be feeling**
- **what you'll know**
- **how you got to where you've got, and**
- **what you've learnt in order to get where you've got.**

Start small

Some of you will find it difficult to visualise a future far ahead. Start small and keep practising. If six months ahead is the furthest you can go, stick to that. You can use visualisation for anything. For example, if your goal is to get fit, but you find it difficult to motivate yourself, or perhaps you don't think you could stick to a regime, then simply begin by visualising yourself working out. You'll find the visualisation soon becomes the reality. And, if you want help, cut out photos of people who look as fit as you soon hope to be and stick them on your fridge or by your desk as a collage.

How often?

Visualisation used to be called 'daydreaming' and put down. Daydream as much and as often as you can. Allow yourself to be inspired by your daydreams – so long as they're motivating you rather than an excuse for procrastination.

Project: Experiment with visualising. Start with these ideas and build up from here:

- A happy memory from when you were young
- The last time you felt good
- A wonderful afternoon
- Walking through your dream house/flat
- Achieving the next goal you've set yourself.

If you'd like to, write down what you experienced. Include any sounds, smells, noises, pictures, feelings you had. Make your visualisations as gloriously colourful as you can.

(See also Body/Heart/Mind Types, Intuition, Life Ambition, Role Models)

Work/Life Balance ● ● ● ● ● ●

I'm very lucky because my work and life are (to me) the same thing. My work is my way of life – I live and breathe it and would be lost without it. Similarly I love the non-work part of my life. The other day, as we were walking to pick up my car from the garage, my 10-year-old said to me that he wanted to be an entrepreneur like me because then 'I could take time out of my day to go to the garage or do anything I wanted.' I think that sums up my life – when it's going well.

Work/life balance is about ensuring that you spend enough time at work and at home so that you have a good balance of both.
'My work/life balance is rubbish – I don't have a job I like and yet I'm spending almost every waking hour at it.'

Classic work/life balance
When we think about work/life balance we tend to think about working too hard. We remember how the precious few hours we have in which to see friends and family, cook and eat dinner, let alone getting stuck into some creative endeavour, can seem impossibly short, as though a huge hour glass were suspended over us, the sand slipping away like quicksilver. Conversely, sometimes we feel that work is working for us and it's our home life that feels flat in comparison.

Why work?
There are lots of reasons why work takes over:
- **Passion: your work is more than just a job to you and you love working hard at it**
- **Fear: maybe you live in fear of what will happen if you stop working as hard – will you lose your job?**
- **You don't want to be at home: are you getting on badly with your partner or feel lonely when you're at home? Have you forgotten what you enjoy doing other than work?**
- **Worry: are you concerned that if you don't 'finish' your work you'll worry about it, even when you've left your workplace?**
- **Boredom: is it a fear of being bored or alone that keeps you at work?**

When I'm 64...
And what if you really love work and just want to do it 24/7? Play this perspectives game: imagine yourself 20 years from now, or find a few people who remind you of yourself but are 20 years older. See what you can learn from them as they are now. And then make the decision as to how you want to live your life.

Use your work strengths
Instead of simply wanting to stay at work and use your strengths there, why not use them at home too? If you're very sociable at work, arrange regular gatherings – neighbours, friends, books clubs, football clubs – in your free time. If you're competitive, start getting into competitive sport and play matches. Organise your home life as well as your work life or it may start to lag behind.

Moving skills around

Think about all the skills, talents and strengths you use at work and then work out how you could use them more in the other parts of your life.

Work skill

....

How do I use this skill at home with family?

....

How can I use this skill with friends in my social life?

....

How can I use this skill with my health and fitness?

....

How can I use this skill for me?

....

Ask a busy person

When truly busy people leave work for the day, they are often very good at getting into the present and leaving their cares behind. Has it occurred to you that you too could do some mental acrobatics so you worry about work at work, rather than all the time? If you have only an hour to read, or play with your children, or do all your shopping, you focus. You find you're there mentally as well as physically. And, ironically, you're then more likely to have that 'lightbulb moment' about work by focusing on the present rather than by worrying about the future.

What would you like to do?

What could you apply yourself to that would bring you great pleasure if you gave it a chance? What talents have you got that you haven't employed for ages? If you don't know, start exploring and seeing where it takes you. There may be things you'd enjoy learning, either just for fun or possibly as potential work in the future, and interests (such as German literature, flower arranging and scuba diving) that have taken a back seat due to your lack of time.

Your Lightbulb Moment:
How would you know when you had a work/life balance that suited you?

(See also Absorption, Accountability, Balance, Planning, Talents, Time Management)

Worrying ● ● ● ● ● ● ● ●

I'm not a great worrier, but sometimes I can worry for the whole family. It's a 'skill' I inherited from my mother, but even at my worst moments I'm still an amateur compared to her. Mummy worried about everything we did, from climbing on walls to crossing the road by ourselves. I think her worrying stopped me from confiding in her as I got older. I was worried that she would worry too much. So who was the worrier?

Worrying: to be in a state of anxiety or uncertainty over real or imagined (past, present or future) problems.
'I'm so worried about my boiler – it's been making funny noises for weeks.'

Tackle your worries

One way of paring down your life is to get rid of your worries. Just writing them down can be liberating and helpful because you've literally spelt out what it is that's really worrying you. Describing your problem as clearly as you can allows your mind to process the information in order to begin solving it.

Three types of worries

There are three categories of worries:

1 those that will get better anyway, given time
2 those that you can't do anything (or very much) about
3 those with a practical solution.

The first category: those that will get better anyway, you needn't worry about as their end is in sight – even though it might not be immediate.
The second category: those that you can't do anything about – at least anything right now – are also not worth worrying about as they are out of your control.
The third category: those which do have a practical solution are worth worrying about. Work out what that practical solution is and solve it.

Going through her life, Sasha was worried about so many things. She worried about the gathering clutter in her house and the mess her fridge was in. She hadn't time to be creative right now and that was stressing her out. Sasha had no idea what she wanted to do in order to get fit, she felt she was overweight, but didn't know how to start losing weight. Sasha was also tired: unusually for her she hadn't been able to get to sleep easily recently even though she had never thought of insomnia as one of her problems. Maybe it was because she was worrying about global warming as there'd been so many hot days recently. On and on it went: would her boss make her redundant, how much money would she need for her holiday and how long would her best friend not talk to her for? When Sasha divided up her worries, she was amazed how much simpler they felt. She wrote them down into the three categories and this is what happened:

WORRIES
I like the idea of us throwing our worries away
and skipping off down the street.

- *Worries that will get better anyway, given time (not enough time to be creative, not being able to sleep, best friend not talking to her)*
- *Worries that Sasha couldn't do anything (or very much) about (global warming, would her boss fire her)*
- *Worries that had a practical solution (clearing the clutter, mess in fridge, how to get fit and lose weight, how much money needed for holiday).*

The next day Sasha decided to start with something small, so she set about tackling the mess in the fridge and thinking about how she wanted to get fit and lose weight. She also made a note of where she wanted to go on holiday so she could start searching for cheap ways to get there. Sasha's problems had become controllable. She soon started sleeping better too.

Worry lines
Take each of your worries and go through this flow chart working out what you're dealing with.

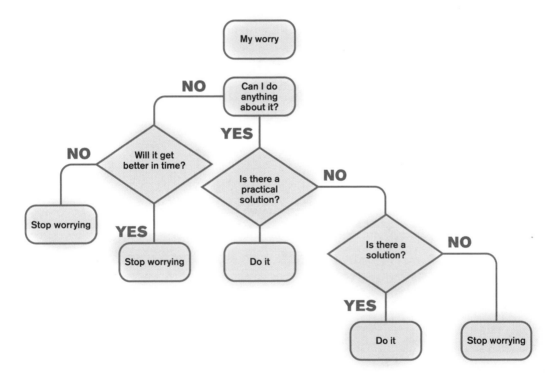

(See also Depression, Procrastination, Sleep, Stress)

'All happy endings are beginnings as well.'

What next?

I like the idea that the ending of this book is the beginning of something new in your life, and maybe something new that *The Life Book* can support you in.

I hope it has inspired you to new heights or into starting off on a new adventure – either digging deeper into certain parts of you and your life or doing something new in the world. At the very least it will, hopefully, have given you a feeling of control over your life and a clearer way of thinking.

What happened for me when writing this book was that I became aware of how three things (Assumptions, Balance and Forgiveness) kept on coming up over and over again as the keys to living a fulfilled life.

Assumptions are so important because our assumptions block off every part of our lives. We make assumptions about who we are, about other people and who they are, and about life and what it is. Then, to make things even more complicated, we make assumptions about what other people think about us. You know how it feels when you meet someone and you say something which you thought was amusing and they don't even smile. You are only too likely to assume 'they don't like me' and to go on from there to 'well, if they don't like me, I'm not going to like them – I don't want to be hurt'. But in fact what they were thinking was how intelligent and fun you were but at the same time had just remembered that they had forgotten their notes for the meeting or had left the oven on – and that was the only reason they weren't smiling with you.

There's more about Assumptions on page 67, but to me becoming aware of the thicket of assumptions which faces us is the best place to begin the journey of self-examination. I was very struck by the passage in one of Barack Obama's speeches where he talks of the assumptions that his white grandmother made about black teenagers – ignoring the fact that her own grandson was one of them. Yet all we have to do is fact-check. 'I've got a black teenager in front of me and he's a good boy, so are all black teenagers to be feared?' Answer 'No'. Start becoming aware of all the assumptions you're making and then question them and you'll soon be able to see through the thicket.

Whilst I've been writing this book a very old and dear friend of mine has been in hospital slowly recovering from the progressive collapse of one organ of his body after another. He's led the most amazing life – intense, hard-working, hard-playing – and it's finally taken its toll. It struck me visiting him, and at the same time writing about life, just how important Balance (page 75) is. If we can get the balance of our lives right for us, then we'll feel more in control and happier within ourselves. As my mother (and Aristotle) always used to say 'Everything in moderation'.

The final topic that kept on coming through was Forgiveness, page 148. If we can forgive ourselves for anything and everything we've done wrong – or just can't do – we'd be so much freer and lighter. And if we forgave everyone else for everything they did 'wrong' to us, either intentionally or unintentionally, we'd also be free of those feelings of blame and 'poor little me' which just hold us back.

I learnt so much about myself and life writing this book. I really hope you did the same.

Nina Grunfeld

Index

Page numbers in **bold** indicate the main entry for that topic.

DISCOVER THE COMPLETE
RULES of RICHARD TEMPLAR

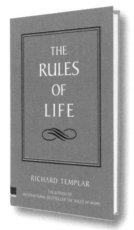

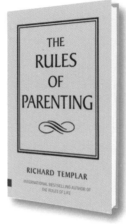

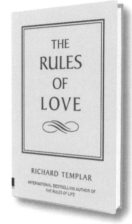

9780273706250

9780273711476

9780273720256

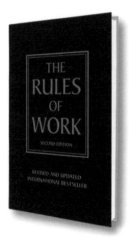

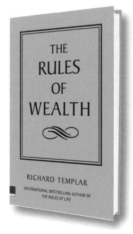

9780273662716

9780273710196

9780273695165

INTERNATIONAL BESTSELLERS
Available online and at all good bookstores.